D1560224

The Harkis

The Harkis

The Wound That Never Heals

VINCENT CRAPANZANO

The University of Chicago Press
Chicago and London

Vincent Crapanzano is Distinguished Professor of Comparative Literature and Anthropology at the CUNY Graduate Center. Among his books are *Tuhami: A Portrait of a Moroccan* and *Imaginative Horizons: An Essay in Literary-Philosophical Anthropology*, both published by the University of Chicago Press.

The University of Chicago Press, Chicago 60637
The University of Chicago Press, Ltd., London
© 2011 by The University of Chicago
All rights reserved. Published 2011.
Printed in the United States of America

20 19 18 17 16 15 14 13 12 11   1 2 3 4 5

ISBN-13: 978-0-226-11876-5 (cloth)
ISBN-10: 0-226-11876-2 (cloth)

Library of Congress Cataloging-in-Publication Data

Crapanzano, Vincent, 1939– author.
     The Harkis : the wound that never heals / Vincent Crapanzano.
          pages ; cm.
     Includes bibliographical references and index.
     ISBN-13: 978-0-226-11876-5 (alk. paper)
     ISBN-10: 0-226-11876-2 (alk. paper)   1. Harkis—France—History.
2. Harkis—Ethnic identity. 3. Algeria—History—Revolution, 1954–1962.
I. Title.
     DC34.5.A4C73 2011
     965'.0461—dc22

                                                      2010047872

♾ The paper used in this publication meets the minimum requirements of the American National Standard for Information Sciences—Permanence of Paper for Printed Library Materials, ANSI Z39.48-1992.

For Garrick
to make a kinder world

CONTENTS

ACKNOWLEDGMENTS

There have been so many people, strangers sometimes, acquaintances, friends, students, and colleagues, whose incidental remarks have helped crystallize a thought, uncover a new perspective, point to an omission, or reveal a blind spot in my thinking. To all of them, whoever they are, I want to express my gratitude. There are, of course, many others who have directly helped me in my research and writing. I list them in alphabetical order: Raja Abillama, Laure Bejawi, Elizabeth Alsop, Hacène Arfi, Talal Asad, William Beeman, Louis Begley, Ramu de Belscize, Fatima Besnaci-Lancou, Mary Blume, David Brent, Joseph Brown, Edward Carpenter, Susan Chace, Song-eun Choi, Aleksandra Crapanzano, Adelaide de Menil, Ellen di Riso, Walid El Hamamsy, Giulia Fabbiano, Maurice Faivre, Nabile Farès, Erika Fischer-Lichte, Steven Foster, Ferial Ghazoul, Saygun Gokariksel, Frédéric Gueron, Yousef Hazmaoui, Larry Hirschfeld, Jonathan House, Elizabeth Hsu, Maurice and Betoule Imbiotte, Rohan Jackson, Lila Kalinich, Banu Karaca, Dalila Kerchouche, Abdelkrim Kletch, Louise Lennihan, Shana Lessing, Tanya Luhrman, Susana Maia, Chowra Makaremi, Shea McManus, Lucy McNaire, Karin Merveille, Jeannette Miller, Caroline Moorehead, Saïd Mrabti, Christine Ockrent, Stephan Palmié, Mariella Pandolfi, the late Paul Parin, Maria Pia di Bello, Christine Pinnock, Linda Pitcher, Barbara Posposil, Zahia Rahmani, Aseel Sawalha, Noam Scheidlin, John Burnham Schwartz, Jonathan Shannon, Jonathan Skinner, Susan Slyomovics, Dimitrina Spencer, Ann Stoler, Nomi Stone, Jesse Tandler, Stuart Taylor, Yunus Telliel, Ana Maria Vinea, Jimmy Weir, Kee Yong, and Mohammed Zaïdat—as well as all the Harkis and their children, who must remain anonymous. I thank them all. I assume, of course, all responsibility for the contents of this book.

I want also to thank Tanya Luhrman and Stephan Palmié for arranging for me to deliver the Rapapport Lecture at the joint meeting of the Society for Psychological Anthropology and the Society for the Anthropology of Religion in 2009, as well as Jonathan Skinner and Rohan Jackson for arranging for the Firth Lecture I gave at the meeting of the Association of Social Anthropologists in Belfast in 2010. Those lectures gave me the opportunity to air my thoughts on the Harkis—on destiny and forgiveness—and I benefited enormously from the discussions that followed them, as I did from talks I gave at the City University of New York Graduate Center; the University of California, Los Angeles; the Université de Montréal; the University of Minnesota; Oxford University; and the Humboldt University in Berlin.

I am especially grateful to my friends Jean-François and Martine Brun, who were my gracious hosts in southern France for far longer than anyone could reasonably expect and whose conversation contributed greatly to my thinking about the Harkis and France.

Finally, as always, I am indebted to my wife, Jane, for encouraging me, for listening to—and contributing to—my thinking aloud at dinner over the five years of my research and writing, and, of course, for her fierce red editorial pen.

The research for this book was supported by grants from the City University of New York Graduate Center (PSC-BHE award), the National Endowment for the Humanities, and the Guggenheim Foundation.

Different versions of chapter 1 appeared as "Die Wunde die nie Verheilt" in *Auf der Schwelle: Kunst, Risiken, und Nebenwirkungen*, edited by Erika Fischer-Lichte, R. Sollnick, S. Umatum, and M. Warstat (Munich: Wilhelm Fink, 2007), 206–26; and as "The Wound That Never Heals" in *Alif* 30 (2010): 57–84.

As Michèle Baussant (2004) has noted, both the juridical and the popular classification of the peoples of Algeria have presented problems that reflect the precarious relations between Algeria and France and among their inhabitants. The names—the categorization—of different populations have been inconsistent, at times contradictory, and have often changed over the 132 years of French colonization. As these changes are not of direct importance to this study, for the sake of readability I have adopted rather arbitrarily the following usage. I refer to the native peoples of Algeria, whom the French called *indigènes*, as *Algerians*. (The European settlers, but not the *indigènes*, were called *Algerians* until the 1930s.) They include both Arabs and Berbers. Although the Algerians have often been called *Muslims*, I have avoided the term except when I am referring specifically to their religious identity, for there are also Christian and Jewish Algerians. I refer to the European settlers as *settlers*, *colons*, or *pieds-noirs*, a more recent term meaning literally "black feet." Though there has been much speculation, the derivation of *pieds-noirs* remains obscure. The *pieds-noirs*, though popularly assumed to be of French origin, are, in fact, the descendants of French, Spanish, Italian, Maltese, and other immigrants; nearly all of them became French citizens, and most remained so. (The Algerian Jews were given French citizenship in 1870 by the Crémieux decree.) I use *French* to refer to the citizens of France who either lived in the métropole, that is, continental France, or were temporary residents in Algeria, military officers, for example. For lack of a better term, and in full recognition of the fact that the Harkis are French citizens, I also use *French* to refer to the European population.

I use *Harki* (pl. *Harkis*) in the narrow sense to refer to an Algerian and his immediate family who sided with the French during the war of independence and served as an auxiliary (*supplétif*) in the French army. I follow

Harki usage in referring to their offspring, regardless of age, as *the children of the Harkis* (*les enfants des Harkis*). The term, at least among those Harkis who are anxious to preserve their Harki identity, now includes their grandchildren. At times, again following Harki usage, I sometimes refer to the Harkis, their children, and their grandchildren collectively as *Harkis*. My usage should be clear from the context. Finally, I refer, at least on first occurrence, to those Harki children who spent at least part of their life in one of the camps or forestry villages in which their parents were housed as *Harkis of the hinge generation* (*les Harkis de génération charnière*), an expression first used, I believe, by General Abd-El-Aziz Meliani (1993). As Harkis of this generation were the focus of most of my research, I often refer to them simply as *Harkis* or *children of the Harkis*. Again, my usage of *Harki* in this sense should be clear from the context in which the term occurs. I should note, however, that, as *Harki* has popularly come to refer to all those Algerians who worked in one capacity or another for the French military, I also use the term in this extended sense when the people I am writing about do so. When the context seems appropriate, following French bureaucratic usage I refer to those Algerians who sided with the French and settled or were settled in France as *repatriated French Muslims*.

A number of words are commonly used for Algerians who opposed French rule. I use *nationalist* for those who took a political stance in opposition to the French. For those who fought for independence, I generally use *freedom fighter*, *independence fighter*, or *maquisard*. I have elected to use the common French spellings of the Arabic terms for these fighters since they are used in many but not all English accounts. Hence, *moudjahid* (pl. *moudjahidine*) for the Arabic *mujâhid* (pl. *mujâhidûn*), *jounoud* for *junud* (pl. *jundiyy*), *fediyyine* for *fidâ-iyyûn* (the plural of *fid-iyy*, "a self-sacrificer, the member of a commando unit"), and the pejorative (albeit frequently used by French soldiers) *fellagha* for *fallâqât* (bandit). I have avoided using *rebel*, *revolutionary*, or *outlaw* (*hors-loi*) except where the context requires it. The meaning of other Arabic and Berber terms will be given on first usage.

All translations from the French are mine unless otherwise indicated.

In the late 1980s, I was visiting friends in the south of France, in the mountains above Grasse, and, jet-lagged, I went to bed very early. It was still light. Several hours later, now in darkness, I awoke from a dream, dimly remembered even then, in which, lulled by the music, I was struggling to stay awake at a Moroccan marriage ceremony. I had had this experience several times when doing fieldwork in Morocco in the late 1960s. As I fell back to sleep, I sensed that the music I had heard in the dream was, in fact, real, coming through the half-opened window in my bedroom. In the morning, I asked my host whether I could have heard Moroccan music. He said, Yes . . . well not exactly . . . it was probably coming from the Harki village across the valley. He had got so used to the "racket" they were always making that he no longer heard them. "Moroccan, Algerian music, it all sounds the same to me." He knew nothing about the village. "Sometimes, you see the men, drunk out of their minds, staggering down the road to their village." That seemed to be the extent of his knowledge of the Harkis and their village. Several days later, on my way back to the house, I made a wrong turn and ended in a cul-de-sac that gave onto the Harki village. Men, women, and children, countless children, were sitting in the shade under a couple of sickly trees at the entrance to the village. I made a quick U-turn and drove away as fast as I could. I can still see them glaring at me, their faces frozen in hostility, suspicion, and fear.

I knew little about the Harkis other than that they were Algerians who had fought on the side of the French in Algeria's war of independence, the bloodiest of anticolonial struggles, which dragged on from 1954 to 1962. I had heard that, at the end of the war, tens of thousands of them had been killed by the Algerian population at large. Most of those who managed to escape to France were incarcerated in camps and forestry hamlets, some for nearly two decades. As my sympathies had always lain with the FLN, the Front de libération nationale, which had led Algeria to independence, I thought of the Harkis, if, in fact, I had ever thought about them, as traitors, opportunists, sellouts, *collabos*. I remembered protests against the war in Paris; the revelations of torture by the French army, including that of Djamila Bouhired, who was sentenced to death for bombing a restaurant in Algiers but whose execution was finally stayed because of public pressure; the bombing of Le Drugstore on the Champs Élysées; and a massacre by the Parisian police (effected, in fact, on October 17, 1961, by the chief of police, Maurice Papon).[1]

The French army and the *pieds-noirs* (Europeans settlers in Algeria) were the enemy; de Gaulle himself just managed to escape being the enemy, at least in my eyes (though also in the eyes many of those who supported Algerian independence). He was not, however, free from opprobrium. My heroes were Jean-Paul Sartre, Simone de Beauvoir, and Frantz Fanon. Though I read about the atrocities committed by the FLN, I never took them seriously, or, if I did, I saw them as inevitable brutalities for a greater good. Though, in school, we learned to condemn the doctrine that the end justifies the means, we were—at least I was—excited by the ruthless pragmatism necessitated by revolutionary struggles. We saw the Algerian War as a revolution and not as a civil war or, as I now see it, as a mixture of the two. But, to be truthful, as an American living in the protected atmosphere of a Swiss boarding school through the early years of the war and then visiting France during its later years, I did not pay that much attention to the war. The events I recalled, the antiwar slogans I repeated, the Sartre and Fanon I read, were, I am afraid, mainly icons in the narrative called *finding oneself*.

I remember driving with my mother and sister through the south of France one Sunday afternoon in 1956 and being stopped several times by an army train that snaked its way through one town after another picking up troops on their way to Algeria. They were not much older than I. They were scared, drawn with anxiety, prideful, tough, lost in themselves, angry, committed, and alienated at the same time. They were being seen off by their families and friends, by whole towns, and by mayors who made pompous speeches extolling bravery, glorifying France, recalling those who had died in the Great Wars or in Indochina. The mayors' high rhetoric—it seemed to come from the same speechmaking manual—was always undermined by the tinny bands that played patriotic songs without verve or concordance. It was only when the trains arrived and everyone sang the *Marseillaise*, as the recruits climbed on, that the send-offs achieved a patriotic high that obliterated, for the moment, the fear, anxiety, and anger that the recruits and their families and friends had been feeling. Of course, the emptiness that followed the train's departure turned the tear-jerking patriotism into sadness and prescient mourning.

I marched a couple of times in Paris toward the end of the war. I was caught in a brawl between the police and a group of Algerians who seemed to have done nothing but be Algerians. I was moved to tears by a French soldier who described how he was made to torture and then kill FLN fighters. By this time, I could sympathize with the French troops, who, however much they were against the war, had no choice but to fight. I shared a train compartment with two soldiers on their way to Algeria, a middle-aged couple who were returning home from a commercial fair in Paris, and a French journalist who wrote for a Marxist review. For an hour or two, the journalist was in deep discussion with the soldiers, condemning the war, praising the FLN, and preaching the evils of colonialism. I felt sorry for the soldiers. The last thing they wanted to hear, I thought, was about the futility—and the danger—of the war they were about to enter. Then suddenly, about a half hour before we were to arrive at the soldiers' destination, the journalist ordered the couple and me out of the compartment. "I want them to have a last fuck," she said clinically, without realizing the force of *last*. When we returned to the compartment, neither soldier could look us in the eye.

It was more than twenty years later that I again heard about the Harkis. This time it was from a team of French psychiatrists who were on some commission or other looking into mental illness among university students. If I remember correctly, the commission had been divided in imperial fashion into five divisions, each concerned with an area of the world from which there were a substantial number of students. Given my work on Moroccan ethnopsychiatry, I was asked to consult with the division devoted to the Maghreb—North Africa. I remember the psychiatrists' arrogant pragmatism, their lack of sensitivity to the situation in which their patients found themselves. They tended to equate the North African students with immigrant workers. (Of France's population of 61 million, more than 5 million are Muslims.)[2] I was struck by their observation that many immigrant workers showed schizophrenic symptoms after they had been working in France for about thirteen years. Treated with drugs, they recovered nicely and then, eligible for a disability pension, returned home. Otherwise, they would not have been eligible for a pension, the psychiatrists told me, until they had worked in France for fifteen years. They laughed dismissively, collusively. One woman pointed out that the children of the Harkis often suffered the same symptoms but were not responsive to any drugs. "Ah, the poor bastards, they have nowhere to go," one of the psychiatrists said. Another, more sympathetic, added that they suffered the silence of their fathers and went on, in Lacanian fashion, to say that, unlike their fathers, they had nothing—no trauma—to foreclose. It was at this point that I intervened, observing angrily that, as far as I could see, no one French, or Algerian for that matter, could possibly treat them successfully or even do research with them. They were too embedded in their history. Frankly, I had no idea whether what I was saying made sense. I was just angry. On my way home, I thought that the Harkis would be an interesting group to study, but I had no time.

Again, I did not think much about the Harkis until the summer of 1991, when I read in *Le monde* that Harki protesters had occupied the tollbooths on the autoroute that led to Spain. I was not sure what they were protesting, but I thought them clever since the French government was losing tens of thousands of francs a day as the Harkis let the German and English tourists through the tollgates free. I remember overhearing a couple of German tourists gloat at how much they had saved in tolls. They had no idea who the protesters were and what they were protesting—they were just a bunch of Arabs.

It was only in 2004 that I decided to work with the Harkis. I had discovered that Harki children—the expression refers to the generation that follows that of the Harkis themselves—had begun writing memoirs, histories, and novels. I read one, Hadjila Kemoum's (2003) *Mohand le Harki*, which I found so filled with contradictions—naive and cynical at once, insightful and without insight, expressing great loyalty to France and at the same time a fury that led the protagonist to sacrifice his life—that I decided I had no choice but to learn about the Harkis. They were like figures in Greek tragedy, betraying (perhaps) and betrayed, abandoned, ostracized, and exiled to an alien land where they would always remain strangers. I knew, of course, that I would probably not find tragic heroes among them—at least of the sort one finds in the Greeks or, for that matter, in Racine. Our world, however tragic it may seem at times, has grown too small for such heroes. I expected to find people caught in their history, their pain, and the petty details of everyday life that would, no doubt, undermine them. It was the contrast between the ordinariness of everyday life and a suffering that was, by that ordinariness, reduced.

I have written in this personal manner less to situate myself in my research than to indicate the fragmented nature of personal historical experience that is tangential to, at times indifferent to, at times vicariously engaged with, that experience. I want to emphasize that historical experience, indeed, any experience—at some level even the most petty—is rooted not only in its empirical context, which we make so much of in the human sciences, but in a transcending reality that we tend to ignore. By *transcending reality* I mean, not transcendent reality in the religious sense (though that may be part of it), but that most often dimly recognized, certainly never entirely grasped bypassing of experience in its immediacy that lends itself to story, drama, and invention, to their possibility, affording us not so much a vantage point as an ever-changing, subtly insistent temporal perspective. Though I do not share the faith of the anthropologist Michael Jackson (2002, 14) in storytelling as "a vital human strategy for sustaining a sense of agency in the face of disempowering circumstances," if only because silence may sometimes be an even more vital strategy, I believe that he does evoke this dimension of experience when he writes: "In spite of being aware that eternity is infinite and human life is finite, that the cosmos is great and the human world small, and that nothing anyone says or does can immunize him or her from the contingencies of history, the tyranny of circumstance, the finality of death, and the accidents of fate, every human needs some modicum of choice, craves some degree of understanding, demands some say, and expects some sense of control over the course of his or her own life."

This craving certainly figured for me and, I believe, for the Harkis in our meetings and in the stories they told me or refused to tell me and my implication in those stories. The demand for voice and understanding hovered, however, between realism and an optative that was cast, as if by magic, in a cloak of realism. Stories may ground action, but, as Jackson (2002, 15) also acknowledges, they are "equally vital to the illusory, self-protective, self-justifying activity of individual minds." To this I would add "individual minds engaged with one another."

I have written about imaginative horizons, which are essentially of a perceptual nature or so metaphorized (see Crapanzano 2004). Here, I want to stress the fuzzy horizons of understanding. Just as each of my experiences of the Harkis and the Algerian War of Independence in its fragmented iconic way evokes a transcending drama, which, even if it is given concrete, textual expression, as in a history of the Algerian War or in what I am about to write about the Harkis, bypasses that expression in, yes, its grandeur. I want, in the text that follows, to evoke that grand, though ultimately inexpressible, context that surrounds the Harki experience and is essential to it. The Harkis may formulate it in terms of destiny, their children in terms of chance, and

I as the result of colonial domination and the irresponsibility that accompanies that domination and its aftermath.

I find that the Harkis both confirm and defy our traditional modes of understanding. It is easy (however painful it may be) to write the Harkis' tale, to place them sociologically, to describe their culture, and even to delineate certain of the psychological dynamics they display, but, without wishing to privilege the Harkis and their situation, I find that none of these modes of understanding can do them—their subjectification—justice. Their understanding—their experience—of themselves, their world, and their past is constrained by complex, often contradictory, certainly paradoxical plays of power. As (political) subjects, they, like all of us, are subjugated by and through the very power that constitutes both their subjectivity and the discursive formations through which they articulate that subjectivity, their subjugation, and their being subjects (see Foucault 1980; Butler 1997; and Fassin 2008). What is often forgotten is that the subjectification of the individual is always ill-fitting—never so complete as to preclude conflict and struggle. Indeed, I would argue that it is precisely through conflict and struggle that subjects and subjectivities are (politically) molded. They instantiate both the reality and the illusions of agency or, as I would prefer, freedom. While recognizing the constituent role of power in the lives of the Harkis, I have preferred not to speak of them in the generalizing terms of political subjectification. Rather, I want to describe its effects in a singular case that has, nevertheless, general relevance.

I have taken a loosely phenomenological approach that seeks to uncover the structures of experience that arise from the Harkis' existential situation and *their* understanding of that situation. But, unlike traditional phenomenological approaches, which are centered on the subject's consciousness, mine insists on the role of the researcher's engagement with the subject in his or her informed construction of the subject's experience. However empathetic, however intuitive the researcher's construction is, it can never achieve the goal he or she sets, for the mind, the subjective experience, of the other always remains opaque. Our constructions must be judged in terms of the relations—the possible understandings and misunderstandings— that arise from our engagement with other people. They are mediated by language and our perception of language, by translation and our understanding of translation, by narrative and descriptive conventions and our critical acknowledgment of those conventions, and by our projective capacities and our appraisal of those capacities.[3] They are also mediated by our interlocutors' understanding of these same factors. They are at best informed evocations of the subjective experience of the other. As epistemologically dubious as such evocations are, they are a prerequisite for (successful) social relations. Indeed, their epistemological dubiety affords the play—the ambiguity—that is necessary for the maintenance, indeed, the creativity, of such relations.

The Harkis are caught in a drama they did not understand at the time they made the decision to join the French. The decision was often enough no decision at all but a necessity of the situation in which they found themselves. No doubt, they have suffered ever since the massacres at the end of the war from the thought that they might have "chosen" otherwise, as many Algerians did in similar circumstances. They fought alongside the French a war in which both sides committed acts of inordinate violence, often less for immediate strategic advantage than for psychological reasons, and they participated in this brutality at times with fervor, at other times out of fear, and most often simply because they were carrying out orders. Like all soldiers in times of war, they were proud of, and at times angered and disgusted by, what they were ordered to do.

At the war's end—and during the war itself—the Harkis were turned on brutally by their people and witnessed the slaughter of others who had made the same decision they had. They were the survivors stigmatized by their people as traitors and betrayed by those for whom they risked their lives. They found themselves apart in an alien society that was forced, however reluctantly, to take them in but would have preferred if they had simply disappeared. Not only did they remind the French of their defeat in Algeria, but, like other non-European immigrant groups, they challenged France's republican values and highlighted its racism.

What is it to be apart in a society? Though the Harkis are marginalized, alien and alienated, I do not want to reduce apartness to these prêt-à-porter categories, which offer us, though not necessarily the people they purport to describe, some conceptual solace. I want, rather, to stress the existential condition of being apart—a condition that is constantly undermined by the reality of being among a people who would prefer you were not there and never had been there as they have to accept you or at least give you a place that is yet a no place. Apartness implies the desire not to be there and to be there, to remain unwelcomed and to be welcomed, to recognize and to misrecognize what sometimes even the host society would prefer not to recognize, to be a symbol, both revealing and mystifying of precisely that which resists recognition, and to suffer its implication—the effects, say, of loneliness, shame, humiliation, guilt, anger, dishonor, and defeat—as it is at times empowered by that implication.

In the autobiographical novel *France: Récit d'une enfance*, Zahia Ramani

(2006, 38), the daughter of a Harki, describes growing up apart in a French village:

> Outside I have no past. No history. No relatives. My father, my mother mean nothing. They are useless. They are alive, breathing, but without quality. One takes account of their presence only in terms of expenses and costs to society. They are uneducated! A child, it is this that one inflicts on me, and I swallow it. Ashamed of them. They have nothing to hand down. And of them there is no trace. They did nothing good. Shame on them, the awkward, the stutterers. I live surrounded by that. No one who says I love you, I know who you are. I'm hardly allowed on the sidewalks. They mount guard with dogs. At fifty meters, on the way to school, all the children in one family make fun of my fear of a German shepherd on a leash. Bite, bite her. Once they let him go. It bit my knee. They hid to listen to me scream.

Ramani captures the emotional tone—the heated frustration and anger—of many of the childhood accounts I heard from Harki children. They never seemed to have lost that sense of separation, of being an outsider who was rarely, if ever, invited into the uncomprehending and incomprehensible world in which, without explanation, they found themselves.[4] Like Ramani, as we shall see, they often cherished the rare moments in which they were befriended by a French neighbor. Such moments were infused, I often felt, as they described them to me, with a longing that they could never really satisfy.

The Harkis are apart, in all the above ways and others too, and they inspire in the French, and, no doubt, in the Algerians, memories they would prefer not to remember and judgments they would prefer not to acknowledge. Yet a poll conducted by the television network France 2 in November 2003 found that 68 percent of the French thought that France had treated the Harkis badly (see Sabeg and Besnaci-Lancou 2004, 10). As one French diplomat confided to me, "The Harkis are our shame. We treated them shoddily. We would prefer they disappeared. But I have to admit that, though they fought for us, they were after all traitors to their people, and, no matter how much I try, they bear that stain." I heard similar, though often less honest, comments from other French people with whom I talked. They provide the surround of Harki apartness.

Like the French and the Algerians, the Harkis also prefer to forget the war, but they cannot, however hard they try, because it has molded their identity. Nearly everyone who has worked with them, including their children, reports their refusal to talk about their war experiences. "I am in exile, friends, but do not ask me," Oedipus asks at Colonus (Sophocles 1959, 88 [line 207]). "What's the point?" the Harkis ask, if they say anything. "It's over. It's best forgotten." They say this with a telling stubbornness. Their memories are too insistent to be forgotten. Their silence speaks the presence of their memories. Despite our psychologies' stress on forgetting, repression, and foreclosure, forgetting is often far harder than remembering. We recognize the bleeding of what is forgotten and repressed and perhaps even foreclosed back into our experiences in disguised form. But what of memories that resist forgetting, repression, and foreclosure? They memorialize themselves.[5] They haunt us in their clarity. They mark a fate we cannot avoid, if only because our social surround—which we cannot avoid—is a constant reminder. The Harkis, I will argue, have been doubly ghettoized—by the French (and the Algerians) and by themselves as they retreat into themselves, hoping to isolate themselves from precisely what has led to their retreat. Their silence, their retreat, is not without effect on their families, especially their children. A product of violence, it does violence. In its emptiness, silence can resist forgetfulness more strongly than can the fullness of the articulated, if only because it offers nothing to be forgotten. The children of the Harkis, particularly those who were raised in the camps, suffer a double wound: that of the pain they themselves suffered and that which arises from their father's stubborn silence. It is with them, particularly the activists among them, that I did the bulk of my research.

I have used the term *Harki* thus far and will continue to do so with the disquiet that comes with generalizing and, thereby, objectifying a people who, like all people, are composed of individuals with distinct characters and unique histories despite the fact that many of them have had similar experiences. As we will see, some Harki families have retained their Harki identity over, by now, three generations. Some of the children have assumed an activist, even a militant stance; others simply identify themselves as Harkis. Still others—some say the majority—have disappeared into French society or, more likely, into one or another of its marginal populations. Some few have become historians, sociologists, writers, journalists, businessmen or -women, doctors, lawyers, or politicians. Others are bureaucrats or teachers or have small businesses of their own. And still others are laborers. Many, if not most, of the grandchildren are unemployed, living on welfare, mostly in drab subsidized housing (*habitation loyer moderé*, HLM) among immigrant workers and their children, who, envying their citizenship, often distrust them.[6]

Though I am forced to generalize, as is required in any social description, I hope my references to individual Harkis will remind the reader that each Harki is a singular individual whose individuality resists its subsumption, not only in the inevitable stereotypes of social description, but also in the collectivized identity demanded by political action. The Harkis and their children have (to struggle) to find their place in this imposed identity. I will often quote from their published or unpublished testimonies, memoirs, and autobiographical novels, most of which have, as Giulia Fabbiano (2007) notes, a strong, seemingly inescapable testimonial quality. Though they may depict the Harkis' experiences with exactitude, they must also be read as symptoms of and reactions to those experiences. By referring to them as well as to French who have known and worked with the Harkis in one capacity or another, I want, not only to supplement my own research, but also to triangulate it so that, at least implicitly, the reader will recognize the effects of my own style on the material I collected and that of others who have been far more deeply immersed in the "Harki experience." What I have written is a result of my understanding and misunderstanding, my empathy and my lack of empathy, my sympathy for them and my failure to be sympathetic. I admit to a certain impatience, a troubling irritation, that some of the Harkis and especially their children produced in me at times. It stemmed less from what seemed to me to be a justificatory indulgence in their story, however real and painful that story was, than from the way in which they had politicized and manipulated it for their own ends. This is, of course, understandable given their present-day circumstances, and I am certainly in no position to judge their reaction to what they have experienced. But it does diminish the force of their story and, in diminishing it, ends up adding another distressing dimension to their struggle to come to terms with themselves. The individual stories that are subsumed in *the* Harki story have become what the Harkis themselves refer to as *testimonies*, *témoignages*, evidence of what they experienced that they use in the demands they make on the French government (and, often enough, in justifying their own particular circumstances).

The activists among them and others too used these conventional stories in an attempt to elicit my sympathy and to recruit me politically. Even though I explained that I was powerless to do anything for them besides tell their story, as I saw it many still believed that I could obtain American support for their cause. This expectation governed much of what they said to me and my response to them. I certainly felt their expectation as a burden. It was difficult, I must admit, to break through their conventional story to their particular ones, and I often failed. I am not altogether sure what it means—and even what value it has—to break through the conventional. What did I expect to find? The Harkis' submergence of their own stories into a collective one seems to be the telling social fact. It was not until I talked to an Algerian woman, a former *résistante* who insisted on calling my attention to the gap between what she called *imaginary* and *real* constructions of the Harkis by themselves and by others, that I realized that, like the Harkis and other participants or nonparticipants in the war and its aftermath, I was caught in a hall of conflicting imaginary constructs, each demanding my allegiance and, in consequence, the renunciation of others. Put in today's jargon, the Harkis were attempting to find and fix an identity from within the variously empowered perspectives—the multiperspectivalism—of modernity, and I was made to play a role in their endeavor. Although I have tried to consider the Harkis from several different perspectives—for example, those of French officers and soldiers who fought in the war, of bureaucrats, of former members of the FLN, of Algerians living in France, of the Harkis themselves, and, perhaps most interesting of all, of casual acquaintances of all backgrounds whom I met during my research—I have certainly not succeeded in eliminating the perspective(s) that derived from the role the Harkis offered me and my resistance to that role. So intense and prolonged is ethnographers' engagement with the people they study that they can never fully abandon the commitment and consequent obligations to them that come with their research.

Though an outsider, I share despite myself something of the ambivalence of the French. It is troubling in ways that my research more than twenty-five years ago with whites in apartheid South Africa was not disturbing. There I was troubled by friendships or near friendships I made with people whose values I despised. I do not despise the values the Harkis have expressed. Though they suffer their mistreatment and, at times, perpetuate that suffering in ways that seem indulgent, the act of siding with the French, that betrayal if it can be so-called, has not inflected their values in the way in which the privilege of the white South Africans inflected theirs. I liked many of the Harkis I met and became friends with some of them. I admired the resilience and forbearance that many of them demonstrated in circumstances so crushing that I often asked myself whether I would have had their strength were I to find myself in a similar situation. My meetings with many of them challenged moral assumptions I had never bothered to examine seriously and uncovered deeply embedded attitudes that I had never recognized in myself.

I hope that I will be able to produce in my readers similar recognitions while still being as true to the Harkis as I can. Many of the themes and concerns I will treat in this book are those of literature, philosophy, and religion—themes and concerns that hover at the edge of our human sciences. As I have often argued, anthropology is torn, not only between the perspectives of the people the anthropologist studies and his or her own, but also between an intellectual or, if you prefer, scientific perspective and a moral-existential one that is at times so disquieting as to be nearly obliterated in our sheltering ourselves from them in the discipline's scientific goals. It would seem that we should recognize the implications of this division of knowledge and its effect on our research. It is difficult to recognize that reason and rationality, however reasonable and rational they may (appear to) be, can also serve unreasonable and irrational purposes. I want to stress the challenge to our moral presumption that people like the Harkis and their situation pose.

While the Harkis' story is, like all stories, unique, it is not so unique as not to resonate with—in Georgio Agamben's (1998) terrifying words—the "vita nuda" of tens of millions of people in refugee camps, the ghettos of the marginalized, and the *nonlieux* of the displaced. Those people are the remains of the ever more frequent local wars and those grander ones that justify self-interest in terms of one ethnocentric value or another—such as democracy American style or an overly rigid Islam. Their stories, inevitably of violation and violence, become allegories of human experience. In this age, not unlike other ages, perhaps all ages, in which violence seems to insinuate itself into every facet of life—war, hatred, and indifference but also peace, love, and concern—we ought no longer to seek relief in the particularization of violence but to recognize in its recurrence its ubiquity.[7]

The Wound That Never Heals is divided into seven chapters. The first, which serves as an introduction to the Harkis, discusses a play, *Le nom de père* (The name of the father), by an Algerian playwright, Messaoud Benyoucef, whose protagonist is a Harki. The Harkis found the play offensive and tried to stop its performance in protests and through the courts. Not only does *The Name of the Father* represent the contradictions in the life of the son of a Harki and, by extension, in the lives of many of the Harki children; it also describes the Harkis in a context they tend to ignore, namely, the confusion, pain, and suffering of many, if not most, Algerians during the war and its bloody aftermath. By introducing the Harkis through the writings of an Algerian, I hope to provide the reader with an edge on my own description of them and to offer, insofar as it is possible, an intimation of how they are affected by—and protect themselves from—one of the many reconfigurations imposed on them that threaten their self-stipulated identity and the story that supports that identity. They are not immune to the effects of the invasive multiperspectivalism that characterizes modern life.

Chapter 2 provides a historical background to the struggle for Algerian independence. It is directed to those readers who are unfamiliar with Algeria's history. Other than my own particular perspective, it offers little that will be new to readers who know that history. I should warn readers that many of the French histories, particularly those concerned with the war and the auxiliaries, that I and other scholars have had to make use of reflect, at times unconscionably, the political position of their authors. I have tried, as best I can, to extract a reasonably accurate account. That the French histories are so politically invested should be taken as a symptom of the French reaction to the war, the divisiveness it has caused, and the stain it has produced on France's hypersensitive and deeply defended nationalism. Chapters 3–6 are organized in roughly chronological order, from the formation of the *harkas* (Harki units) at the beginning of the war to the Harkis' life in France today. Chapter 3 is concerned with the role of the Harkis during the war. Chapter 4 describes their abandonment by the French and their massacre by the Algerians. Chapter 5 focuses on life in the camps and forestry hamlets of those who managed to escape to France. Chapter 6 is concerned with the way in which the Harkis see themselves now and how they struggle for recognition, compensation, and apology from the French.

In the final chapter, I return to many of the themes laid out in a provisional way in chapter 1 and throughout the book. I discuss the role of the wound in the formation of identity and its passage from generation to generation. I am particularly concerned with how that passage is hardened by a misrecognition, less of its particular circumstances, than of the ontological differences in the way in which historical experience is understood, that is, of the change from an understanding configured by a sense of destiny to one determined by chance. I focus, as I have said, on those Harki children who were raised in the camps and have suffered the effects of their father's silence as well as the indignities of camp life and its sequel. How do they—how does anyone live with an onerous heritage for which one is not responsible and yet respect those (the fathers) who were responsible for that heritage? How does one live with a marginalization, a racism, discrimination, and accusation that constantly recall that heritage—a heritage that is both imposed by others and self-imposed? How does one live with what is, in essence, a double trauma: the silence of the father—the dead but alive, the live but dead father, as I have characterized him (see Crapanzano 2009a)—and the wounds one has experienced oneself? How does one live with an unknown that has dramatically affected oneself? How does one preserve a memory—a nonmemory—that gives one definition and yet has no particularity? How is it to be haunted by memories of nonmemory? What role does the Harkis' story—their activism—play in this? Can a story that has become frozen regain the vitality it loses with each repetition? Or is it destined to produce only the pain that lies behind it and the pain that comes with its increasing loss of vitality? Are the Harkis lost in that story, that pain? Would apology, forgiveness, or revenge free them from that story, that heritage? Or does their tragedy ultimately lie in the impossibility of tragedy and the consequent debilitation of meaningfulness? Is there no escape? It is this possibility that offends the Harkis, as we will see in the next chapter in their reaction to *The Name of the Father*.

ONE

The Wound That Never Heals

On March 3, 2005, Mohammed Haddouche, the president of AJIR pour les Harkis France,[1] wrote to the president of the Conseil régional de Haute Normandie protesting its coproduction of a play, *Le nom du père* (The name of the father), by the Algerian philosopher, translator, and playwright Messaoud Benyoucef. After playing in Fécamp from February 22 to February 25 without incident, the play moved to Canteleu and Louviers, also in Normandy, where, under the direction of AJIR and another association, Génération mémoire Harki, Harki protests were launched in which tracts were distributed demanding the cancellation of the play and its publication.[2] Though there was no violence, there was, as *Le monde* (April 30, 2005) put it, "considerable pressure." The Harkis tried to prevent the audience from entering the theater, and Claude-Alice Peyrotte, the play's director, received a menacing telephone call. While insisting on the right of free speech, the mayor of Louviers tried to calm the protestors and finally managed to clear the house so that the play could be performed.[3] In early March, the two Harki organizations brought a case for defamation against the publisher of the play, Les Editions de l'Embarcadère, its author, and its director. Protests continued. At the beginning of June, however, when I saw the play at the Théâtre de l'Epée at the Cartoucherie de Vincennes in Paris—it had been playing there for nearly a month—there were no protesters. Before the play opened in Paris, Smaïl Boufhal, the president of Génération mémoire Harki, told Brigitte Salino of *Le monde* (April 30, 2005) that the court case has "permitted us to act as citizens. We will not intervene when the play is performed at the L'Epée-de-Bois."

Neither Benyoucef, Peyrotte, nor Alice Yvernat, the director of the publishing house, ever imagined *The Name of the Father* would cause an outcry. Though the protest and the ensuing case are of little significance in the annals of French law, they do raise a number of questions about the Harkis. Who were the protesters? Why did they protest? What did they expect to gain from their protests? On what grounds did they base their case? On what grounds was it rejected by the court? The text and its performance were clearly not neutral. Was the reaction they generated simply a question of content? The power or the failure of representation? Or was it fired by breaches of theatrical convention or everyday etiquette? Was it a question of publicity? Of exposure? By an outsider? To me, as to many members of the audience, its author, its publisher, and the director, *The Name of the Father* did not depict the Harkis pejoratively. I found it sensitive to the paradoxical situation in which they find themselves. Both the play itself and the Harkis' reaction to it raise questions about the identity of an ostracized people living in a modern nation-state. The Harki response points to the role of memory, wound, and pain in the struggle to preserve that identity. Possession, I argue, is one of the ways in which memory resists the treachery of its historical existence—the ultimate failure of its own memorialization. As Albert Camus (1951) observed in *L'homme révolté*, "Le gout de la possession n'est qu'une autre forme du désir de durer" (The taste of possession is just another form of the desire to last"). Clearly, memory—its representation and memorialization—must be understood in terms of both its origin and its own history.

Part 1: The Harkis

> At the end of ten years of this regime, the people in the camp saw a judge arrive: he came to see whether the Harkis were mature enough to become French. He questioned them one by one and asked them the same question: "Well, do you want to remain French?" Our fathers, they were really worthless! If not, they would have answered him: "But, sir, if you ask us if we want to remain French, that means that we are already French? Well, if we are French, why haven't you treated us as French?" But all they could say was, "Yes, sir, we want to remain French."
>
> —Seif-El-Islam El Mansour in Messaoud Benyoucef's *Letters to Jeanne*

Strictly speaking, *Harki* (from the Arabic for "movement, military movement") refers to the approximately 260,000 Algerians of Arab or Berber descent who served as auxiliary troops (*supplétifs*) in the French army.[4] The term is, however, often used loosely for any Algerian who served in or with the French military or police forces during the war.[5] The Harkis have been called *les oubliés de l'histoire* (history's forgotten), for, until recently, they have been ignored by both scholars and the press and have lived, for the most part, in abject silence. Although some of the Harkis sided with the French because they believed that Algeria would be better off under them than independent or because they and their fathers had served in the French army, most of them, poor, illiterate peasants, did so because they desperately needed what money they could earn to survive in an impoverished, war-torn country. Many had suffered at the hands of the militant and often brutal FLN, which led Algeria to independence and, according to the Harkis and many other critics of the Algerian government, has been responsible for the ensuing poverty, disorder, and violence.

Despite warnings of likely bloodshed from officers who had fought alongside the Harkis, the French government ordered their demobilization after the signing of the Treaty of Evian on March 18, 1962, and sent them back to their villages. The treaty, which gave Algeria its independence, offered the Harkis little protection, and, in the months surrounding its ratification on July 3, 1962, between 60,000 and 150,000 Harkis were tortured, mutilated, or killed by the Algerian population at large. Overwhelmed by the arrival in 1962 of more than a million *pieds-noirs*, or Algerians of European origin, many of whom supported the terrorist Organisation armée secrète (OAS), which had attempted a coup in April of the previous year, de Gaulle's government did almost nothing to halt the bloodbath. As little sympathy as he had for the *pieds-noirs*, de Gaulle had even less for the Algerians themselves. As a result of public pressure, from June 23 to September 28, 1962, 48,625 French Muslims were given entry to France. By 1967, another 60,000 arrived (Jordi and Hamoumou 1999, 49).

In France, most Harkis were sent to camps, forced to live in miserable conditions, subjected to abusive discipline and constant humiliation, and offered, if any, the lowliest of jobs. Fourteen thousand families were eventually moved into seventy-five isolated forestry villages scattered across southern France, where they worked in an enormous reforestation project. Those who could find work outside the camps and villages left as soon as they could. Many of those who remained—some for more than sixteen years, until the last of the camps was closed in 1978—suffered the pathologies associated with abjection: identity loss, anxiety attacks, delusions of persecution, idées fixes, depression, bouts of violence, suicide, and, among the men, alcoholism. The women lived in a sort of double purdah: that imposed by tradition and that stemming from the fear of venturing out into a threatening world they could not understand. Children not only suffered discrimination at school, that is, when they were able to leave the camp schools, but also lived under their father's silent and often violent regime.

They did not understand why they were treated as they were, nor were they told what their fathers had done or why. Yet, despite their parents' silence, the children came to know, if only by indirection, the Harkis' story and experienced, at a step removed, their parents' ambivalence.

Today, though there are still concentrations of Harkis in the south of France, often near the camps where they were incarcerated, and in the industrial north, many Harki families are scattered across France. They, and to a lesser extent their children and grandchildren, have remained a population *à part*. Condemned as traitors by the Algerians, abandoned by the French, anxious not to be identified with Algerian immigrant workers, who reject them in any case, they have lost their bearings, their country, but not their dignity and pride. Those who were able to leave the camps and hamlets found themselves in a country where they were treated as half citizens (though they have the rights of any French citizen), mistrusted, marginalized, and subject to often virulent racism. They did not speak up; they did not write. For the most part, they lost themselves in their despair. The Harki novelist Zahia Rahmani (2003) refers to them as *soldatsmorts*. Yet, as we shall see, their children have assumed the wounds they suffered and articulate their identity in terms of those wounds. They share, if vicariously, their parent's sense of having been betrayed, abandoned, and humiliated. Unlike most of their parents, many have begun to take an activist stance, forming political associations, like AJIR and Génération mémoire, lobbying for the recognition of the sacrifices their parents made for France, and demanding compensation for the losses their parents sustained. In the last few years, they have begun publishing memoirs, novels, testimonies, and histories, all of which express their ambivalent loyalty to France.

Part 2: The Complaint

> We cannot accept this play because it puts our history in serious question.
>
> —Smaïl Boufhal, president of Génération mémoire Harki

The case for defamation was based on article 5 of the law of February 23, 2005, prohibiting "toute injure ou diffamation commise envers une personne ou un groupe de personnes en raison de leur qualité vraie ou supposée de Harki," which may be roughly translated as prohibiting "all insult or defamation of a person or group of persons because of their real or supposed identity as a Harki." The law's promulgation was the product of years of lobbying by Harki associations.[6] The French minister of culture and numerous writers, intellectuals, and artists opposed the Harkis protests of Benyoucef's play because, as they found nothing injurious or defamatory in it, they saw the charge as a breach of freedom of speech.

The Harkis' position is best described in Mohammed Haddouche's letter to the regional council.[7] He begins by stating that the author of the play is an Algerian who wants "to display the alienating surrender [*déshérence*] and rottenness [*mal être*] of Harki children."[8] The play is "a malicious and underhand attack" on the Harkis and "casts opprobrium and discredit" on their community. By "insidiously planting clichés [*des poncifs et des clichés*]," the playwright arrives at his "hidden goal: to revive the scars of the Algerian War and to wound a community." He takes up anew the insult of treason and affirms that "it is found in the genes of the Harkis and is inherited from generation to generation." He forgets that the Harkis were against, not independence, but the terror imposed by the FLN. He revives the rumor that the Harkis formed battalions of the GIA (Groupes islamiques armés, the most uncompromisingly militant of the Algerian Islamist groups that tried to take control of Algeria in the 1990s). The rumor, it is said, was spread by the Algerian government to turn the Harkis into a scapegoat to justify its own failure. Haddouche argues finally that Benyoucef "pushes ignominy to the point of writing that treachery is perpetuated through blood and by crime since the son 'must sacrifice the father' and betray in turn." By negating the identity of the son—that is to say, the Harkis and their descendants—whom he dubs SNP (*sans nom patronymique*, "without a patronymic"), he renews the idea of "the traitor always under the skin."[9] Haddouche points to the paradox: even though France is in the process of working through the painful memories of the Algerian War as well as its racism and anti-Semitism, it supports *The Name of the Father*. He demands that its performances be stopped immediately.

The language of the complaint is hyperbolic and, at times, falls out of grammatical constraint, but it does reveal the pain the Harkis and their children feel today. It reflects their exceptionalness—and the way in which that exceptionalness is perpetuated by their sense of being betrayed and abandoned by the French. It is noteworthy that Haddouche begins his letter by stating that Benyoucef is an Algerian without adding any qualification. He does not try to situate the play in the body of Benyoucef's work. It is the third play in a trilogy dealing with violent contradictions in Algeria's struggle for independence and its aftermath. The picture Benyoucef draws of the French, the Algerian government, the FLN, the *pieds-noirs*, and Algerians in general is hardly more flattering than that of his Harki protagonist. Haddouche fails to see the play's terrible irony, its cynicism, and the occasional relief that comes with humor—humor, as often as not, vested in the cliché. He does take up the argument, which has gained currency in recent years, that the Harkis were against the FLN but not against Algerian independence. This was certainly true of many Harkis, perhaps the majority, but there were others who were, if not opposed to independence, then fearful of what it would bring.

Part 3: The Play

> And I want to make of it a literary space for memory. Not a memory riveted to what one believes was the original reality; a memory that will be only a worn-out rehearsal of the past and a loan word for nostalgia: but an active memory that will ceaselessly reaffirm the primacy of the present—an essential condition for the correct understanding of the past—and will permit a better apprehension of the future.
>
> —Jeanne in Messaoud Benyoucef's *Letters to Jeanne*

The Name of the Father is the third work in a loose trilogy that is united by a notion of active memory, which Jeanne describes in *Lettres à Jeanne* (Letters to Jeanne), the epistolary novel (later adapted for the theater) that begins the trilogy.[10] The book consists of letters by Jeanne's French and Algerian classmates to whom she had written decades later, presumably in the 1990s, asking for news. They illustrate the social and cultural complexity that lay behind the Algerian struggle for independence and how that struggle affected the destiny of French and Algerians alike. Though Benyoucef is clearly critical of all the parties involved, he projects enormous sympathy for the individuals entrapped in its history. Violence and its effects figure in each of the letters: in murder, exploitation, political and moral bankruptcy, disorientation, language (an Islamist curses Jeanne), the loss of a homeland, impossible love, suicide, sex, madness, the revelation of truth (a *pied-noir* discovers her husband took part in the gang rape of an Algerian woman and killed her when she became pregnant), and, most terrifying of all because it has no fixed referent, pervading menace. Benyoucef notes the lack of distance between the past called up by Jeanne's letters and the present that the letters put into question. Past and present "telescope each other, they reflect in an implacable game of mirroring the grotesque effigy of that goddess who drinks the blood of her victims in their own skulls, the terrifying midwife of history, violence" (Benyoucef 2002b, 6). Can memory ever get beyond this violence, even in its active stance, toward the present and the future?

In the second play, *Dans les ténèbres gîtent les aigles* (The eagles live in gloom), from Hölderlin's poem *Patmos*, the "goddess" of violence appears mysteriously as Tergou, a white woman, a woman in white, who walks on stilts and clacks the reeds that extend her long fingers, announcing the death of those she will devour. *The Eagles* is the most philosophical of the trilogy. Its two protagonists are Frantz Fanon, the Caribbean psychiatrist who became an Algerian revolutionary and wrote *The Wretched of the Earth* and other works on the psychology of colonialism, and Ramdane Abane, a leader of the FLN who was assassinated in Morocco by his rivals in the movement. The play asks which should have priority in a revolution, in a struggle for independence, the political or the military? It follows the trajectory of its two protagonists during the most violent phase of the war, from January 1956 to December 1957, though it incorporates Fanon's death in Washington, DC, on July 12, 1961. Fanon, who had hoped to reform psychiatry in Algeria—which, under the influence of Antoine Porot, was deeply racist (see Berthelier 1994, 71ff.; and chapter 2, n. 9, below)—comes to recognize the futility of his project when he realizes that the delusions of one his patients, a French Algerian woman who believes that her husband is plotting a massacre of the Algerians, are, in fact, true: "If to cure a patient is to restore their ability to choose, it is still necessary not to have any illusions of freedom for a subject whose very being is denied. What is the use of returning to a deadening colonial order those who have fled it, seeking shelter in madness?" (Benyoucef 2002b, 25–26). He gives up his hospital position and joins the FLN. Abane, a political pragmatist with little subtlety but considerable, indeed, stubborn, integrity, insists in the play, and insisted in reality, on the priority of the political over the military: "A revolution cannot be led by shepherds bearing arms" (45). He recognizes that "symmetry in the use of violence does not generate an equality of political benefits for the protagonists" (50–51). He tells Fanon: "[A] politics in arms is as dangerous and incongruous as military politics. At the limit there is no difference between them" (94). Fanon is more open to the possibility of military leadership in the struggle against colonialism.[11] His fear is the creation of a postcolonial neobourgeoisie. Though committed to the political, Abane, a realist, must acknowledge the inevitable role—the temptation—of violence in the political. Indeed, it leads to his assassination—to his refusal, an act itself of perverted violence, to heed warnings of his assassination.

Although *The Name of the Father* takes places decades after the end of the war, its protagonist, SNP, can be described in terms of Fanon's observation in *The Eagles*: "Since it is a systematic negation of the other, a fanatical decision to refuse any attributes of humanity to the other, colonialism drives a dominated people to ask continually: Who am I in reality?" (Benyoucef 2002a, 89). This is the question that SNP constantly asks himself in word and through deed. He is caught in an ever-widening arabesque of being bullied, being tempted, refusing, withdrawing, and engaging. The play, which is the most dramatically successful of the trilogy, begins with a song by a rapper[12] who, emerging from darkness, scrutinizes and then challenges the audience by telling them what they should not expect from the play: no hip-hop, no face-splitting clowning, no alexandrines (rather, *un style malandrin*, "a thug's style"), no tear-jerking, no sex, no intellectuals who puff up (*se péter*) their heads, no facile psychology, no introspection . . . It's a question of the torments of memory, of life buffeted by history: "You know that profane divinity who drinks the blood of its victim[s] from their skulls" (6). As he sings, the title of the play is projected on a screen in its several Lacanian versions: *le nom du père, le non du père, le nondupe erre, the name of the father, the no of the father, the nonduped who wanders, who errs*.[13] The Lacanian pun captures SNP's dilemma—and, by extension, that of the Harkis—for it calls attention to the question of identity as it is vested in the father's name, in his authoritative no, his refusal (in the Harkis' case) to talk, in the negation of having been duped, in wandering, indeed, in erring, as disillusioned. Those who are not duped wander; in wandering do they err?

The play takes place in France and then in Algeria sometime in the 1990s when the Algerian government is caught in a violent struggle with competing Islamist and other political factions. It consists of a series of scenes that follow one another autonomously, without any necessary connection, like a picaresque tale, figuring destiny in all its terrible absurdity, yet motivated in the instance by the insistent reality of history, its violence, its violation, ultimately, by Tergou. She never actually makes an appearance, as she did in *The Eagles*, but her effect is omnipresent. At first paralyzed, if at times self-indulgently, by his camp experiences and, more realistically, by the prejudices of French society, SNP is forced into conflicting roles by Islamists and their warring factions; by a "special" branch of the French army that bullies him into infiltrating the Islamists; by the Algerian army, which wants him to reinfiltrate the Islamists and, eventually, return to France to continue the war against them (i.e., as it was put to him, "to take advantage of the military aid Paris gives to the apostate power in Algeria" [Benyoucef 2002a, 70]);[14] and by his love for a French schoolteacher named Christiane, who wants him to move in with her.[15]

There is, as the rapper says, no introspection. How can there be in this whirl of identities? SNP can only act out, despairingly at times, with bitter irony at others, that which is prescribed and once prescribed, inevitable. The line between inner motivation and outer coercion is never clear. Indeed, inner and outer are reflections of each other. Not only does the life space reflect the self, as Agnès, a psychologist, tells SNP in the first scene, but the entanglements of plot or lack thereof also reflect the confusions of motivation and nonmotivation, of strategy and thoughtlessness, in—for lack of a better term—SNP's soul space.

As the play opens, we find SNP in a slovenly state in a room in a Harki camp that is littered with empty beer cans and a plate overflowing with cigarette butts.[16] He is talking to Agnès, who shakes her head in a gesture of disapproval and helplessness. He is in his thirties, immature, trapped in and by the camp. Whenever he tries to leave, he always ends up returning. In lines that are reminiscent—though less delicate and more critical of the father—of those that I heard from many of the Harki children with whom I talked, he describes his experience in the camp:

> We didn't know anything but the camp, the camp school, the camp teachers, the camp guards, the camp director, the camp curfew, the glacial wind in the camp in winter, the molten heat in the camp in the summer. . . . And nothing else to do but walk around the camp looking at our mothers muffled up in their covers, with their dresses on top of each other. . . . And our fathers . . . the shame of our fathers, sitting, sheltered from the wind, under the barrack walls, smoking and looking out in front of themselves. . . . But it's not the future they see because here there is no future. It's not there for anyone. It's their past that they do not stop looking at and ruminating on! Because their past—they can never swallow it [*Parce que leur passé, il ne leur est jamais passé*]! It lies across their throats. . . . And it's their past that has prevented us from having a present and that eats up our future. (Benyoucef 2002a, 9)

SNP resists all Agnès' efforts to make him to do something with his life. He says that all his efforts to get the better of the camp have failed. He joined Harki associations, participated in all their protests, burned the camp at Bias, occupied Saint-Laurent-des-Arbres, another camp, went on hunger strikes, fought with the CRS (Compagnie républicaine de sécurité, the French state security police), and went to prison. He left the camp three times, looking for work, but even with his diplomas in soldering and mechanics he could never find anything. It's not that he didn't try, he tells Agnès: "Thanks to you, I learned that I must question my thoughts and actions and try to understand what they mean [*riment*] because finally everything makes sense. And it's that way that I discovered that there's absolutely nothing in us. The camp has eaten up our insides. . . . Of course there are moments when you believe that you're free, that you can change the order of things, build a splendid future. . . . But that's a dream, delirious, not real" (Benyoucef 2002a, 11). Does SNP grasp the implication of his observation? Does Agnès? Fanon, the Fanon of *The Eagles* at least, would have appreciated the role of introspection, real or not, in displacing, indeed, in eliminating, consideration of real-life impediments.

As SNP describes his search for work, he tells Agnès that his name had been changed from Ali Lakjaa, "the lame" in Arabic, to Alain Boiteux, "the lame" in French. (Many Harkis had their names changed by the authorities when they filed papers in France; others changed their names voluntarily; and still others, the majority, kept their Arab or Berber names.)[17] But, later in his conversation, SNP asks her not to call him Alain any more. "I don't want to hear myself called by that name," he says excitedly. "It not my name. It's a name [*sobriquet*] others have chosen for me. Without asking my advice." He doesn't want to be called Ali either because his father gave him that name and he does not want to owe him anything. "It's a little late to kill the father," Agnès observes dryly before asking him what she should call him. He answers, SNP. "So you have decided to become nobody," she says, leaving him. "You know where to find me if you want to talk" (Benyoucef 2002a, 15).

By referring to himself as SNP, the protagonist recalls the enormous task the French Algerian administration took on at the beginning of the war. Up until then, the majority of Algerians lived in relative anonymity from an administrative point of view. "For one hundred twenty-four years," Michel Roux (1991, 290), who wrote the first detailed account of the Harkis, observed, "they could be born, live, and die anonymously without any one caring about their civil status [*état civil*] or bothering to know whether they had one." It was only when the French intelligence service, the Deuxième bureau, needed a means of keeping track of potential *fellaghas*—literally, "bandits, freedom fighters"—that a census was taken and identity cards issued. Most Algerians were simply known by their name and the name of their father and, if necessary, their paternal grandfather: for example, Mohammed ben [or ould] Ali ben [or ould] Mohammed (Mohammed son of Ali son of Mohammed) or Fatima bent Ali ben Mohammed (Fatima daughter of Ali son of Mohammed). It was decided that, to ensure identity, it was necessary to include both the father's and the grandfather's name in the census and on identity cards. These names were preceded by SNP. Many of those auxiliaries who made it to France were given (or had to choose) a last name.

SNP takes on various names as he moves from one identity to another.[18] Before asking him to choose a name, the French commander who recruits him observes: "To name is too important to leave in the hands of parents or immigration authorities. To name something is to give it life. And it's the same with human beings" (Benyoucef 2002a, 30). On this occasion, SNP names himself Elias because it sounds like *alias*. "Up until now I was only an alias," he says as he accepts the role the commander gives him. With the Islamist, he is given no choice. He is told that his new name is Abou-Chafra, the son of the sword (39). The Algerian commander also gives him a name, Lieutenant Lyès, after asking him what his real name is. "The brothers finally gave you a name?" the commander asks. "I thought I could find an identity among them," SNP answers. "So you dumped your old name," the commander says, noting that that is perfectly understandable, especially for those (by which he means the Harkis) who had to take on a French name. "But you have rejoined your camp, the true one, the only. The camp of your blood, of your earth" (68–69). Of course, the commander misses the irony. He offers SNP no choice of name. It is not clear that SNP catches it either.

The name changes are symbolic of SNP's inability to assume a permanent identity. They are like the costumes he wears: ordinary Western clothes, those of an Islamist, and those of a *maquisard*, a guerrilla fighter. They are also like the several languages he uses. At times he speaks near-schoolbook French, at others one argot or another (rap, Beur, military). When he mixes them, the result is incongruous, revealing an absence of a fixed perspective. When he tells the Algerian commander that he thought he could find an identity among the Islamists, we (and, it would seem, SNP) do not know whether he means what he is saying. Does he mean he really thought he could find an Islamist identity? Or is he acting the role of a French spy? Or is he simply speaking strategically to save his neck? He is, after all, in enemy territory. Can there be any introspective certainty in such a position? Or are there only multiple and contradictory introspective stances? Our deepest psychological assumptions that center around a fixed point, as illusory as it may even be, are challenged.

Not only are the events, the roles and identities, that befall SNP arbitrary and autonomous, as though they are the debris of a fractured destiny, but so are many of his own acts. He does not have to accept the identities offered him, but he does. Suddenly, in one of the most brutal scenes in the play, he kills, without any apparent need to, an old man who has been pleading for the life of a young Algerian recruit who has been condemned by Abou-Laala, the leader of the Islamist faction SNP has joined. The scene, one of the longest in the play, is so filled with black humor, so grotesque in its depiction of Islamist justice, that one wonders how the Harki critiques of the play could not appreciate Benyoucef's condemnation of all sides in the Algerian War and its violent aftermath. Abou-Laala arbitrarily condemned to death one innocent villager after another—for adultery (a man and a woman who were simply seen alone together, the man turning out to be gay), for writing plays (presumably referring to the assassination of the Algerian playwright Abdelkader Alloula, whom Benyoucef has translated into French), for being a Westernized widow who wears pants, drives a car, and had a demographer husband whom Abou-Laala had had executed. At first, Abou-Laala confuses *demographer* with *democrat*, and then, when he is corrected, he says, "Ah, I see. Those who prescribe pills and other satanic measures to fill garbage cans with fetuses" (Benyoucef 2002a, 51). The recruit is condemned simply because he was drafted. The old man defends him. He knows the family; he saw the police carry him off to the barracks. Abou-Laala threatens the old man with death and then, in a twist worthy of the most Orientalist of tales, ends up marrying the old man's daughter. When the old man asks Abou-Laala not to announce the marriage (for, if he does, the old man and his family will be killed by his fellow villagers for siding with the Islamists), Abou-Laala says, "If I were not your son-in-law, I'd send you to Cairo [put you to death]." It is at this point, in a highly stylized, entranced fashion, that SNP shoots the old man. Abou-Laala praises SNP, and the imam who has been present all along says that he will issue "a postmortem fatwa" (56). As a reward, Abou-Laala divorces the old man's daughter and gives her to SNP as a wife, despite his protests.

Now, overcome by the murder he has committed, SNP tries to lose himself in a massive dose of opium and marijuana. Sakhr, his friend and foil, warns him that the combination will send him through the stratosphere to a meeting with Azraël, the angel of death. SNP ignores his friend's warning. He has a terrifying vision of a past he does *not know* and does not want to acknowledge. A ghost describes how, when the French executed all the young men in his village, the ghost's elder son accused his younger brother of treachery and shot him in cold blood with a revolver lent by the commanding officer. He was rewarded with a combat uniform; that is, he became a Harki. Despite SNP's pleas to stop talking, the ghost, who now identifies himself as SNP's grandfather, tells him that he is now mature enough to take on the burden of his history. "A great rift in the soul [*une grande faille de l'âme*] never finds the path to forgetfulness," the ghost says. "Always identical to itself, it passes from generation to generation. All one can do is try to live with it." The ghost goes on to tell SNP that only one of the two sons could have children and that that son gave a son (SNP) to his childless brother. When SNP asks the ghost who his real father is, the ghost refuses to tell him. "It is a family secret sealed in iron by words pronounced over the Holy Book." "I give you at least the possibility of choice," the ghost says, and, before disappearing, adds, "Don't forget that a man is never more than the sum of his murders. How I pity you little one, adieu" (Benyoucef 2002a, 65).[19]

Real or not, the ghost's revelation reinforces the failure of the father's name, his authority, his ability to name in turn, for there is no certainty in even the father's identity. Was SNP's father killed by his brother? Was he, as his brother maintained, an enemy of the French? A member of the FLN? Or was SNP the son of the murdering brother? A Harki? Had the murdering brother himself been an FLN operative? Had either brother been involved in the war at all? Whoever his real father was, SNP ended up in a Harki camp because he was identified, if not with his real father, then with the father who assumed his paternity. Of course, all these questions rest on a drug-induced vision. There is no certainty. There can, therefore, be no nominal stability.

In the following scene, after SNP has gone over to the Algerian side, to be sent back to the Islamists, he tells the commander, speaking more to himself than to him, that he had come back to Algeria to find his own people, his land, his origins. "Am I permitted to be stupid?" he asks. The commander does not trust him. He wants to know whether SNP has crossed over from the Islamists on an intelligence mission for them. SNP tells him he made the decision after a terrifying night and starts to tell the commander about the vision he had, which, he says, made him conscious of his debt to Algeria. "Perhaps the commander can save . . ." Confusion follows. The commander tells him, "Where there is a debt, there is guilt, and that's a destructive sentiment that can be abolished by the payment of the debt. You have then the historical opportunity to erase your shame no less historic than that of your father" (Benyoucef 2002a, 71). The commander brushes off with a gesture an objection that SNP starts to make. He argues that SNP has no choice but to do as he is told, for it is only by joining the Algerian army as an operative among the Islamists in France that he will make up for his father's treason and the two betrayals he himself has made—to join the French and to join the Islamists. SNP says he agrees (72). But does he?

Trapped, back in the *maquis*, SNP calls Christiane in desperation on an emergency phone the French commander had given him. He tells her of his treachery (the only defect from which he thought himself immune), his entrapment, his love for her, his blindness, which came from pride and the desire for recognition, and the certainty that he will not escape alive. She responds with sentimental clichés about love and the need for self-compassion and at the same time takes the situation in hand. She will contact the French commander Zacharie; SNP should get to the nearest French consulate. As he finishes his call, he is caught by his old Harki friend Sakhr, who wants to arrest him and take him to Abou-Khadra, the leader of an Islamist group, financed by American money, who opposed Abou-Laala's group and through Sakhr's treachery facilitated its destruction. SNP has to talk his way to safety. He convinces Sakhr, always the dimwit, that he has an important meeting in town and will join up with Abou-Khadra the next day. As proof of his word, he gives Sakhr the cell phone and a code word and tells him to have Abou-Khadra call at "eleven o'clock universal time." Abou-Khadra will be rewarded. Reluctantly, Sakhr agrees.

The finale of the play—or is it?—is a projection of an explosion that goes off the following morning when Abou-Khadra makes the call and gets the nasalized voice of an American. Exalted, SNP cries out, "Bingo! Adieu Sakhr! Adieu Abou-Khadra! . . ." and then hysterically, "A man is the sum of his murders! A man is the sum of his murders! Are my sacrifices acceptable, Babylon? Are you going to open your gates to me?" (Benyoucef 2002a, 84). As he runs offstage, shouting, "Christiane wait for me," the rapper reappears and sings, "There you have it. We'll stop here the trials of these poor guys, but you have the right to choose another ending." A happy ending Hollywood style, as in a third-rate Indian film with syrupy music at dawn, or as in a journalist's uncovering the truth of the affair. The rapper starts to leave, hesitates, turns back, and in a confidential tone says, "Not to give you a donkey's kick, we like the Christiane ending" (85). He winks at the audience and sends them kisses with both hands.

Part 4: Discussion

> That which is lived at the moment that it occurs is not History. History is that which is endlessly written and rewritten. It is from this alone that you draw your legitimacy as an actor.
>
> —Abane, in Messaoud Benyoucef's *The Eagles*

Despite the humor, as black as it often is, and the cute ending, which some French reviewers took seriously as a resolution to the play (e.g., Jaulin 2005), *The Name of the Father* is in its relentlessness a terrifying play. Though some critics saw it as *Bildungstheater*, as a growing-up play, it seems to me that it has rather to be understood in terms of the picaresque—a dark, violent, cruel picaresque that puts into question the possibility of *Bildung*, not just for the Harkis, but for all Algerians who have suffered the brutality of colonialism, the violence of the War of Independence, and the carnage that has ensued.[20]

Contingency aside, the events recounted and enacted are motivated by historical circumstances and, as Benyoucef sees it, the violence that always lurks behind the movement of history. The contingency of individual life is, as it were, subsumed under ever-greater contingencies that we call *history* and seek to understand in terms of one narrative or another, often forgetting that the understanding we have is a refraction of the narratives we have created. These narratives, particularly when they are centered on the individual, promote, if not the reality, then the possibility of resolution—of an ending that makes sense. But is there ever resolution? Is there ever an ending that makes sense? It is the picaresque, at least as I see it, that calls attention to the artifice of resolution and meaningful endings, indeed, of any endings. It plays on destiny, which in its boldest formulation resists the seduction of explanation. It is, as the Algerians say, *mektub*—written, a word that Harkis, less so their children, often used. By speaking of the contingencies of their lives in terms of the "written," they avoided explaining what they could not or would not want to explain.

Of course, the Harkis could blame de Gaulle and his ministers for their abandonment, the Algerians for the slaughter of their people, and French racism for their subsequent treatment. It was my impression, however, that they found little satisfaction—I am tempted to write *moral*, indeed, *metaphysical*, satisfaction—in such blame. Specific in its focus, blame could not do justice to the magnitude of their change of fortune and the complexity of their own involvement in that change. However enraged they were by their treatment in Algeria and in France, they had, at some level, to recognize the consequences of their own decisions, however forced on them, and, what was no doubt even more devastating, their impotence before these forces. There lay deep within them a hurt, a wound, a lesion, what the ghost called "a great rift in the soul" (Benyoucef 2002a, 65). They were at once responsible and not responsible for that wound. They knew and did not know what they were getting into when they joined the French.

Did they suffer guilt for the "treachery" they had committed. One Algerian psychiatrist I talked to, who had little sympathy for the Harkis, insisted that they were overwhelmed by such guilt. I did not find evidence of this. If there was guilt, it was contorted by the real pressures put on them by the war. Perhaps SNP expressed it better when he described the fathers of his generation: "The shame of our fathers . . . smoking and looking in front of themselves," not at the future, for they have no future, but at a past "they can never swallow."[21] The past "lies across their throats." One might well add "like a knife." Suicides were frequent, drunken stupors even more so, and depression was a constant. As the ghost remarked, the riven soul will never find the path to forgetfulness.

The Harkis, at least those I talked to, were ashamed of being duped. Though Benyoucef does not develop Lacan's third play on *le nom du père*, *le nondupe erre*, "the nonduped wanders" (and, in my reading, errs), it would seem that Lacan's formulation is not irrelevant to the Harki situation. They were duped by the French, and, in suffering the consequences of their dupery, they were "unduped" and (rather more, perhaps, in reality than Lacan may have meant) have been forced to wander—to live, homeless in their new home, unable in fact and in psyche to return home. That they may have erred sounds, I believe, like a *basso continuo* in their ruminations. But here, in my presumption, I trespass the limits of anthropological understanding.

The name situates the subject within the tissue of signification, within language, within the linguistically classified, if not constituted, world. Naming is, as the philosopher Saul Kripke (1972, 96) observes, a baptism. "An initial baptism takes place," he writes. "Here the object may be named by ostension, or the reference of the name may be fixed by a description. When the name is 'passed from link to link,' the receiver of the name must, I think, intend when he learns it to use it with the same reference as the man from whom he heard it." Kripke is, of course, talking about the names of objects, but he could also be talking about proper names. They too must be used as they are given, and, as they are used, they, like all names, recall the initial baptismal event and the authority that lies with it. To name is a performative act, and the name giver must have the authority to name. In patriarchic societies like Algeria at least, that authority lies, as Lacan would no doubt have stressed, with the father—in his name (for he is already incorporated within the linguistically endorsed universe), in his ability to say no, that is, in his identification with the law. "We must recognize support for the symbolic function in the *name of the father*, who since the beginning [*orée*] of historical time identifies his person with the figure of the law" (Lacan 1966, 278).[22]

In his silence, has the father lost the ability to name? It would certainly appear so in SNP's case.[23] He rejects the name his father gave him. He refuses the debt imposed on him by that name. "I don't want to owe that man anything," he tells Agnès, the psychologist, and she understands his rejection in Oedipal terms. "It's a little late to effect the murder of the father," she says.

"But if you have to follow that route . . ." (Benyoucef 2002a, 14). She interrupts herself with a gesture of helplessness. She recognizes that the murderous desires of the son will not free him from the debt he owes his father. Rejected or not, the name will adhere, if only through negation. *Sans nom patronymique* still evokes the name SNP's father has given him as well as his father's own name and all it symbolizes and demands.

That SNP made no effort to find out the circumstances that led to his father's joining the French, that he refused, as the ghost would have it, to accept the burden of history, would have been rare, in my experience, among Harki children. That he knew nothing about his father's fratricide (if we are to believe the ghost), that he had no idea of his father's sterility (if, indeed, his father was sterile), and that he will never know his father's true identity are exceptional circumstances, but they dramatically symbolize the faulted role of the father, *le père barré*, for Harki sons and their children, as Benyoucef expresses it in his insistent but teasing Lacanianism.[24] That the information is conveyed by a ghost suggests the phantasmatic dimension of such knowledge that resists as it insists on the reality of the father—his authority. The paradox—resistance and insistence—is mirrored, not only in SNP's inability to escape the effect of his father's name, but also in the replay of his father's paralysis in his own paralysis as he sits in the beginning of the play drinking beer and smoking cigarettes in his room. Wittingly or unwittingly, he takes on the burden his father has bequeathed him. Is SNP destined, then, to repeat his father's history? When Zacharie, the French commander, explains SNP's mission, SNP stands up, pale, and says, "Ah, I understand! After the father, it's the son's turn to be used against his fellow men [*congénères*, suggesting "genus, tribe, of the same birth"]! (*He hits his head with his fist.*) But what can I be, weak . . ." (Benyoucef 2002a, 32). Zacharie, who always plays the tough guy, ignores him and continues to explain the mission.

Is the murder of the father or father substitutes the only means of escape? The ghost suggests this when he tells SNP to remember that "a man is only the sum of his murders." SNP repeats these words hysterically after Abou-Khadra and his friend Sakhr are blown up in the final scene of the play. Is our destiny inexorably determined by the Oedipal drama? It should be remembered that SNP shot the old man—a father figure—who was defending the young recruit. He seems never to have been protected by his own father, whoever he in fact was. We must also remember that, for Benyoucef, violence is the midwife of history, and one of the Islamists in *The Name of the Father* refers to the "mother of battles" (Benyoucef 2002a, 17). Is violence, the murder of the father, then, inspired by women—by the mother? Women too, it would seem, inspire their own murder. In the penultimate scene, as SNP leaves for the French consulate in Algiers, the old man's daughter, whom Abou-Laala gave to SNP as a wife, suddenly appears, demands her marriage rights, informs SNP that she is pregnant, and, though SNP has never slept with her, insists that, according to the sharia, he is legally the father. SNP kills her. It would seem that such a mechanistic, indeed, stereotypic, conclusion does not do justice to the complexity of the events recounted and enacted. Fanon of *The Eagles* would certainly find it unsatisfactory, for it fails to take account of the historical reality in which the drama is played out. Of course, Benyoucef tantalizes us with the possibility of escape. Women—two women at least, both of them French, one, in particular, named significantly Christiane—offer the possibility of escape from the real and psychological entanglements of history, as the rapper, with a wink and kisses blown to the audience, says he would prefer to end the play. But the action of the play does not end that way. The rapper stops it arbitrarily. "There you have it. We'll stop here the trials of these poor guys."

Part 5: A Return to the Complaint

> The facts that I am going to evoke leave no place for any type of distance. . . .
> Impossible to be clever with them or to count on the artifices of performance
> [*représentation*] to hold them at a respectable distance.
>
> —The Writer in Messaoud Benyoucef's *The Eagles*

Even a cursory reading of Mohammed Haddouche's letter of complaint reveals the pain that *The Name of the Father* inspired in him and other Harkis and their children who attended or read the play. It is obvious that many more joined the protest without having any firsthand knowledge of the play. In fact, several Harki activists with whom I spoke claimed to know nothing about the play or thought the protests to be a waste of time. The principal goal of associations like AJIR and Générations mémoire Harki is to advance the Harki cause. They lobby the government for compensation for their losses and recognition of their sacrifices for France. They are particularly sensitive to any slur on the community and do their best to call attention to its injustice in as public a manner as possible. For them, Benyoucef's play—and, particularly, its subvention by the government—was an insult.

It is of significance that Haddouche opens his complaint by noting that Benyoucef is of Algerian origin. Jacques Lévêque, the president of AAAAS, another association of Algerian repatriates, which joined the complaint, wrote plainly in the newspaper *Paris-Normandie* (March 18, 2005), "It is absolutely intolerable that an Algerian author comes to insult on French soil the Harkis who have remained faithful to France." Though many of the younger Harki children are beginning to associate with Algerians living in France, the two groups do not identify with each other (Fabbiano 2006). Memory of the slaughter in Algeria as well as the violence directed toward the Harkis by Algerians living in France when they first arrived are very much alive. Both the Harkis and their children continually complain, often enough with little justification, that the immigrants are treated better than they are. "We are the traitors in the eyes of the French, despite all we have done for France," I have heard them say. Despite the intensity of their resentment of the Algerians, it would be a mistake to dismiss the Harkis' reaction to Benyoucef's play on the grounds of his being Algerian. They are distressed by the disparaging, cliché-filled image the play presents of them without realizing that Benyoucef is using SNP and his foil, Sakhr, as figures for conveying the ruinous effects of the war and its aftermath. Their reaction to the play is, of course, familiar in a multicultural world that is rife with sensitivities.

I do not want to diminish the pain felt by one discriminated-against group or another here. Rather, I want to call attention to one important characteristic of such reactions. They are responses to a pejorative image, often intensely visual, that is so powerful that it effaces, if it does not obliterate, most of the historical circumstances of its occurrence. Distance—critical, aesthetic distance—is nearly impossible under such circumstances. Put in technical terms, the iconic power of the image is so strong—the pain that lies behind it, in this case, is so intense—that the indexical force of the image, to call up its context, is redirected to the image itself, extinguishing or at least dramatically reducing the relevance of the image's surround. There follows a series of often stereotypic associations with the image that appear to be unconstrained by context, genre, convention, and prevailing norms. Haddouche's protest contains the usual litany of Harki complaints: accusations of treachery, the failure to recognize that the Harkis were opposed, not to Algerian independence, but to the terror of the FLN, the Algerians' refusal to respect the Treaty of Evian, the perpetuation of the rumor that Harkis' sons attempted to destabilize the Algerian government by supporting the militant Islamists (the GIA) and, implicitly at least, impugning the Harkis' loyalty to France. Now, I am not questioning the truth of this list of complaints—they are incontestable—but are they the subject matter of Benyoucef's play? Did he intend to slur the Harkis? Or did he simply figure them rhetorically, as he did the Islamists, the French secret service, the Algerian military, and even Agnès and Christiane, to dramatize his argument?

So removed is Haddouche's litany of complaints from even the text that he accuses Benyoucef of arguing that the Harkis and their children are possessed of genes for treachery. This is not the case. It is true that the ghost speaks of the passage from generation to generation of the riven soul. The Algerian commander also speaks of his camp as being the camp of SNP's blood (Benyoucef 2002a, 69). But these views are voiced by characters in the play and must be treated as such. They are figures of speech. The same claim cannot be made, however, for Haddouche's use of *genes*, but his usage is, I think, a response to Benyoucef's pessimism—his stress on the repetition of trauma and its effect, on the inevitability of the son's patricidal desires, and on the role of violence as the "midwife" of history. Haddouche wrote, it will be recalled, that the playwright "pushes ignominy to the point of writing that treachery is perpetuated through blood and by crime since the son 'must sacrifice the father' and betray in turn." Entrapped, SNP cannot escape his heritage; he is destined to slovenliness, confusion, murder, conflicting commitments and loyalties, and an identity imposed on him by others—his father, the French, the Algerians, and, ultimately, Tergou—that precludes the cultivation of his own identity. It is as though his insistent heritage is the symbolic equivalent of the incarceration of the Harkis in the camps. The image is devastating, and it certainly does not do justice to those Harkis and their children who have been able to overcome or are struggling with the impediments of a crushing marginalization. What the Harkis found most disturbing about this play is, I believe, its representation of their indelible inscription within a sweep of history that they can neither erase nor escape.

TWO

The Historical Background

The fact is that none of our colonies was ever treated as Algiers. In one form or another all of them were allowed agency [*action*] by the local population or at least the administration of local revenues by the local authorities. Algiers is unique in wrongdoing [*mal*], even in the middle of our detestable colonial system.

—Alexis de Tocqueville (1841)

The Harkis like to say that they are France's conscience—its guilty conscience, its shame. However insightful these observations may be, they have become an easy way for the Harkis to describe their situation. Like all clichés, they are not without some truth. And, in fact, I have heard French of both the Right and the Left make similar remarks. They tended to distinguish themselves, sometimes with disgust (particularly those on the Left) and sometimes with anger (typically those on the Right), from that France, those French, as they acknowledged their own, their critical "Frenchness." They showed, in my experience, little collective guilt or sense of responsibility. It was simply a sad fact of history.

What was this sad fact—these sad facts—of history? The Algerian War of Independence was certainly one of the bloodiest, most savage of the struggles for independence that followed World War II. It was deeply disturbing not only morally and politically, as all wars are, but also in terms of the self-image, the honor, each side wanted to preserve. Algeria has always had a special relationship with France. Unlike its other colonies, Algeria had been, legally, part of France since 1848, was administered at first by the military and then by the Ministry of the Interior, and had over a million European settlers, most of whom were French citizens. The war was both a revolution, as the Algerian nationalists like to say, and a civil war that threatened France itself. I use *revolution* with some hesitation since the Arabic word, *thawra*, which has been translated as *revolution*, is perhaps better translated as *uprising*, though no doubt it has, and had, taken on the ideological connotations of "revolution."[1] The war has certainly been cast as a revolution by the Algerian government that followed independence (Liauzu 2004, 167–170). The French never referred to it as a *revolution*; in fact, it was not until June 10, 1999, that the French National Assembly officially recognized it as a war. Until then, the French had referred to it as *les événements* (the events) or "police operations." They made it clear that the proper name of the war is the Algerian War (*la guerre d'Algérie*), not the war in Algeria (*la guerre en Algérie*). It was for not just ideological reasons that the French refused to recognize the "events" as a war but, as the historian Benjamin Stora (2004, 215) points out, budgetary ones. Were it declared a war, the French would have had to indemnify the thousands of wounded and traumatized among the 1.4 million soldiers who had fought in it.

As a revolution, the war was, on the surface, simply a struggle for independence. The "revolutionaries" were not united in their vision of what an independent Algeria would look like. The civil war was more complicated. It was a war between French and Algerians whose legal status, in practice at least, was at best ambiguous; between the Algerian people and the *pieds-noirs*, as the French residents came to be known at about the time the war started (Baussant 2002, 110–16); between the *pieds-noirs* and, toward the end of the war, the ultranationalist OAS and metropolitan France; and, of course, between the liberation forces and those Algerians, like some of the Harkis, who wanted their country to remain French but under conditions that were more favorable to them. As in the wars in Iraq and Afghanistan, which are being waged as I write, relations between these factions were complex, shifting, and often contradictory.

The aftermath of the war was, in some respects, as troubling as the war itself. I cannot speak of the Algerian response except to note that for nearly fifty years Algerians have lived in often violent, at times anarchic, conditions and in ever-increasing poverty under one ruler after another who has identified his government with the FLN. During the 1990s, violence reached civil war proportions as the secular regime supported by the army fought various Islamist groups vying with one another for power. As many as 200,000 Algerians were killed. This violence, as we have seen it depicted in *The Name of the Father*, became a silent but insistent accompaniment to the conversations I had with the Harkis, echoing, no doubt, memories of the war, the death of relatives, the precarious situation of others, and, perhaps most difficult to admit, a justification for their "betrayal" and, despite their hardships, a sense that, living in France, they may have been favored. When I ask them what they thought about what had happened in Algeria since they left, most of them shook their head in despair. It seemed to me that they preferred to live with their memories—an observation that was seconded in far stronger language by one of their children, a politically engaged university student, who had married an Algerian woman and often visited Algeria. He argued that the Harkis finally had to move in the reverse direction: to ally themselves with Algeria.

The Algerian War and its aftermath lie heavily on the French. Both during and since the war, the French have failed to reconcile themselves with their conduct as a nation and as individuals (Harbi and Stora 2004; Stora 2004; Liauzu 2004). Particularly for those, mostly on the right or extreme right, who were pro–French Algeria to the war's end and even afterward, but, at some level, for most French, the loss of Algeria, following soon after their surrender to the Germans during World War II and their defeat in Indochina, was a severe blow to their national pride.[2] They have been burdened by the acts of violence—torture and summary executions—their military forces committed. How those who fought have come to terms with their engagement in the war is couched in silence. Many are distressed by the shoddy way they treated the million or more *pieds-noirs* who fled to France; by their failure to integrate—or even to save the lives of—those Algerians, like the Harkis, who sided with them and those who, since the war, have immigrated to France; and by the difficulties of reconciling, on at least a political level, supporters and opponents of Algerian independence. France, it should be remembered, was on the brink of civil war toward the end of the war. Rarely, in my experience, do the French refer to the disabled soldiers, some of whom are still lying in military hospitals. Though many French stress the need to work through their experiences, few have made any public claim to have done so.[3] They seem always to refer to others. They argue that most people's response to the war has been one of denial— "a forced amnesia," as one woman put it.

Recently there has been a flood of books, articles, documentaries, and colloquia on the war from all sides of the political spectrum. Benjamin Stora (2004) estimates that over three thousand works (*ouvrages*) in French on the war were published between 1955 and 2002. He notes that a lull in their appearance from the end of the war to 1982 has been followed by "massive and multiform work" on the memory of the war.[4] I am tempted to argue that, through this near-obsessive textualization of the war, the French are seeking, if not achieving, distance and disengagement—they would say perspective—on the war. They are, in other words, seeking a story: a self-affirming narrative of reconciliation with an idealized self-image. Of course, they would stress the importance of "objective accounts." I do not want to deny the good faith in which most of these accounts are made, but, as in all moral and moralizing discourses, there are, in attempts at coming to terms with one's past, manifest and hidden dimensions to their production and circulation. Through revelation, one usually seeks expiation.

Violence is contagious, and no war has been without its abuses. From the moment France invaded Algeria in 1830, the relationship between the French and the Algerians has been a violent one, at times dramatic, as in the war, but most of the time banal, as in the *colons'* daily show of superiority over their workers as they exploited them and, less forceful to be sure, the petty resistance, the refractoriness, of the Algerians to the *colons'* demands. It has been argued that reasons for this violence lie in the character or social organization of the Algerians; one could, of course, say the same for the French, at least the *colons.* Such arguments are as dangerous as they are fallacious since they fail to acknowledge that violence is always relational and, as such, dramatically produced, through the engagement, as asymmetrical as it may be, of all its parties. By casting blame on the other, on their character, their social circumstances, such arguments are simply exculpatory. This is not to say that there is not an initiator of violence. It was the French who invaded Algeria but in response to Algerian corsairs attacking their ships. Any initiation is never really a beginning, for it is embedded in history. It has a past; it occurs in a context that, paradoxically, it helps frame. The declaration of an event as the origin of violence figures violently in that violence. An artifice, however socially necessary it may be, and it seems always to be so, it perpetuates the violence by casting blame, by assuming a morally superior stance, by oversimplifying the situation, ultimately, by turning an event, the postulated beginning, into a figure of political and moral rhetoric. An easy moralism substitutes for a rigorously realistic morality.

We often speak of the theater of war, referring to the arena in which the war is carried out, but there is another sense in which a war can be regarded as a theater. It displays the social and political assumptions, the structural contradictions, and the tensions that prevail in each of the warring parties and in their relations with one another. Arising out of violence—the violence of war—the displays themselves are violent in effect. In contrast to highly ritualized wars, in which the assumptions come to be celebrated and the contradictions and tensions appear for the moment at least to be resolved, much as myths give the illusion of resolving the paradoxes of social and cultural life, the less ritualized modern wars, in which civilians are subject to attack, have a more devastating effect on the societies at war.[5]

I am referring here, not to their massive destructive capacity—that is obvious—but to their barely constrained, barbaric violation of what used to be recognized as the rules of war as well as the social and political etiquette, the symbolic forms, that preserves any social formation from the acknowledgment of its artifice—the fragility, the arbitrariness of that artifice.[6] In remembrance of René Claire's brilliant film *La grande illusion*, we may speak of illusions and illusions of illusions. These violations are, I believe, among the reasons why wars have become so morally and politically destructive of the societies that engage in them even when they themselves lie outside the theater of war. Put another way, we can say that modern wars, at least, are deconstructive in a double sense. They literally deconstruct, that is, destroy, the warring societies, and they deconstruct, that is, expose the artifice of, those warring societies and their relations with one another. Unmediated by ritual, or mediated only by empty ritual, the interplay between these two deconstructive modalities appears to be particularly lethal.

The revolutionary wars of independence, as they were figured in military treatises of the time of their occurrence, had rules of engagement that were different from the Europeans' conventional ones.[7] The independence fighters did not have organized armies that could engage with the trained armies of the colonial powers. In Algeria, it was not until well into the war that the FLN was able to mount a trained army, but that army remained, for the most part, across the border in Tunisia and Morocco and, despite continual skirmishes, served primarily as a potential threat—a reminder of the FLN's increasing strength. To the end, the war was an asymmetrical one in terms of not only the relative number of combatants but also their different strategies and counterstrategies.[8] The Algerians, like other independence fighters, depended on small-scale attacks, ambushes, acts of terrorism directed at both their enemy and their own people. They bombed important and, perhaps more significantly, strategically unimportant targets, like post offices, cafés, and marketplaces. What is most characteristic of these wars of independence was their exploitation of contingency and unpredictability. One never knew when and where the independence fighters would strike next and what tactics they would use; they depended less on winning battles than on creating fear, ultimately, on the erosion of their enemy's morale and will to fight, producing, thereby, the conditions for a political settlement. Their strength lay in their Marxist-inspired ideologically vested commitment to national liberation.

The colonialist armies had, on the other hand, to depend largely on their size, sophisticated weaponry, and seemingly infinite materiel, the cultivation of informers, the sweeping clearance of enemy-infested areas—what the French call *ratonnage*, or "rakings"—and tight policing activities to maintain order. In Algeria, they depended on quick helicopter raids and the frequent use of torture in their interrogations. They moved whole communities, thought to be harboring or supporting the FLN, into enormous camps far removed from their villages. These camps became hotbeds of anticolonialism.

I am not a military expert and make these observations in a tentative manner to call attention to some of the features of anticolonial wars that are conducive to their atmosphere and the reinforcement of their mission and its accompanying ideology or, more accurately, at least in the case of Algeria, ideologies. One of the most salient characteristics of these wars was that, for the colonial powers, the wars took place abroad and, for the colonized, they were waged at home by powers from abroad of incalculable, near mythic strength. The homelands of the colonial powers were not usually threatened by war, and their citizens were often quite indifferent to it. The Algerian War was exceptional. There were violent protests in the métropole, terrorist incidents, internecine fighting among the Algerians living there, mass arrests, a real threat of civil war, and a coup d'état.

Caught between the colonial homeland and their own homes in the colony, in, as it were, enemy territory, the colonists found themselves in a particularly vulnerable position. They risked losing everything and were blinded by that risk. Their attitudes toward the colonized (as primitive, racially inferior, and incapable of governing in any civilized manner) led them to hard-line policies of defeat and total and arbitrary control.[9] In the Algerian case, given their number (over a million) and the length of their settlement—some families had been there for over a hundred years—the *colons'* position was so uncompromising that, toward the end of the war, the ultranationalists—the *ultras*, as they were called—viciously terrorized the Muslim population, randomly their own, the metropolitan French, the army, and those in their own ranks whom they suspected of sympathizing with the Algerian cause or having concluded that Algerian independence was inevitable.

Just as the Algerian War of Independence displayed some of the organizational features of colonialism, so too did it display some of the structural conflicts of Algerian society that predated the arrival of the French in 1830 and their annexation of "Algeria" on February 24, 1834. At the time, Algeria was under weakening Ottoman rule, which never seriously aimed at transforming Algerian society but sought to extract as much wealth as it could through taxation and expropriation. There was at the time no nationalist feeling or even a concept of the nation. It was the French who named Algeria Algeria in 1839. As elsewhere in the Ottoman Empire, each ethnic group was represented by a guild that exercised control over its own population, thus preserving the social character of each.

Like other North African societies, Algerian society was organized into lineages, clans (Arabic *firis*; Kabyle, *adhrums*), and tribes, which were the weakest unit (Evans-Pritchard 1949; Montagne 1930; Ruedy 1992, 4). These various segments united when faced with a common enemy or cause. Their relationship is reflected in the common saying, I against my brother, my brother and I against our cousins, and so on. Not only was this segmentary organization conducive to vendettas that could last for decades, but it limited alliances, under most circumstances, with other similarly organized tribal groups, for they did not share common ancestors. One group could conquer another, but it could not integrate that other group. Intertribal relations were, in consequence, unstable and short-lived. The remnants of the segmentary system, and the feuds associated with it, which were still particularly strong in remote areas of the country, played a significant role during the war in the recruitment of both liberation fighters and Harkis and their respective pursuit of the war.

The ostensible reason for the French invasion of Algeria was to halt the piracy carried out by Algerian corsairs; its immediate justification concerned the payment of debts owed France by the dey of Algiers, who had lost his temper over these debts three years earlier and had struck the French consul with his fly whisk, calling him "a wicked, faithless, idol-worshipping rascal" (Horne 1987, 29).[10] The French invasion produced, as Alexis de Tocqueville (2003, 47), who visited Algeria in the 1840s, noted, anarchic conditions as the Ottoman government collapsed and the French military had not yet had time to "pacify" the country.[11] In fact, there was considerable debate in Paris about whether France should limit its occupation to the Algerian littoral, expand inland, or abandon its presence altogether.

The French encountered unexpectedly strong resistance from the Algerians, particularly from the legendary Abd al-Qadir, who, in 1832, at the age of twenty-five, began a struggle that was to last fifteen years before he was finally defeated, imprisoned in France, and then exiled to Damascus.[12] (France's military presence in Algeria increased rapidly. By 1840, it numbered 108,000 men, or nearly a third of the entire French army.) Fighting was so brutal that many of the young and idealistic officers, just graduated from Saint Cyr, expressed enormous shock in their letters home at the way in which they were ordered to treat the indigenous population. Lucien François de Montagnac wrote on March 15, 1843, that the way to make war on the Arabs was to "kill all the men above fifteen, take all the women and children, load them on ships, send them to the Marquesa Islands or elsewhere, in a word, annihilate all of them who do not grovel at our feet like a dog" (Montagnac 1885, 299; see also Sullivan 1983). Pillage, rape, burning homes, and scorching fields were rampant. The governor-general of Algeria, Thomas-Robert Bugeaud, Duke of Isly, was called back to Paris in 1846 because word of his cruel repression of the Kabyle Berbers had shocked Paris.[13]

Though I am not willing to push the parallel too far, I note striking similarities between the war of conquest and the war of independence.[14] I remember making this observation to a Harki novelist who was quick to stop me. "Be careful," she said. She assumed that I was attributing violence to the Algerian character, when, in fact, I was suggesting that, from the start, the relationship between France and Algeria rested on violence. I was, I explained to her, wondering whether there was ever a way to escape such initiatory violence. She would not hear of the failure of escape, any more, I suppose, than did those Harkis who protested Benyoucef's play and the intergenerational entrapment it proposed. As I was to find, any expression of cynicism and pessimism on my part usually upset even the most pessimistic and cynical Harkis, as did expressions of intense sympathy. It was as though their objectification in the words of an outsider was too painful in its confirmation of their own position. What the Harkis wanted, I often found, was agreement with what they themselves said, as cynical and pessimistic as it was, in the form they gave it, but not its reformulation from the perspective of an outsider. I was often corrected.

In the 1840s and early 1850s, the French encouraged the rural settlement of Algeria. In 1830, when they entered Algeria, there were about 5,000 Europeans living there. Despite the violence of Arab resistance, the number of settlers increased sevenfold to 37,374 by 1841 and continued to grow rapidly throughout the nineteenth century, reaching 131,283 in 1851, 279,691 in 1861, 412,435 in 1881, and 633,850 in 1901. Growth slowed in the twentieth century, reaching 984,031 in 1954 at the outbreak of the war (Ruedy 1992, 69). Only half the settlers were French; the others were mainly from Spain, Italy, and Malta. Many of the French were impoverished farmers who, looking for work, had fled to Paris and other cities and were responsible for the civil unrest that characterized French urban life from 1830 to 1870. The majority settled in the coastal cities. The rural *colons*, including both small and large landholders, had the most direct influence on the Arab and Berber populations.

The French, especially the *colons*, thought that the Algerians were incapable of governing themselves. "Arab society is not viable; a society whose organic system is fatalism can only perish," one observer reported (quoted [without reference] in Ageron 1979, 14). Such an attitude justified the segregation, exploitation, and domination of the native population as well as the landgrab that followed annexation. As early as 1833, a parliamentary commission reported the abusive treatment of the natives. It spoke of the despoiling of the heirs of men who were arbitrarily executed without trial, the massacre of people carrying safe conducts and of whole populations later found to be innocent, the transformation of mosques into barracks, the occupation of buildings without indemnity, the seizure of religious property (*habous, waqf*), and the destruction of cemeteries (quoted in Ruedy 1992, 50). Attempts by the military and the government in the métropole to put a halt to such abuses encountered the enmity of the *colons* and encouraged in them attitudes of mistrust, suspicion, and a stubborn, collusive opposition that were to last until independence 130 years later.

Aside from the million hectares (2.45 million acres) of dominion land and huge tracts of forest that they inherited from the Turks, the French expropriated still more land on often flimsy grounds. Private purchases of land from the Arabs and Berbers were frequently fraudulent. In 1841, 20,000 hectares were owned by Europeans. In the following decade, that number quintupled, to more than 115,000. By the century's end, it had reached nearly 2 million and, in 1954, at the beginning of the war, over 2.8 million (Ruedy 1992, 69).[15] Already in 1900, the *colons* produced more than two-thirds of all the crops in Algeria, and nearly all those crops were exported to France.[16] Bugeaud's statement to the French National Assembly in 1840 sums up the attitude of many *pieds-noirs*: "Wherever there is fresh water and fertile land, there one must locate a *colon*, without concerning oneself to whom these lands belong" (Horne 1987, 30).

During the first forty years of French occupation, Algeria was run by the military, and, even after the installation of a civilian government in 1870s, the military continued to play a significant role in the administration of the country.[17] It has been argued that confusion between military and civilian rule lasted until the end of the war, culminating in the Generals' Putsch of 1961 (Boulbina 2003, 15; Peyroulou 2004; Thénault 2004). Relations between military and civilian rule were, of course, only one arena in the struggle for power. The local European population seems to have been in constant conflict with the French government. In 1871, after an uprising by the European population (then around 280,000) for greater administrative control, Paris yielded, instituting an administrative structure similar to that in the métropole—one that was to continue until independence and in modified form thereafter. The French historian Charles-Robert Ageron

(1979, 9) argues that the insurrection marked the real beginning of *Algérie coloniale*.[18] A governor-general, who was by tradition never a *colon*, was always appointed by the French minister of the interior.

Unlike Morocco and Tunisia, which were protectorates and, therefore, under the French Ministry of Foreign Affairs, Algeria was administered by the Ministry of the Interior after 1896. This difference of status made it difficult to integrate policies with the protectorates and other colonies, which were under the Ministry of the Colonies. It also posed legal problems that were never fully resolved until independence and even thereafter. As Laure Blévis (2001; see also Langelier 2009, 2–3) argues, the judicial categories— *national, citizen, subject,* and *having the quality of a French citizen* ("ayant la qualité de citoyen français")—remained vague, flexible, and changing as the French attempted to reconcile republican values with colonial practicalities. As French nationals or subjects, but not citizens, Algerians had few rights and virtually no meaningful representation in the civilian government well into the twentieth century.

The decree of July 22, 1834, which declared the annexation of Algeria, made all its inhabitants subjects, but not citizens, of France and, as such, subject to their own laws and customs. The application of Islamic law was, however, limited by decree in September 1842, when local justice was subordinated to French law. Ever-greater restrictions on Islamic law continued throughout the century and well into the twentieth, but, in reality, this legal situation was far removed from the everyday life of most Muslims, except insofar as it facilitated the landgrab (Miège 1992, 103). The jurisconsult of July 14, 1865, granted non-French *colons* French citizenship and recognized Muslim and Jewish Algerians as having "la qualité de Français"; that is, they officially became French nationals of the French Empire. Muslims could become French citizens if they renounced Islam. Few did. On October 24, 1870, the Crémieux Decree granted the Algerian Jews French citizenship. The marginalization of the Muslim population was hardened under the Code de l'indigénat of 1881, which, among other restrictions, prevented Algerians from leaving their villages without permission from French authorities. Restrictions were removed in 1914. It was not until September 20, 1947, that Algerians were finally declared French citizens. In practice, however, rules of personal status (i.e., subject to French or Islamic law), which were promulgated in 1889, remained in effect, thereby preserving the distinction between European and Algerian citizens.[19]

The Algerians who could not find work on the colonists' farms, some of which had been their own, either retreated into the infertile hinterlands or moved to the cities. At times, relations between this proletariat and the poor *pieds-noirs*, the *petits blancs*, "the little whites," as they were called, were fraught.[20] The rural Arab and Berber populations were administered by the Bureaux arabes, which had been started by Bugeaud and run by the military. The administrators had enormous powers and were, for the most part, protective of the people in their district. In 1875, the Bureaux arabes was replaced by a new administrative unit, the *commune mixte*, under powerful colonial administrators.[21] These mixed communities became hot spots in the struggle for independence in part because their administrators were responsible for areas and populations far too big to govern. Both the French and the FLN recruited support from these communities. Many of the Harkis I talked to came from them.

Though the French had educated a small elite, from which this opposition arose, the majority of the indigenous population remained uneducated. On the eve of war in 1954, after nearly 125 years of French rule, 86 percent of the men and 95 percent of the women were illiterate (Ageron 1979; Deming 2006, 533). The figures were a bit lower in the cities. Demands for education were resisted by the *colons*, who argued shamelessly that education would reduce their pool of labor and raise their costs dramatically. Between 1860 and 1870, thousands of mosque schools were closed. In 1892, the French spent five times more on the education of European children than on Muslim children, who were five times as numerous. It has, in fact, been argued that, at the time of annexation, the literacy rate in Algeria was about equivalent to that in France.

Colonization and the impoverishment that accompanied it produced dramatic changes in Algerian social life. By 1914, 32 percent of the rural population had become sharecroppers and 16 percent wager laborers. Forty-eight percent still farmed their own land, but, with the fragmentation of their holdings, the majority of their farms were too small to support them (Ruedy 1992, 98). Pauperization accelerated during World War I and continued until independence and in the years that have followed it. From 1930 to 1955, the gross national product of Algeria increased on an annual basis by only 1.8 percent, while the population of the country increased by 63 percent (Ruedy 1992, 186). By 1954, roughly half the rural population of working age were usually unemployed (Ruedy 1992, 123). The Muslim population in the cities more than doubled as the rural poor fled to the cities, the majority ending up in shantytowns and overcrowded "native quarters." Urban unemployment reached 28 percent in 1954. True, an economically active urban middle class (around 200,000) also grew but at a far slower rate. They were deeply resentful of the small Algerian elite (roughly 5,000–6,000) and the European middle classes. By the 1940s, they had become a fertile field for the recruitment of nationalist militants. After World War II, the middle class replaced the Algerian elite as the dominant force on the political scene (Ruedy 1992, 125).

This is not the place to discuss in detail the rise of nationalist opposition that was to lead to the war. It is, of course, difficult to date the beginning of any social movement. But among the roots of the nationalism of the interwar years were the Jeunes Algériens—the Young Algerians—which was started in the late nineteenth century. A modernizing movement that idealized French culture and demanded equality and assimilation with the French, the Young Algerians were what the French call *les evolués* (the evolved), that is, those who had recognized the superiority of French culture and had adopted it as best they could. They were opposed to the Vieux turbans (the Old Turbans), traditionalists who, at the extreme, believed in the immutability of Islam and held the French responsible for just about all the wrongs in Algeria (Ageron 1979, 228).

These two groups represented the two principal directions that Algerian nationalism was to take: religious traditionalism and secular modernism. In 1931, the traditionalists created the Association of Algerian Muslims, headed by Sheikh Abdulhamid Ben Badis. His puritan teachings were inspired by the Salifi reformists and resembled those of the Wahabis and the Islamists today. Given their desire for an Islamic society, the traditionalists may well have been the first to give momentum to the struggle for independence (Horne 1987, 38). In the 1930s, their main concern was to combat the assimilation with France advocated by Ferhat Abbas, among others. Abbas, a pharmacist from Sétif, took a liberal, secular position, not dissimilar to that of the Young Algerians, advocating a progressive assimilation of the Frenchified Algerian elite with France. By *assimilation*, he meant, not the total abandonment of Algerian culture, as some of his opponents argued, but the integration of French and Algerian culture. Abbas's position, welcomed in Paris, was ruthlessly attacked by the *pieds-noirs*. As one attempt to reform after another failed, stifled by the *pieds-noirs* and the indifference of the metropolitan French, Abbas lost faith in the possibility of assimilation and eventually affiliated himself with Ahmed Messali Hadj, one of the earliest and most determined proponents of Algerian independence. A brilliant orator in both Arabic and French, vain, fearless, often imprisoned, Messali appealed to the Algerian proletariat. More cautious than Messali, Abbas in 1956 joined Messali's enemy, the FLN, whose armed branch wiped out Messali's followers in Algeria but not in France, where the majority of the quarter of a million Algerians living there at the time remained loyal to him (Derder 2001, 13). The two parties fought one another in what came to be known as the Café Wars because each side bombed the cafés the other frequented (Fytton 1961). Over five thousand Algerians were killed in these "wars." With the intensification of FLN assassinations on French soil in August 1958, the government instituted repressive methods—"to defeat the enemy within"—that involved the collaboration of military and civilian authorities. As we shall see in the next chapter, the Harkis were to play a controversial role in this effort.

Ironically, the FLN developed out of the terrorist wing of Messali's party: the OS, or Opération secrète, started in 1948 by Hocine Ait Ahmed and Ahmed Ben Bella, who was to become Algeria's first president. In many respects, the shift from a political to a violent solution to the Algerian problem was the result of the massacre in May 1945 of Algerians in the small, largely Muslim town of Sétif about eighty miles west of Constantine. Rioting broke out at the VE Day celebration (May 8), resulting in the deaths of 103 Europeans; another 100 were wounded. Many corpses were mutilated, women's breasts slashed off, men's genitals stuffed in their mouths. The French response was massive. Planes and ships fired on the Algerians over the next few days, and the area was raked for supposed dissidents. In all, 5,460 Muslims were arrested. Officially, the French claimed that 1,500 Algerians had been killed, but other estimates run from 6,000 to 45,000. (Such enormous statistical discrepancies were frequent during the war. The figures must be taken less as facts than as indices of the intensity of the positions of those who advanced them.) Though shocked, the *pieds-noirs* assumed that their retaliation had ended the dissidence. In fact, it hardened the nationalists' position. Ben Bella, who had fought for the French in World War II, wrote, "The horrors of the Constantine area in May 1945 succeeded in persuading me of the only path: Algeria for Algerians" (quoted in Horne 1987, 28). On November 1, 1954, Ben Bella and Ait Ahmed, who had taken refuge in Cairo, formed the FLN.

It is difficult to describe any war, especially one riven with as many factions as the Algerian. It is conventionally described in terms of a series of battles and other events deemed significant, a procedure that allows its everyday experience—the countless little gestures, the acts of courage and cowardice, the individual deaths and wounds that disappear in the immensity of numbered casualties—to slip away. The battles and significant events give war a shape it certainly does not have as it is pursued. They suggest an inevitability that betrays individual experience, enveloped by a hope or a fear that defies realistic expectation and perspective. During the war's pursuit, the articulation of its course is either (immediately) retrospective and, as such, subject to elaboration and forgetting or projected forward—speculative, probable, hoped for, or dreaded—from an ever-shifting perspective as circumstances change. Rarely accurate when viewed after the fact, these projections do figure in retrospective understanding and the accounts that follow. They are also subject, as I found in talking to the Harkis and others who fought, to narrative capacity. The experiences of those who can tell a story (and have the opportunity to do so) weighs more in our historical understanding than those of the inarticulate and those who prefer to remain silent. The latter are the majority.

The Algerian War is said to have begun on All Saints' Day, November 1, 1954, when the leaders of the *maquis* in Cairo declared a national struggle for "the restoration of the Algerian state, sovereign, democratic, and social within the framework of Islam."[22] They had divided Algeria into six autonomous districts, or *wilayas*, each with its own leader, that became the organizational framework of their struggle. That day, they launched a series of attacks on military and police bases, warehouses, communication centers, and public utilities in several of the *wilayas*. One event in particular has come to mark the passional onset of the war for French and Algerians alike. Two young schoolteachers, Guy and Janine Monnerot, both sympathetic to the nationalist cause, were attacked in the Tighanimine Gorge, high in the Aurès Mountains in eastern Algeria. They had taken a bus that day to visit friends. The bus was ambushed, and they were shot, along with a *caid*, Hadj Ben Saddock, who refused to ally himself with the nationalists. The bus driver, who had been alerted to the ambush, took the *caid* to a hospital, where he died the next day. The teachers were left on the roadside, some say, as a lure for a second ambush. They were not discovered until the following morning. Guy had died, but by some miracle Janine survived. The episode received little attention at first, but it soon became a resonant symbol. For years, the French press has commemorated it by publishing Janine's account or that of the anthropologist and reserve officer, Jean Servier, who had come to their aid.[23]

To illustrate the ardor with which this incident has been incorporated into the French war narrative, let me quote from Janine's testimony published in *La figaro* in 1994. After describing how they were shot, Janine goes on: "I did not understand. I was covered with blood, but I was not suffering. I tore my dress to make a tourniquet. Guy was in coma. He was groaning. I did not know what I could do to help him. He had been hit in the chest. I pulled him tightly against me. Birds of prey began circling around us" (*Le figaro*, October 29–30, 1994, quoted in Boulhaïs 2002, 70–71). Servier's account ends with irritation: "We brought the couple back to Arris. The teacher was cared for. I never received a word of thanks from her. I only know that afterward she never stopped saying that her husband, who, like her, was a Communist sympathizer, was 'a victim of colonialism'" (*Le figaro*, October 29, 1994, quoted in Boulhaïs 2002, 72).

The Toussaint Rouge, as the date came to be called, is equally important for the Algerians. Monuments have been erected and stamps printed with the effigy of the insurrection, and Mustafa ben Boulaïd, who ordered the attack, has become a revolutionary martyr, his name having been given to many public places throughout Algeria. The local Berbers still argue among themselves about who did what and why, sometimes relating the murder of the *caid* to long-standing feuds—feuds, I should add, that played a role in the recruitment of Harkis by Servier (Faivre 1995, 35). These were, in fact, the first Harkis to be employed by the French.

More important was the reaction of the French government. François Mitterrand, who was the minister of the interior at the time and, therefore, charged with Algerian affairs, declared: "The only negotiation is war." Pierre Mendès-France, who was prime minister, established the judicial parameters of the war for France: "One does not compromise when it comes to defending the internal peace of a nation, the unity and integrity of the Republic. The Algerian departments are part of the French Republic. They have been French for a long time and they are irrevocably French. . . . Between them and metropolitan France there can be no conceivable secession" (quoted in Horne 1987, 98). Mendès-France ordered the military to restore order. Over two thousand suspects, mostly followers of Messali Hadj, were arrested. Though he remained in office for only three more months, Mendès-France set the main lines of France's Algerian policy, policy that was to last until the autumn of 1959. It combined rigorous repression of the rebellion with economic, social, and political reform in Algeria and in its relationship with the métropole. Confronted with resistance from the settlers as well as budgetary considerations, reform was to play second fiddle to repression.

Just before his government fell, Mendès-France appointed the anthropologist Jacques Soustelle governor-general. Soustelle had been one of de Gaulle's most trusted lieutenants during World War II. Known for his intelligence, tough-mindedness, and liberal views, he favored reform. He had, however, to temper this with the stubborn demands of the *colons*. Discovering the poverty in which most Algerians, particularly those in the Aurès, were living, he initiated a series of reforms, one of the most important of which was the creation in September 1955 of the SAS (Section administrative spécialisée), or *képis bleus*—a sort of military Peace Corps, as John

Talbott (1980, 117) characterized it—which was to protect the inhabitants of remote areas who might otherwise join the rebels.[24] Each of the four hundred detachments was headed by an officer, fluent in Arabic, familiar with the local culture, and capable of handling rural problems ranging from those in agriculture, education, health, and building to those concerned with the administration of justice. These SAS officers figured in many of the Harki accounts I collected. Many had worked for the SAS or received help from SAS officers and admired them for their evenhandedness.

In the aftermath of the Toussaint Rouge, the FLN continued its terrorist activities on a smaller, more sporadic scale, attacking pro-French Muslims rather than harder targets like military bases and power plants. Often, they terrorized villages in order to gain adherents. Several Harkis told me that they knew of cases where, to prove the loyalty of a recruit, they would send him back to his village to kill someone there, even a relative. At the end of June 1955, frustrated by its lack of progress, the FLN changed tactics and began attacking French civilians regardless of age or sex. On August 20, 1955, a second massacre, which punctuates the war narratives, occurred in and around the coastal city of Philippeville (present-day Skikda). As Alistair Horne (1987, 120) puts it: "Muslims of both sexes swarmed into the streets in a state of frenzied, fanatical euphoria. Grenades were thrown indiscriminately into cafés, passing European motorists dragged from their vehicles and slashed to death with knives or even razors." The carnage was especially intense in El Halia (Ain-Abid), a nearby mining town in which the Algerians miners turned ruthlessly on the *pieds-noirs*, slitting women's necks, slashing their bellies, bashing the brains out of little children, and disemboweling a mother and stuffing her five-day-old son, who had been hacked to death, back into her womb. The outrage was enormous, and France responded, as it had done in the past and would do in the future, with a violence that undercut its own moral position. In this case, orders were given to kill every Arab in sight. Europeans were allowed to defend themselves with arms and formed vigilante groups. In the end, according to Soustelle, the FLN killed 123, of which 71 were Europeans, and the French 1,273 insurgents. Again, the figures are disputed. The FLN claimed, perhaps more realistically, that 12,000 Muslims were killed in retaliation.[25] What makes Philippeville different from previous massacres was that it had been planned. The carnage so shocked Soustelle that he did an about-face and eventually became a staunch supporter of the ultraconservative OAS.[26]

At the beginning of February 1956, the newly elected socialist prime minister, Pierre Mollet, tried to replace Soustelle with a liberal, octogenarian Arabophile, General Georges Catroux, but so violent was the *pieds-noirs'* reaction to the appointment that within a week Mollet was forced to accept Catroux's resignation and appoint Robert Lacoste, his minister of the economy, in his stead. Lacoste was a tough, stubborn bureaucrat, known for his earthy language, who would not even hear of the possibility of an independent Algeria. In March, during a wreath-laying ceremony in Algiers, the *pieds-noirs* pelted Mollet with rotten tomatoes, an insult he never forgot and, some claim, hardened his policy toward Algeria. On March 16, the French National Assembly adopted a law that granted the executive administration "the most extensive powers for undertaking any exceptional measure required by circumstances with a view to the reestablishment of order, the protection of persons, and property, and the safeguard of the territory" (quoted in Talbott 1980, 62).[27] Lacoste dissolved the Algerian assembly, ruled by decree, granted the military and police exceptional powers (Peyroulou 2004, 175), and stepped up military operations. By the end of the year, more than 400,000 troops, roughly twenty soldiers to every FLN guerrilla, were stationed in Algeria. Lacoste's attempt to install a new administrative structure that would give the Algerians some autonomy was blocked, as usual, by the *pieds-noirs*.

Weakened by internal strife, lack of coordination, and mistrust among its leaders, the FLN started calling the war a *jihad* at the beginning of 1956 and prohibited smoking, drinking alcohol, and working for *colons* or the administration. Torture, mutilation (the cutting off of noses, the slicing of lips), and imprisonment for breaches of these rules were not infrequent (Heinis 1977). FLN members who were mistrusted by one faction or another were assassinated. The most notable would be Ramdane Abane, who was one of the protagonists of Beyoucef's play *The Eagles Live in Gloom*.[28] Opposed to the exiled members of the FLN, the so-called exteriors, among them Ben Bella, Abane sought to privilege the political over the military and the "interiors" over the exteriors. To remedy the situation, the principal FLN leaders on both sides called a secret meeting, which took place in a forester's cottage in the idyllic countryside above the Soummam Valley in Kabylia in late August and early September 1956. Ben Bella, who was waiting in San Remo until he could be smuggled into Algeria, arrived only after the meeting was over. Abane, who had probably arranged Ben Bella's delay, took charge of the meeting, which produced a forty-page document that synchronized the movement's political and military activities. The highest authority of the FLN was vested in the thirty-four-member National Council of the Algerian Revolution (Conseil national de la révolution algérienne), within which the five-man Committee of Coordination and Enforcement (Comité de coordination et d'exécution, CCE) formed the executive. In September

1958, the CCE transformed itself into the Provisional Government of the Republic of Algeria. On October 22, the French forced a plane from Morocco carrying Ben Bella and three other organizers of the Toussaint Rouge, Mohamed Boudiaf, Hocine Ait Ahmed, and Mohamed Khider, to land in Algiers, where the four leaders were arrested, transported to France, and imprisoned for the remainder of the war.

By 1957, still weakened by internal strife, which was to continue until well after the war's end, the FLN began an international campaign for support, which was to play an important role in finally ending the war five years later. By this time, the ALN (Armée de libération nationale, the armed branch of the FLN) had become a highly disciplined army of about forty thousand, thirty thousand of whom were stationed abroad on the Moroccan and Tunisian borders. The main ALN tactics were ambushes and night raids. Nearly all the Harkis with whom I talked had at one time or another to fight themselves out of an ALN ambush. The FLN pursued its terrorizing plan, instilling fear in both the *colons* and the Algerians who either were opposed to them or preferred to remain neutral. Kidnapping was common, as were ritual murders and the mutilation of military personnel and *colons* and, later, Muslims who did not support the FLN. The most common form of execution was slitting the victim's throat, which, aside from terrifying the surrounding population, had deep religious connotations. Rémy Valat (2007, 28) suggests that it sacralized the war in the militants' unconscious. Often, the victim was tortured before his execution and mutilated after his death with a bladed weapon (*arme blanche*) that referenced a pre-Islamic belief that anyone so mutilated would never find peace in the afterlife (Valat 2004, 28–29, quoting Meynier 2002, 538).[29] Within two years, over six thousand Algerians and a thousand Europeans had been killed.

Despite these tactics, the FLN did not have the support of most Muslims. To this day, many Harkis claim that their number was always greater than that of the FLN. Gradually, the FLN managed to gain control of large sections of Kabylia, the Aurès, and other mountain areas. The ALN established military administrations in these areas, but they were short-lived for strategic reasons. The "taxes" they collected and the food they requisitioned were resented, even by their supporters. Many Harkis claim that they joined the French because of these strong-arm tactics. Elsewhere, clandestine groups were formed. Still, confusion reigned in the FLN. There were defections, political purges, the settling of old scores, feuds, private wars against rivals, and the establishment of fiefdoms, all of which led at times to near-anarchic conditions. The CCE decided to bring the war to Algiers, where Muslims and European alike were terrorized in order to instill fear and mistrust in both. The FLN stronghold was the Casbah. With over eighty thousand inhabitants, 50 percent of whom were under twenty, it was one of the densest slums in the world at the time (though not by today's standards). With more than 50 percent of the men unemployed, it was an ideal recruiting ground. Still, the FLN was often forced to use intimidation to recruit members and extract funds from its population.

No doubt the most significant encounter of the war was the Battle of Algiers, memorialized by Gillo Pontocorvo's film of that name, which, if its start can be dated, began on September 30, 1956, when three Muslim women planted bombs in the Milk Bar and the Caféteria, locales popular with the *pieds-noirs*.[30] (A third bomb, planted in the Air France terminal, failed to go off.) Violence in the city was increasing daily. With the assassination of the mayor, Amédée Froger, on December 28, Lacoste lost patience and, on January 7, 1957, ordered General Jacques Massu, the commander of the elite Tenth Division of parachutists, to use all necessary measures to destroy the FLN infrastructure. Massu carried out illegal searches in the Casbah and used many of the FLN's tactics, torturing prisoners and instilling terror in the Muslims in the city. The battle finally ended more than ten months later, with the capture of the FLN leader, Saadi Yacef, and the killing of his chief lieutenant, Ali la Pointe.[31] The Battle of Algiers was not, however, a complete loss for the FLN since it proved its power and the fact that the French had to resort to illegal searches and torture.

In November 1956, General Raoul Salan, an intelligence officer with years of experience in the Far East, was appointed commander in chief of the military forces in Algeria. He developed a system of *quadrillage*, that is, forming sectors with permanent garrisons throughout the country. Though successful in limiting insurgency in these areas, it was, in effect, static. The French army began applying a principle of collective responsibility in those villages that were suspected of supporting the FLN. They were bombed. Innocent men, women, and children were killed. Whole villages were moved to barbed-wire encampments where they were subject to continual surveillance. Michel Cornaton (1967/1998, iii) estimates that, by 1961, at least 2.35 million Algerians (or 26 percent of the entire population of Algeria) had been forcibly resettled in nearly twenty-four hundred *camps de regroupement*.[32] Some were hastily built and considered provisional; others, particularly as the war progressed, were planned as permanent villages. Conditions were atrocious. The surrounding land was overgrazed. Several of the Harkis whose families had been forcibly moved to these *regroupement* camps compared them to the transition camps. They described how confused and tired they were as they were forced to march in endless lines for hours, sometimes days, carrying as many of their possessions as they could. In words reminiscent of many of the descriptions of the French camps I heard, Zoulikha, one of the Harki women the Harki activist and writer Fatima Besnaci-Lancou (2006a, 109) interviewed, talked of "being torn from the land of her husband's ancestors" and "packed together like sheep" with strangers: "Night and day, soldiers circulated, checking and arresting suspects and sometimes imprisoning them." As they had no tools, Zoulikha says, they could not cultivate the land. What food they were given, mainly powdered milk for the children, was insufficient. "Hunger weakened [*fragilisé*] a lot the children and old folks. Some lost their lives." Although Zoulikha refers only to men who became Harkis to feed their families, many of the men in the *regroupement* villages escaped across the Tunisian and Moroccan borders to join the FLN.

In 1958, Salan's successor, General Maurice Challe, replaced the *quadrillage* system with a more dynamic approach. He created mobile forces who would be flown by helicopter into areas where insurgents were operating and carry out search-and-destroy missions over and over again until the insurgents were destroyed or had lost the will to continue fighting. To this end, despite de Gaulle's opposition, Challe managed to increase the number of Harkis under his command dramatically, from twenty-six to sixty thousand, for they were familiar with the areas in which the mobile forces were sent and could serve as "trackers."[33] This strategy was so successful that, by the end of 1958, some historians have argued, the French had won the war from a military but not a political standpoint.[34]

It took four more years until Algeria finally gained its independence. Although there were sporadic fighting, ambushes, and acts of terror during these years, the route to independence had become political and diplomatic. The two greatest obstacles were France's initial refusal to negotiate directly with the FLN and the ever-more-insistent, indeed, violent, resistance of the *pieds-noirs*. This is not the place to rehearse the progress of the negotiations; though their outcome affected the Harkis profoundly, they were far removed from the negotiations themselves.[35]

The *pieds-noirs* (and, to a lesser extent, the FLN) took advantage of the weakness of the Fourth Republic and were instrumental in its fall and de Gaulle's assumption of power in June 1958. The sequence of events is complex and confusing. Put simply, rioting broke out in Algiers on May 13 at a ceremony (following a general strike) honoring three prisoners of war shot by the FLN in retaliation for the execution of three FLN terrorists by the French military. Government headquarters were occupied, and a committee of public safety, dominated by the ultras, was formed with Salan at its head to replace civil authority and force René Coty, then president of France, to ask de Gaulle to form a national union invested with extraordinary powers to prevent the abandonment of Algeria. De Gaulle waited until May 29 before agreeing to form a government. His French Algeria position changed over the years. At first, he felt that a special relationship between France and Algeria was still possible, but, as the FLN hardened its position, as foreign pressure for an independent Algeria mounted, and as opposition in France increased, especially after torture by the French army was made public, he was forced in September 1958 to change his position on self-determination. The *pieds-noirs* felt betrayed and mounted an insurrection in January 1960. With the aid of Challe, de Gaulle was able to diffuse it, but the *pieds-noirs* formed vigilante groups that attacked the government and proindependence Europeans.

Far more serious but also short-lived was the so-called Generals' Putsch in April 1961. Supported by the OAS and by the French Foreign Legion, high-ranking military officers, including Challe and Salan, seized control of Algeria, aiming to topple de Gaulle's government. The revolt was quelled within four days, but it left its effect.[36] It has been claimed that one of the reasons Challe joined the putsch was de Gaulle's lack of sympathy for the Harkis. Challe feared (quite rightly, as it turned out) that the eventual peace agreement would not give them any protection (Horne 1987, 537).

As de Gaulle, who was now convinced that Algeria would have to become independent, began serious negotiations with the FLN, the OAS unleashed a terrorist campaign to break the truce that de Gaulle and the FLN had negotiated. It attacked the French army and police, the FLN, Muslims indiscriminately, schools, and hospitals. The carnage was terrible. In March 1961 alone, it threw 120 bombs a day. Finally, in June 1961, it concluded a truce with the FLN, and the way was set for independence.[37] That same June, over 350,000 *pieds-noirs* left Algeria mainly for France, and, within a year, over 1 million had fled. Many pro-French Muslims, including those Harkis who managed to escape slaughter, also fled despite the obstacles to immigration that the French government had created. Only 30,000 Europeans remained. The wealthiest *colons* had already managed to transfer much of their wealth abroad, but the majority of them, especially the *petits blancs*, arrived in France penniless.

On July 1, 1962, 6 million of the 6.5 million eligible voters in Algeria voted for independence. In France, 90 percent of the electorate had already voted in April to ratify the Treaty of Evian. Though the treaty was signed on July 4, 1962, the Algerians celebrate their independence on the following day, July 5, when 132 years earlier France invaded Algeria. It is said that the war cost France more than 50 billion francs. The cost of human lives is still controversial. The French military estimated in 1962 that 227,000 Muslims were killed in the war; in 1985, *Le monde* raised the figure to between 300,000 and 500,000. The Algerians claim that 1.5 million died. More recently, the historian Guy Pervillé (2004, 694) estimates that there were 1.5 million victims. Of these, more than 500,000 soldiers, civilians, women, and children were killed or disappeared, and 1 million were wounded. What is clear is that the FLN killed more Algerians than Europeans—some claim as many as 140,000 (Talbott 1980, 246; Pervillé 2004, 716). The French lost between 17,000 and 25,000. As many as 55,0000 *pieds-noirs* are said to have died in the war. Put in terms of the total population of each group at the end of the war, the Algerians lost between 2.5 and 2.7 percent, the *pieds-noirs* between 0.5 and 0.6 percent (including the missing), and the French 0.05 percent (Pervillé 2004, 715, quoting Ageron). The actual figures will never be known.

Violence did not end with the ratification of the Treaty of Evian. On July 5, between two and three hundred *pieds-noirs* were killed in the city of Oran.[38] Sporadic killings continued for several months. The massacre of the Harkis, which had begun in March after the Evian agreements, increased dramatically in late August. On August 22, de Gaulle escaped an attempted assassination by the OAS at Petit-Clamart, which intensified France's fear that the OAS, aided by the Harkis, would continue its terrorist campaign in metropolitan France.

THREE

The Harkis

Since the French first colonized Algeria, the juridical and popular classification of the peoples of Algeria, including European settlers, has presented
problems that reflect the precarious relations between the two countries
(Baussant 2002). The names—the categories—of different populations have
been inconsistent, at times contradictory, and have often been changed over
the 132 years of French colonization and in subsequent years.[1] The many
names that have been used to designate those Algerians who sided with the
French in one manner or another during the war are particularly revealing of their ambiguous status. None of them are particularly satisfactory.[2]
One of the most common, *Français-Musulmans rapatriés* (repatriated French
Muslims), which has been criticized because its acronym, FMR, sounds like
éphemère (ephemeral), is inaccurate on two counts. There are hundreds of
thousands of French Muslims who do not come from Algeria or even North
Africa. *Repatriated* suggests a return to one's country of origin. But, as every
Harki will ask, How could we be repatriated to a country we had never even
visited? Which was never ours? Which didn't want us?

Following a long colonial tradition, the French in North Africa made
use of *indigènes* as auxiliary troops (*supplétifs*), known in Morocco and more
generally in the Maghreb as *goumiers* ("troops," from the Arabic *qum*, "to
stand up"), in their military operations.[3] In 1856, they created for each of
Algeria's three provinces a regiment of indigenous *tirailleurs* (skirmishers)
that participated in campaigns in Italy (1859), Senegal (1860–61), Mexico
(1862–67), Alsace-Lorraine (1870–71), and Tonkin (1883–86). The French
began drafting Algerian Muslims in 1912 and had regular corps of *zouaves*,
spahis, *turcos*, and *tirailleurs* in World War I. Of the eighty-one thousand
troops who took part in the war, twenty-five thousand died. A *corps d'indigènes*
of seventy-six thousand (excluding volunteers) fought in World War II

(Langelier 2009, 6).[4] In 1954, there were twenty thousand indigenous career soldiers in the French army as well as thousands of draftees, most of whom were stationed in Indochina (Jordi and Hamoumou 1999, 23). The French army had, in fact, only twenty thousand men in Algeria at that time.

As large contingents were still in Indochina and others in Morocco and Tunisia, it took time to build up a military presence in Algeria. Not only were troops transferred there, but, over the course of the war, military service was extended from eighteen to twenty-four, then twenty-seven, and finally thirty months. The number of troops stabilized at around 450,000 in 1957 and 1958 and was reduced to about 400,000 from 1959 to 1961 (Charbit 2006). In November 1954, Jean Vaujour, then director of the Sûreté générale (the Algerian equivalent of the French security branch of the national police), started recruiting auxiliary troops whose juridical and administrative status was not clear (Faivre 1995, 28).

It is, in fact, necessary to distinguish two principal categories of "repatriated" Muslims: those who were subject to French civil law (*droit commun*, not be confused with Anglo-American common law) and those who were subject to local civil law (*droit local*).[5] The former, which included bureaucrats, elected officials in the colonial administration, and certain elites, were beneficiaries of the French civil code; the latter had no such benefits and were subject to often ill-defined local laws. Essentially, local law was exclusionary in function. The distinction played an important role in the treatment of the two groups in colonial Algeria and in their arrival in France.

At different times during the war, the French created five principal auxiliary groups as well as several unofficial pro-French militia, each with its own status and ostensible mission. Many Harkis (in the restricted sense) and the French often refer to all the auxiliaries as *Harkis*. Sometimes, they include regulars in the French military and in the police force. The political scientist Tom Charbit (2006, 21) suggests that this "semantic slippage" attests to the simplification of history. No doubt it does, but it also results from the Harkis' incorporation for political purposes of other auxiliaries into their fold and the acceptance of this enlargement by politicians and administrators when it served their purposes. Often in my research, one Harki would refer me to another who turned out to have been a member of one of the other auxiliary units or a regular or a conscript in the French army (Chauvin 1995).

The auxiliary groups were formed primarily to supplement the French army, at lower cost, with men who were familiar with the local terrain and population in a war, like all guerrilla wars, of dispersed and often changing zones of combat. They were also meant to serve a psychological purpose. The French hoped that, by recruiting a large number of Muslims, they would demonstrate how strong their support was among the Algerian population. At the very least, they would keep the auxiliaries from joining the *moudjahidine*.

In order of creation, the five auxiliary groups were as follows:[6]

1. In January 1955, the GMPR (Groupes mobiles de protection rurale) was created, charged with reinforcing existing forces policing the countryside (*bled*).[7] Organized like the Moroccan *goumiers*, but more disciplined and hierarchized, the rural guard were a permanent Franco-Muslim rural police force made up primarily of veterans. They were recruited by the civil administration, placed under the authority of the Sûreté nationale, ranked in nonmilitary terms, uniformed, and commanded primarily by reserve officers and volunteers in active service, few of whom were Muslims. Their salaries were higher than those of the Harkis. In March 1958, they were renamed the GMS (Groupes mobiles de sécurité) and attached to the CRS, the tough French security police whom one sees in France today guarding government buildings and maintaining order at demonstrations. In 1962, there were 114 GMS units, numbering thirty-four hundred men.

2. Also in 1955, the *mokhazni(s)* or, more commonly, *moghazni*, members of a quasi-military organization charged with protecting the SAS and, later, the SAU (Section administrative urbaine) were created.[8] Though attached to the administration of the French Affaires algériennes, they were at the disposition of the officers who directed the SAS and the SAU. Their mission was defensive, but they could be—and were—called on to participate in offensive operations. They were given renewable six-month contracts and salaries that were higher than the Harkis' but lower than the rural guards' (except at higher ranks). By 1960, they numbered twenty thousand. The Harkis with whom I talked respected them, and many had fought alongside them.

3. In May 1956, the Unités territoriales (UT), which were made up at first of *pieds-noirs* under forty-five who usually served one month a year, were created. In 1958, Algerian Muslims were added (3,700 in 1958, 7,300 in 1959, and 620 in 1960). On February 23, 1960, owing in part to strained relations between the European and Muslim "territorials," the UT was dissolved. Some of the units were renamed Unités de réserve (UR), serving full-time. Muslim auxiliaries known as Assas ("guards" in Arabic, sometimes transcribed as Assès or Asses) were attached to them. The UR served primarily as convoy, building-site, and roadwork guards. Falling under the military

budget, their pay was higher than that of other auxiliary units. The UT and the UR were of little military importance. They never numbered more than four thousand (1961).

4. The members of the Groupes d'autodéfense (GAD) can also be considered auxiliaries. At first, they were voluntary, unpaid militia, supported by the French army, whose purpose was to defend their villages. According to Ageron (1995, 8), they first appeared in military correspondence at the end of 1956. Poorly armed, usually with hunting rifles, they were to report "rebel" activities to the army. By 1960, there were over two thousand self-defense groups, numbering about sixty-two thousand Muslims, less than half of whom were armed. Untrained, badly armed, and poorly motivated, their operations were of such little consequence that, in 1959, General Massu denounced "the treasons germinating in the Groupes d'autodéfense, their suspicious apathy in face of the rebels when they don't give them [the rebels] ammunition and supplies" (Ageron 1995, 9). Some villagers even said, "We accepted the arms reluctantly and in fear of reprisals on the part of the forces of order. But we won't use them against our brothers." Their number was nearly halved between 1959 and 1960. In fact, many of them supported the FLN. I did meet former GAD members who claimed to have fought loyally for France and seemed proud of being in the unit.

5. The Harkis were generally considered—and perceived themselves—to be the lowest ranked of the auxiliaries. For the most part illiterate peasants, they were, in effect, journeymen who performed all sorts of tasks, ranging from scouting and combat to menial ones like garbage collection and KP. Some were attached to engineering and transportation units, others to police brigades (*brigades de gendarmerie*), and still others to counterguerrilla units known as *commandos de chasse*. In 1961 only 7500 out 60,000 were commandos. The Harkis were usually recruited by French officers in local command. I was told that they were often pressured into joining a *harka*. Their status was never as clear as that of the other auxiliaries. They served at first on a noncontractual basis and later under short-term contracts, purportedly in accordance with local law (*droit local*). It was not until December 11, 1961, a little less than a year before the war ended, that the French army finally granted them legal status in the form of limited but renewable contracts.[9] They received no guaranty of continued service, no social benefits, no family allocations, and a tiny salary (in July 1957, 750 Algerian francs a day and an additional 400 if they came with a mule or a horse) out of which they had to pay for their own food.[10] They were granted a day and a half paid leave for every month and a half they worked, free medical

care if they were wounded, compensation for a "work accident" if they were permanently disabled, and, if they were killed in combat, compensation for their widows—usually after an inordinate delay—determined, some say arbitrarily, by the administration (Ageron 1995, 6). They were given the poorest of weapons. In 1957, they were supplied with only a hunting rifle and twenty-five cartridges. By 1959, they were equipped with 7.5-millimeter repeating rifles, but many of them complained that they were never taught how to use them.

The first *harka* was created in 1955 by Jean Servier in the region of Arris in the Aurès Mountains, near where the Monnerots and Caid Saddok were attacked on the Toussaint Rouge in 1954.[11] Servier found the area in panicked disorder. The local administrator had armed the Europeans and had machine guns placed on the roofs of houses in accordance with a World War II plan in case of aerial attack. Servier called in all Europeans and asked them to return their weapons. He then ordered the *agha* Abdullah Merchi of the Aît Daoud (Touaba tribe) to form an armed *harka* (with fifty rifles) to defend against a rebellious faction of the Touabas that, under Mustafa ben Boulaïd's leadership, was held responsible for the death of the two schoolteachers and the *caid*. (Others, including many Harkis from the area, insist that the *agha* himself—always loyal to the French—first offered to form the *harka*.)[12] Cursed by the Europeans for arming the Touabas, Servier explained: "in acting so I avoided eventual reprisals by the European population and I explained to the local populations that the French were not confusing them with the FLN outlaws." With considerable exaggeration and manifest self-importance, Servier observed: "The revolt suddenly took on another aspect [with the creation of this first *harka*]. It was no longer a war of liberation led by all the Muslims against the Christians, but an open rebellion against the law. On the side of order and a French peace, there were Muslims; and on the other side, some French were already wallowing [*se réjouissaient*] in the troubles and, in secret, without a doubt aided the rebels" (1955, 24–25).

General Gaston Parlange, who was then charged with the Aurès Region, formed other *harkas* in the area without integrating them with the military units. General Henri Lorillot, who was then the commander of the Tenth Military Region (Algeria), and Jacques Soustelle, the governor-general, encouraged the recruitment of Harkis. Soustelle, who, as we have seen, became a staunch supporter of the ultraconservative *pieds-noirs* after the Philippeville massacre, told General Faivre in 1985, "We can say: 'We lost but we did not fail' ("Nous avons perdu, mais nous n'avons pas failli"; Faivre 1995, 38), thanks to those Arabs and Berbers who supported, indeed, died for, France."

One of the most famous, if not necessarily most effective, *harka* was formed in July 1956 by Saïd Boualam, then the *agha* and later the *bachaga* of the Beni-Boudouane, who lived in the Oursanais southwest of Algiers. Turned in on itself, the tribe was little influenced by the colonial presence. Boualam, the tribe's spiritual and administrative ruler, was one of the most fervent supporters of French Algeria. He became the vice president of the French National Assembly and had been a career officer in the French army, retiring as a captain in the reserve in 1945. He had fought in Tunisia, Italy, France, and Germany during World War II. He demanded unquestioned allegiance from his "people," as he liked to call the Beni-Boudouane, and insisted on their supporting France. "I was under the orders of the *bachaga*," an old Harki told the anthropologist Giulia Fabbiano (2008b, 115). "I had to be submissive and respectful, and thus, if he chose the French camp, we, through respect and by choice and for legitimate defense, were obliged to follow the *bachaga* and become Harkis."[13] In September 1956, Boualam organized a *harka* of 300 armed men (Faivre 1995, 31). A wily character, he tried over the next few years to separate his *harka* from any regular army unit. In May 1958, he was even asked by a local FLN leader to join forces with them, but he refused. In 1959, Maurice Challe asked him to form a *harka* of 2,000 men, and, had General Massu not intervened, Challe might well have let him create an autonomous auxiliary quarter (*un quartier supplétif autonome*).[14] Relations between the *bachaga* and the army remained tense. At the end of August 1959, his 723 Harkis were organized into two groups: a *harka* of 110 men and 5 enlisted officers to be stationed at the *bachaga*'s home and a larger one attached to nearby military units. Although it was feared in June 1961 that the *bachaga* would support the OAS—he in fact flirted with the notion—he finally refused to back their activities in the Ouarsenais (Roux 1991, 220–23).

In April 1956, Soustelle's successor, Robert Lacoste, finally established rules for the creation, organization, and arming of the *harkas*, which he defined as "temporary formations whose mission is to participate in order-maintaining operations." Lacoste wanted to turn the *harkas* into independent counterguerrilla units, with ranked Muslim soldiers under French officers, but Raoul Salan, who was then the commander in chief of the army in Algeria, vehemently opposed the project, arguing that such units would form the basis for an Algerian army, "thus materializing an Algerian nation" (Ageron 1995, 6). On May 20, 1957, he specified that the Harkis were to be recruited for only a limited time and for specific operations and were always to be attached to regular military units.

Salan's position reflects France's ambivalence about the use of auxiliary forces, particularly the Harkis, as the least *evolués* of them. Although some military officers were opposed to the use of any indigenous forces in the war, not only because they feared desertion and betrayal, but also because they believed that a people should not be made to turn on themselves, the army generally found the engagement of Harkis without having to guarantee their continued employment a "convenience" (Ageron (1995, 7). It was continually badgering Paris for more and more funds for their recruitment. Salan himself, supported by the minister of state charged with cultural affairs, the novelist and art critic André Malraux, managed a little more than a year later to have the number of Harkis increased from seventeen to thirty thousand (but not the forty-eight thousand he originally requested). Five months later, Challe, who had replaced Salan, was accorded another thirty thousand. But, as de Gaulle was opposed to "the engagement of Harkis in any operation against their brothers in race [*contre leurs frères de race*]," Challe had to promise the general that they would be used only for surveillance and protection, although this commitment was never kept (Ageron 1995, 7, quoting Horne 1987, 333, quoting Boissieu 1982, 151).[15] The Harkis were, in fact, used whenever and wherever they were needed for any operation, defensive or offensive.

At the end of 1959, the notorious prefect of Paris police, Maurice Papon— who in 1998, after the courts had delayed for nearly seventeen years, was finally convicted at the age of eighty-eight for crimes against humanity involving his role in sending thousands of Jews to Nazi death camps—created an auxiliary police force (Force de police auxiliare) popularly known as the *calots bleus* (blue caps). It was made up of between 250 and 400—some claim as many as 600—Harkis, recruited in Algeria primarily by Captain Raymond Montaner, whose methods, as Betrand Legendre put it in *Le monde*, "left something to be desired."[16] "He appears to have been oblivious of the '*droits communs*.'" The *calots bleus* were armed, provided with special uniforms that resembled those of the CRS, and put under the authority of French officers. Their mission was to maintain order in Muslim sections of Paris (mainly in the thirteenth and fourteenth arrondissements and the outlying shantytowns) and to search out and infiltrate the FLN, which was sending money and arms to Algeria and Tunisia. They were still fighting Messali Hadj's ever-weakening Mouvement nationaliste algérien (MNA) and attempting to create an "idealized Algerian countersociety" (Valat 2007, 25; see also Fytton 1961).[17] Under Montaner, the *calots bleus* were active participants in the massacre that took place in Paris on October 17, 1961, when twenty to thirty thousand Algerians protested a curfew imposed on them by Papon in response to recent FLN attacks on Parisian police officers.[18] Two hundred of the protesters were killed and dumped in the Seine. Through random street killings, torture, and assassinations, the FLN had already managed to extort more than 6 million francs a year from the Muslim population in France. More than ten thousand were eventually killed or wounded, primarily by the FLN, in what some historians refer to as a *civil war*. It was certainly the bloodiest conflict in Europe since World War II (Faivre 1995, 63).[19]

The *calots bleus* were also meant to demonstrate that all–French Muslim units loyal to France could be created and were capable of engaging with the FLN. From June to November 1961, the Harkis in Paris captured 650 automatic weapons, dozens of kilograms of explosives, more than 150 grenades, and forty bombs (Faivre 1995, 63–64). They killed thirty members of the FLN and made 1,189 arrests; perhaps as many as 500 of the arrested held positions of responsibility in the FLN.[20] Their mission was far more dangerous than that of the Harkis in Algeria, Hamoumou (1993, 117) says. According to Faivre (1995, 64), twenty-seven Harkis were killed fighting, nineteen more either had their throats slit or died under torture, and eighty-two were wounded.[21] At the end of the war, the Parisian Harki units were disbanded and their members integrated into the municipal police force.

The methods employed by the *calots bleus* were similar to those of the urban Harkis recruited by General Massu during the Battle of Algiers. In 1961, Paulette Péju, a journalist who wrote for the leftist newspaper *Libération*, published two short books, *Les Harkis à Paris* and *Ratonnades de Paris*, both of which were seized at the printers by the Police judiciare. In *Les Harkis*, Péju documents the brutality of the Paris Harkis, their arbitrary arrests and seizures of Algerians whom they suspected of being supporters of the FLN, the tortures they used, and the executions they carried out as well various government cover-ups.[22] The Harkis, Péju argued (in so inflamed a fashion as to diminish the credibility of her account), were left untrammeled. Like many members of the French Left, who were sympathetic, if only ideologically, to the cause of Algerian independence, Péju (1961/2000, 27) had little use for the Harkis. She refers to them as "mercenaries in service of the occupier who rake [*ratissent*], rape, pillage, torture, and kill":

> The Harkis—they have nothing to prepare for, nothing to lose but their mercenary's uniform and their salary of treason. All they have to fear is a peaceful solution of the Algerian War because, without war and repression, they're

nothing at all: neither Algerian nor French. Scorned by those who make use of them, rejected by the Algerian community, they attack with all the more violence their countrymen whose murder is the murder of their own lost image. They try to efface what they can no longer be; they desperately flee what they have become: false brothers. (Péju 1961/2000, 109)

I quote Péju at some length to illustrate the intensity of the French Left's attitude toward the Harkis. I do not mean to deny the violence the Harkis were responsible for in Paris (or, for that matter, in Algeria)—there is more than sufficient evidence of that—but I should note that Péju does not take as critical an attitude as she might have toward the testimonies she collected (Valat 2007, 12). Some of these accounts were, no doubt, exaggerated, if not confabulated by supporters of the FLN, the so-called *porteurs de valises*, who did so for propaganda purposes.[23] But we must also look with skepticism at the French claim that much of the violence attributed to the Harkis was, in fact, carried out by the FLN. An at times violent propaganda war was being fought in Paris, as in Algeria, by both the French and the nationalists.

More revealing of the Left's attitude toward the Harkis is Péju's complete failure to consider the pressures placed on the them by the military and the police. Papon was—and is—notorious for the killings, the tortures, the mass arrests, and the unjustified imprisonments he authorized, as Péju acknowledges in both her books. But her failure to consider the subjective understanding of the Harkis gives to her account an ideological dimension that does not—and cannot—do justice to the complexity of the situation in which the Harkis, the FLN and its supporters, and the politically disengaged Algerians found themselves. Cast as mercenaries, the Harkis become stock figures—the cruel savage, the Arab, the Berber, who has little, if any, control over his instinctive violence—in Péju's ideologically induced tale, whatever its reality. Ironically, by casting the Harkis as she does, she undermines her own anticolonialist position by assuming its stereotypes. The Harkis can only "murder . . . their own lost image," "efface what they can no longer be," and "desperately flee what they have become." Péju's stereotypy, her failure to consider the "enemy's" subjectivity, and her insistence on understanding their reactions to the situation in which they found themselves in terms of primitive instinctual behavior are also characteristic of the Right's frequent assumptions about the independence fighters and, however sympathetic they may be to the Harkis, about the Harkis themselves.

Even under the best conditions, it would be difficult to determine the number of repatriated Muslim French, if only because many of them served in different auxiliary groups during the war.[24] In fact, as I noted in my discussion of war statistics in the last chapter, accurate figures are impossible to obtain, partly because some archives are still closed, but mainly because the figures have been distorted for political and propaganda reasons by all the participants in the war. On March 19, 1962, when the Treaty of Evian was signed, it was estimated that there were around 260,000 pro-French Algerians, among them 58,000 Harkis, 20,000 *moghaznis*, 15,000 members of the GMS and the Assas, and 60,000 members of the GAD. The remaining 107,000 were Algerians serving in the French army, veterans, elected officials, and bureaucrats. Other estimates for the auxiliary troops as a whole have ranged from 147,000 to 160,000 and for the Harkis from 45,000 to 70,000.

The "decision" to become a Harki must be seen from within the context of violence and terror that pervaded Algeria from the beginning of the war. Saïd Ferdi, whose rather inflated memoir, *Un enfant dans la guerre*, published in 1981, was one of the earliest, if not the earliest, personal account of the war by an Algerian who sided, or, more accurately, was forced into siding, with the French, notes the terror that was felt in his village near the Aurès Mountains when the villagers first learned of the fighting that followed the Toussaint Rouge: "During the following three months, a true terror seized the population. Incredible rumors about the bandits spread. Some said that they were invisible, others that they had the power to transform themselves into animals—sheep, donkeys, or cows—and, thus, present everywhere, they were able to observe everyone. Each was afraid for his life" (Ferdi 1981, 22). Ferdi's use of *bandits* reflects the way in which the revolutionaries were cast for the villagers by the French administration. (Servier referred to them as *outlaws*.) He attributes the rumors to the ignorance and naïveté of the villagers.

Soon afterward, Ferdi goes on, the village was riven with internal strife as some of the villagers sided with the revolutionaries and others with the French. They all suffered murderous violence from both sides:

As soon as the revolutionaries committed an assassination, they claimed responsibility, sending one of them to report it to the [village] population as a safeguard against their eventual collaboration with the French. On the other hand, when the French kidnapped someone, generally at night, you didn't hear any more talk about the abducted, who would be found dead a few days later, left in a ditch or in the market square, with documents that made you believe that he was a victim of the revolutionaries. But it was necessary only to hear the names of the victims to understand who had, in fact, killed them. (Ferdi 1981, 26)

Over the years, violence intensified in Ferdi's village and its environs, most of whose inhabitants supported the FLN. On January 11, 1956, about a hundred French troops—"the red berets" or "leopards"—arrived in the village, and, that night, they raided houses and carried off about a hundred men, claiming that it was only to verify their identity. A forty-eight-hour curfew followed during which the villagers were not allowed to leave their homes. When the curfew was lifted, the villagers were confronted with a horrible sight: "The dead were lying abandoned on the sidewalks, covered with signs of torture, shop doors were broken, kids were crying in the streets looking for their father or their brother" (Ferdi 1981, 31). Of the eighty-five men who were kidnapped, twelve were found dead, and the remainder were never seen again. The *maquisards* retaliated with equal savagery, killing a dozen men whom, on scant evidence, they thought to be collaborators. Several were probably innocent. From this time on, Ferdi (1981, 31) observes, the rift grew between the few villagers who still supported the French and the majority, who wanted to avenge those who had disappeared by rallying with the revolutionaries.

Though I never heard a description of a village massacre as complete as Ferdi's, many of the stories I did hear from the Harkis echoed his. They focused, however, on massacres carried out by the FLN, and they usually referred to the death or disappearance of a family member or friend with little if any context. "In the morning my uncle was found with his throat cut in front of his house. My mother pushed me into a hollow behind our house, which my father had dug. It was hidden behind a stack of hay. I lay there all night. It was terrible. In the morning, there were dead bodies all over." "My three brothers were killed by the FLN. I saw my youngest brother's throat cut."

Most of the auxiliaries did not have any particular political conviction, certainly no strong patriotic feelings for France.[25] (I am excluding those Harkis who were recruited by the *bachaga* Boualam and who seem simply to have followed their leader's instructions.) True, there were veterans who had fought in the French army in World War II or in Indochina and joined an auxiliary unit out of military loyalty.[26] "I was a soldier. What choice did I have?" one Harki said. "I fought in Italy, at Monte Casino, and then in Indochina, at Dien Bien Phu, in the jungles. What was I to do?" By this, I believe, he implied what he could not say, namely, that he did not want the army he had served in to suffer another defeat. He was, in my experience, unusual. Most of the veterans who had become Harkis simply reported that they were "soldiers" when I asked them why. They did not elaborate. That fact was sufficient. A few showed me the ribbons they had been awarded.

(I will come back to this truncated type of explanation below.) Others implied, and a few said, that they missed army life. One man, who was quite histrionic, gestured pulling a trigger with his hands and laughed, as if he enjoyed fighting; he denied ever having tortured a prisoner. "I wasn't in the Deuxième bureau," he said coldly, referring to military intelligence. When his wife, who was also at the interview, shook her head sadly and said that war was terrible, he immediately changed his manner and ranted at the French for having put him in danger and then refusing to acknowledge what he—what the Harkis—had done for France. He went on complaining about the French bureaucracy and especially the mayor's office in Arles, where he lived, which he said was doing everything in its power to prevent him from (as far as I could make out) renegotiating the terms of the government loan for his house.

Other Harkis were recruited forcibly. A chief of an SAS unit wrote in his monthly report that some of his colleagues recruited entire units in an unorthodox fashion "worthy of recruiting sergeants of yesteryear" (Ageron 1995, 12 n. 6). Though no doubt exceptional, given his age, Ferdi's (1981, 49–73) description of his recruitment by the French has become an icon of such methods. Early in the morning, on March 3, 1958, as he was washing in a stream before starting for school, Ferdi, then thirteen, was picked up by five Algerians serving in the French army, beaten, and carried off to a nearby casern. "I immediately had the impression of having entered a world apart, a world of savage beasts from which I would have no chance of leaving" (51). Refusing to answer questions about the political affiliations of various villagers, he was subjected to the *gégène*. He was strapped naked to an iron table, electrodes were attached to his penis and one of his ears, and, each time he refused to answer a question, an increasingly powerful electric charge was sent though his body. "The pain was such that I suffocated and then howled horribly" (55). After about twenty minutes, the base commander entered and ordered a halt to the torture. Ferdi was told that he would not be allowed to leave the base and was forced to tell his father (who, unknown to the French, was sympathetic to the FLN) that he wanted to remain in the casern with the French.[27] He hoped that his father would understand that he was remaining against his will as the French had threatened his family, but he could say nothing and, in fact, never saw his father again. After working in the casern's kitchen for several months, he was sent on operations until the war ended. Luckily, he was favored by the captain and his successor, who, after the signing of the Treaty of Evian, counseled him to go to France and managed somehow to arrange for his transfer. He was still too young to join the army.

The French often gave ALN prisoners a choice: to become a Harki or to be killed. These *ralliés* were rumored to be more ferocious than other Harkis since they had the most to lose if they were ever captured by the ALN. To ensure their loyalty, the *ralliés* were sometimes photographed in the midst of French officers drinking to France or as they were interrogating prisoners; they were told that, were they to desert, their photographs would be sent to the ALN (Roux 1991, 128). Among the most famous of these *ralliés* were those who served in the Commando Georges, a special, all-Muslim unit organized by Captain (later General) Georges Grillot. It used ALN tactics and was known for its terrifying efficacy. The Commando, based in Saïda, was organized into four sections (*katibas*), each headed by a *rallié* and divided into three groups (*sticks*) of ten men as well as other personnel. Thirty percent of the men were *ralliés*, 40 percent highly competent professional soldiers, and 30 percent young men who had been co-opted by the older soldiers. In a unique but risky experiment, the men chose their noncommissioned officers from a list of candidates made up by Grillot. All of them earned the same wages, which were supplemented by bonuses for exceptional service, paid out of funds taken from ALN units they defeated. Morale was exceptionally high, that is, until the cease-fire at the end of 1961, when some of the men attempted to rejoin the ALN. Despite the amnesty the ALN promised them, they were tortured, mutilated, and killed. Grillot managed to have the Commando leaders loyal to him transferred to France (where one of them was later murdered by the FLN). Grillot's friend the banker André Wormser, who had also fought in Algeria and was to play an important role in defending the rights of the Harkis, bought a farm in the Dordogne that became a center for those Harki commandos who managed to make it to France.[28]

Many other *ralliés* were attached to the infamous Operational Detachments for Protection (Détachements opérationnels de protection), whose mission, as General Massu put it, was "the interrogation of suspects who wanted to say nothing" (Horne 1987, 199). They were to obtain confessions by whatever means and to keep records on thousands of Algerians. (It has been estimated that, during the Battle of Algiers, 30–40 percent of the entire male population of the Casbah was arrested and "interrogated" at one time or another [Horne 1987, 199, quoting Behr 1962]). The *ralliés* were said to be the cruelest and most efficacious of interrogators. Indeed, J.-P. Vittori (1980, 55) noted in his *Confessions d'un professionnel de la torture*, "We learned quickly that the prisoners preferred to be questioned by the French, and we used the threat [of employing an auxiliary interrogator] as a means of pressuring [them]." Vittori attributed the ferocity of the *ralliés'* methods of torture to, on the one hand, their need to continually prove their sincerity and devotion to the French cause and, on the other, to their terrible guilt vis-à-vis the militants, who had remained faithful to their ideals. Instead of rendering them less brutal, their guilt led them to intensify their cruelty.

For the majority of Harkis, however, becoming an auxiliary was simply a way to earn a living. But, given the value that some of the Algerian men placed on serving in the army, it also offered, or so many of them thought, a certain prestige. Most were in contact with the French or were from rural areas where they worked on farms owned by the *colons*. Some simply told me (or their children) that they had joined because they needed the money. Others explained that the FLN had requisitioned all their food, even their last sheep or cow, and that they had no other way of feeding their families. Often they would add, coldly, that the *fallaghas* had threatened their lives, raped their women, or killed villagers who had resisted them. One man told the social worker Anne Heinis (1977) that, after discovering that the FLN had slaughtered his cow and his sheep and destroyed his crops, he had run in fury to SAS headquarters and joined up. Another, who had served in Indochina, was arrested by the *fallaghas*, watched them slit his father's throat, and was beaten so badly that they left him for dead. He remained semiconscious for nine days and, when he recovered, enlisted in the nearest *harka*. (He was eventually dismissed because of his violent, drunken rages in which he threatened the lives of the survivors in his family.) Sometimes, as an initiatory test, an aspiring *moudjahid* was sent to a village, even his own, to kill at random someone, anyone (Méliani 1993, 53, quoting testimony collected by Mohand Hamoumou). Ferdi (1981, 29) describes three such killings in his own village. One man, who was ordered to kill a gendarme, panicked and missed. On returning to the *maquisards*, he was shot. A second was executed because he had shot his victim two hours before the prescribed time, when the revolutionaries were still in the village. And a third was killed because he told his friends what he had been ordered to do before he did it. Ferdi explains that the goal of these initiatory murders was to instill strict discipline and to prevent the recruits from backsliding—which would have automatically compromised them in the eyes of the French.

Such stories were so frequent that I sometimes wondered whether they had not become conventional figures for describing the pain the Harkis suffered or simply a way of supporting their decision to join a *harka*. But there is more than ample evidence of the FLN's brutal treatment of the peasants. Sometimes, in fury, the FLN would kill all the men in a village and even the women and children. Of course, the Harkis never admitted the violence they committed in furor. Those Harkis who described such events frequently added, or implied, that they had become auxiliaries for revenge. It sometimes happened, as it did in the formation of the first *harka* after the Toussaint Rouge, that the violent relations between the FLN and the villagers who became Harkis reflected long-standing feuds between different tribal sections or animosities within a single family (Boulhaïs 2002, 33ff.). Often, the members of a whole clan would become Harkis in response to an affront by their traditional enemies. I heard more than one story of a villager becoming a Harki because his brother or cousin had joined the FLN. There seemed to be no love lost between the brothers or cousins. Anger and bitterness seemed to overwhelm family connection.

Thus far, I have discussed only male auxiliaries. In fact, as with the FLN, a number of women served either formally or informally. They worked mostly as medical assistants and social workers (*assistants sanitaire et sociales*) but also as messengers, particularly if their husbands were auxiliaries. The French called them *Harkettes*—a feminine diminutive that is clearly condescending. Many of the women with some education served on traveling medical teams and were highly praised for their commitment and stamina. One French soldier later wrote: "The conquest of the women was easy; they expected everything from me, first understanding and friendship. They were *my women*; I was their *toubiba* [doctor]. No question of schedules; work was continual, hard, and complicated, fatigue secondary, but the compensation was there: in the smile, the extended hand, coffee taken together [*au même sol*], all those little nothings that make for friendship" (quoted in Faivre 1995, 118). One wonders to whom this friendship was addressed: the *toubiba* or his patients.

One Harki succeeded in having his wife transferred to the base where he was serving after she had been threatened in their village. She referred to the anguish she suffered each night as the base was under continual attack by the FLN. Her husband gave her hand grenades, a small pistol, and binoculars. She was to press a buzzer that sounded in the guard post in case of an emergency (Faivre 1995, 119). In Catinat, women—particularly those whose husbands had been killed by the FLN or were in GAD units—were armed and served in combat and as convoy guards. Helmut Ontrup (quoted in Faivre 1995, 120) observed: "The amusement of the soldiers in the garrison when they saw these amazons in skirts go by was short-lived. The women quickly became seasoned sharpshooters, handling a rifle as if they had never done anything else." This was an exceptional case.

Many of the Harkis I spoke with reported that their wives often carried messages for them. Some of the Harki daughters were angered that the role of Harki wives and daughters has been ignored. Celestine Rolland, a Harki activist and feminist, angrily recalls the way her mother was treated. "The villagers spat at her because she was married to a Harki." Celestine told me later that her mother carried messages for the Harkis in her village. The women also spoke about the hardships they endured, the anguish they suffered, the fear for their husbands and sons, and the scarcity of food. They dreaded the arrival of the FLN or ALN in their villages, never knowing what they wanted or whom they would kidnap or murder. In many of my interviews with the old Harkis, their wives were present and listened to their husbands' accounts with extraordinary intensity, as if they were reliving their pasts. They would interrupt, giving expression to the emotional dimension of the experiences their husbands seemed incapable of expressing. They reminded me of the choruses in Greek tragedy.

Often, when the Harkis described how the FLN had killed a relative or requisitioned their family's food, they would become so enraged that they could no longer sustain the temporal gap between the narrated event and its telling. Serving in the army, even as an auxiliary, afforded them some repair of the aggression, the shame, and the dishonor they had suffered. But, clearly, the repair was insufficient, or subsequent events had destroyed it. Once they had expressed their anger, their desire for revenge, many would sink into themselves. Some of them simply stopped speaking. If their children were present, and they often were, they would indicate that the interview was over and later tell me, "You see."

The children's—usually the son's—"you see" echoed their father's truncated speech. Was it that the events were too painful to elaborate? I do not want to minimize their fathers' pain, which was certainly great, but at the same time I do not want to vest this truncated speech with deeper psychological significance than it has, that is, as an inevitable consequence of trauma. I found that, as a group, the Harkis were not given to narrative elaboration.[29] They relied on silence, long pauses, isolated phrases, and single words whose resonance, coming from within, was also directed inward, as if they could not conceive of having a comprehending interlocutor. They depended, far more than their children, on the demonstrative gesture, an expression of disgust, wizened understanding, or a cynicism enforced by an exhausted incredulity.

Perhaps more significant than the pain they felt—and here I must be very cautious—was the paradoxical situation in which they found themselves. The decision to become a Harki was theirs, and they and their families had to bear the consequences of that decision. But was it a decision? At least as they told it, they had had no choice. What were they to do? Let their families starve? Join the FLN, which had stolen from them, threatened them, or murdered those close to them? All they could do, realistically, was to become auxiliaries. But was it their only choice? Any decision, or, for that matter, nondecision, always raises the possibilities of not having made that decision (or nondecision). However realistically evaluated these other possibilities are, they are always optative. Tinged with desire, they justify the decision, or, more torturously, they perpetuate regret. Certainly, many Harkis were caught between having to justify a decision they were *realistically* forced to make and recognizing the haunting possibility, however unrealistic, that they had had a real choice.

Decisions, even those forced on us, are never simple affairs. Not only do they evoke their negation, not only do they reflect the ambivalence felt at the time the decision was made and, even more disquieting, the ambivalence that follows that decision; they call forth at some level, however suppressed, those less than rational, emotional factors that accompany any decision. The peasant who decides quite rationally that in order to feed his family he has to join a *harka* may also be acting out of the desire for revenge, escape from an impossible situation, or even adventure (though I doubt that this played an important role for the Harkis). The Harkis' realism may have been affected by shame, insult, a sense of helplessness, the desire for succor, or the loss of dignity (*mahaba*) and honor (*ird*) that are so important in North African culture. These feelings and sentiments, the fact of their (fragile) repression, if they are repressed—which can undermine the decision and its justification—so haunted most of the Harkis with whom I talked that they had become frozen in outlook and focused on a truncated image—an icon of their experiences that they could not or would not want to develop into a story. Or they dwell obsessively on a tangential but consequential event, most notably, their sense of betrayal and abandonment by the French.

One woman whom the Harki writer and activist Fatima Besnaci-Lancou (2006a, 75) interviewed told her that, after fighting alongside the FLN for three years, her husband joined a *harka* for reasons she still does not know. "I think my husband was disgusted by the conduct of the chief of the *maquis*, who respected no one," she said. "It seems he raped women when he raided the farms at night. I never asked my husband. We do not talk about that. It's sinful."

According to Charles-Robert Ageron (1995, 12), French officers recognized that, for the most part, the Harkis—"those poor wretches," "those rustic journeymen," "those timid and submissive farmworkers"—had joined for "mercenary" reasons.[30] A 1960 study by the *état-major*, echoing a long history of colonialist stereotypes of the Arab, noted: "The Harki has no worry. His situation gives him complete satisfaction in the immediate. He has a journeyman's mentality" (quoted in Ageron 1995, 12). A year earlier, in October 1959, the *Revue militaire d'information* warned that the Harkis were not particularly reliable, that one could not count on their loyalty, and that these attitudes required care in their employment. They had to be watched constantly, weapons had to be locked up or chained, a European always had to be present when they were on guard duty, and a French noncommissioned officer had to be attached to every *harka* (Ageron 1995, 7). The study also referred to those Harkis—the *responsables politiques*—who were paid highly (30,000 Algerian francs per month plus bonuses) to "suppress" those auxiliaries who were, in fact, attached to the FLN.

Georges Buis, who headed the Hodna Section of the Constantine Region from 1957 on, was particularly mistrustful of most Harkis. Out of the thirty *harkas* he administered, he found only three or four to be trustworthy. "It is simply foolhardy," he wrote, "to believe that the Harkis can cut themselves off from the life of their village, to separate themselves totally from the rebellion." They are not, Buis goes on to observe, necessarily dishonest; they did not join up to betray those who pay them. Willing or not, they have been of service to the army in everyday matters. However: "It is obvious that, when a *harka* goes out on patrol with even the best kept secrecy, it is necessary only for a rifle to go off 'by accident' in the night or a pebble, a bit too large, to roll down into a ravine for the whole mountain to know that the post is out on 'mission'" (Buis 1975 quoted in Roux 1991, 80).[31]

According to the Service de sécurité de la défense nationale en Algérie, there were cases of collusion and subversion among the auxiliaries nearly each week in the last years of the war. The service claimed that most of the *harkas* had relations with the *moudjahidine* and that some Harkis were actually members of the FLN or the ALN, to which they gave information and supplied arms and ammunition. In 1959, there were about 20 cases of subversion a month; in 1961, the number increased to 27 per month (Faivre 1995, 132). Between August 1960 and January 1961 in the province of Oranie, for example, the 134 cases of subversion uncovered involved 582 Algerians in the armed services, of which 386 were auxiliaries, and of these 263 were Harkis. Of the 325 cases in 1961, Faivre (1995, 133) found that 53 percent concerned contacts with the enemy and infiltration, propaganda, and demoralization of Algerians serving with the French; they were without concrete effect. Thirty-six percent involved aborted attempts at desertion, 31 percent trafficking in small quantities of ammunition, and 4 percent theft of small arms. Few of the contacts turned out to be treasonous. Many accusations were based, according to Faivre, on testimony from prisoners, who preferred to incriminate their enemies than blame their fellows in arms; others were the result of police errors. Subversives who were caught were imprisoned, and those who abandoned their arms and tried to flee were left to suffer *their* just punishment (Ageron 1995, 15).

I myself met no Harkis who had, or were willing to admit having had, colluded with the FLN or its army while being part of a *harka*. (I did meet several Harkis who had been supporters of the FLN before they joined a *harka*. In each of these cases, it was some atrocity that the FLN had committed in their villages or the murder of a family member that, they claimed, led them to shift their loyalty to France.) In her attempt to uncover the reality that lay behind her father's silence about his experiences as a Harki, the writer Dalila Kerchouche (2003b, 253–54) followed his trajectory from Algeria to France, from camp to camp, only to discover, when she finally visited his village in Algeria, that he had aided the FLN by supplying them with ammunition. When she confronted him with what she had learned, he refused at first to acknowledge it. What follow are excerpts from her imaginative reconstruction of that meeting.[32]

Dalila begins by telling her father, Ali, that she had learned that one of his brothers, Latrache, had worked for the FLN:

ALI: That's not true: they approached him, but he refused.

DK: Everyone confirmed it there. Uncle Ahmed, Tayeb, Djamel . . . And you, did you work with them?

ALI: No, they never came to see me.

DK: Yet they all told me that . . .

ALI: They're mistaken.

DK: What are you afraid of, *apa*? Look, Lakhdar [another brother] was a Harki, and he has lived in Algeria for forty years. No one has blamed him. And you, you have hidden from me that you worked for the FLN? All that's finished. Talk to me now.

ALI: I never worked for the FLN.

DK: However, you were Uncle Ahmed's pal, who collected money for them. And you often saw your brother Latrache and your nephew Mohammed. You brought them ammunition. You carried it on your donkey, hidden in wicker baskets, and Mohammed gave it to the *moudjahidine*.

Dalila's father smiled, "as though a forgotten image passed in front of his eyes." She saw it as a confession. He then turned in on himself. Dalila insisted that he answer. He refused. She told him that she had first heard the story from her mother. "You told her a few years ago. And you know how she is; she repeats everything." He stalled. She insisted stubbornly: "Yes or no. I'm not moving until you tell me." Ali remained silent. He sighed:

ALI: Yes . . . yes, yes, yes. I gave them ammunition. Let's go now.
DK: Wait . . . Why didn't you ever say anything?
ALI: I was already considered a traitor in the eyes of the Algerians. I wasn't going to be one for the French. . . .

Two purportedly objective criteria for judging the fighting ability (*combativité*) of soldiers by the French are the number of deaths and the number of desertions. In the Algerian case, the first criterion—the number of deaths—is generally inconclusive since the figures are inaccurate or, after October 1960, no longer distinguished between French and Algerian casualties. Faivre (1995, 16) estimates that 2.31 percent of the auxiliaries lost their lives in action. It appears that the number of desertions by auxiliary troops (including the Harkis) remained relatively stable at under 1 percent after it had peaked in December 1956 (2.13 percent) and January 1957 (3.6 percent). As might be expected, as the war was nearing its end, the number of desertions increased dramatically, to 9.36 percent in March 1962. The percentage of desertions among the auxiliary troops was far lower than that of Algerians in the French army itself. Ageron (1995, 14) attributes this discrepancy to two main factors. First, unlike most French troops who were conscripted, the Harkis were mostly volunteers. Second, most Harkis who were suspected of FLN connections or who were not considered serious had been weeded out. I would add that their poverty must also have played an important role. Many of those auxiliaries who deserted or resigned did so because they did not want to go on night patrol or because they found their French leaders too demanding. In the late spring of 1961, their number increased out of fear of reprisals in an Algerian Algeria. They did not want to be identified with the French. Others, so Ageron reports, resigned or deserted when offensive operations were halted in May 1961. They complained that they were no longer free to kill captured or wounded *moujahidine*, as they had before offensive operations had been called off. One Harki I spoke to admitted that he had run off. When I asked him why, he simply shrugged his shoulders. Given what had happened to the Harkis, he had no need to explain.

As the war was drawing to an end, the Algerians' hostility toward the Harkis, spurred by the FLN, increased dramatically. They insulted the Harkis, threw rocks at them, attacked them with knives as they sat in cafés, and, on occasion, murdered them. Boulhaïs (2002, 281) records anti-Harki songs—in Chawiya (Berber) and Arabic—from the Aurès Mountains:

> Gather the Harkis
> Gather them together.
> What remedy is there for them?
> The sharpened knife.
> A hail of gunfire will eat them.

And, prophetically, as it were:

> Harkis, be cursed!
> France will not help you.
> The civilians' children will track you down.

It should also be remembered that the FLN barraged Algerian troops and auxiliaries with propaganda urging them to desert, to join the "revolutionaries," and promising them amnesty (*âmân*, "pardon"). The propaganda reflected the several attitudes with which the FLN and the ALN regarded the auxiliaries. On the one hand, the auxiliaries, particularly the *goumiers*, were reputed to be especially cruel—"more cruel even than the French" (Ageron 1995, 17). Though it was recognized that some Harkis fell into violent rages against the *moujahidine*, especially when their villages had been attacked or when the attackers belonged to an enemy clan, it was also acknowledged by both the ALN and the French that, unlike the *goumiers*, the Harkis often spared the *moujahidine*, for example, by shooting over their heads in an attack or failing to report their presence during a reconnaissance mission. Generally, Algerians in the French army were treated by the FLN and the ALN with considerable sympathy. Conscripted, they had had no choice.

Many of the directives from the FLN urged moderation in the treatment of the Harkis. For example, one issued on March 30, 1961, concerning "contact with Muslims enrolled in the enemy ranks," read: "Firmly promise them absolute pardon if they join the ALN with arms and their kits [*bagages*]. The ALN knows that they were tricked by the enemy and that second thoughts [*remords de conscience*] do not stop assailing them. . . . Explain to these strays that the ALN knows their moral suffering, the injustices they submit to every day, and that they are the object of mistrust in the enemy barracks" (quoted in Faivre 1995, 139). But others were menacing. A tract distributed in July 1961 (from Wilaya 2) urged the freedom fighters to slit the throats of most Harkis but to save the lives of the least bad. "Not paid, and submissive 'like pigs,' they will work in your place" (Faivre 1995, 142). A report of a meeting held on July 18, 1961, announced: "All women who decide to marry, or are already married to, *goumiers* [here, Harkis and *moghaznis*] will be condemned to death" (Faivre 1995, 141). And a model letter addressed to officers and noncommissioned officers, distributed by the FLN Press Office in Wilaya 4, stated:

> If your profession of a mercenary of colonialism has not completely killed your honor, if you are still capable of freeing yourself of racism, listen then before it will be too late for you. What merit do you gain in attacking unarmed civilians who have committed no other crime than that of loving freedom and aspiring to dignity. Stop then soaking your hands in the blood of civilian Algerians. This letter is a last and solemn notice. Know that the revolution is vast like the sea. We are aware of each of your words, each of your gestures. If you persist in your criminal activity, our *fediyyine* will strike you at an hour and a place that we will tell them. If necessary, punishment will follow you to the other side of the Mediterranean and strike your family. (Faivre 1995, 139)

I found those French officers (now retired) with whom I talked and who had had Harkis under their command to be quite sober in their appraisal of the Harkis' military role. Some stressed their courage and loyalty, others their disengagement and even desertions, especially as the war was coming to an end. One general was particularly cold in his discussion of the Harkis. He had fought in Algeria but had had little experience of them there. It was only after the war, when he was charged with developing an education program for their children, that he came to know them. He said little about them, seemed to regard them as a bureaucratic problem, a nuisance, really. But even he had reluctantly to admit that the Harkis had been treated shabbily by the French government. I personally did not meet any officer who denounced them as treacherous, but clearly there are some who did.

Several conversations I had with these officers seem to have produced an almost romantic, certainly nostalgic, attachment to the Harkis. I am not sure whether this reaction was the result of my questions, of their actual experiences, of their missing the excitement of war and the bonding that comes with it, or of never knowing what happened to those Harkis with whom they fought. One French soldier, Jean Gouneau, who had been honored by the French government in November 11, 2004, recalled: "One night I was on patrol with a Harki whose father had been killed [in battle] in 1944. At one moment he took my arm and told me not to advance. He saved my life. He was called Sharif. I left Algeria in 1959. He was in the French army, and he remained there. I've never had any news of him, but I often think of him."[33] It may also have been compensation for the guilt they felt for having "abandoned" their men. None with whom I talked admitted this. Nor did they admit to torture or wish to talk about the atrocities of war in any but a general sense. However proud they may have been of their military careers (and they were), however serious they knew war to be (and they did), however patriotic they were (and they certainly gave expression to their patriotism), they were often evasive in conversing with me. It was not, I think, that they had secrets to hide—no doubt, like all soldiers they did—but rather a desire to avoid appraising a war they had lost, a war that compromised their honor, the honor of France, as they might have put it, and the principles of correct, if not moral, warfare that had been instilled in them. I was surprised, for, with the exception of those who were defensively conservative, they were rather less pragmatic than I had expected. Perhaps this was a sign of age. It was, after all, more than forty years since they had served in Algeria. But, I suspect, their evasions were stirred by my asking them about the Harkis, a subject they would have preferred to forget, for the Harkis called up for them, as for many French civilians of their age, especially the conscripts who had been sent to Algeria, the moral complexity of that war. It was, of course, far easier for them to discuss the political dimensions of the war, probably of any war. We sometimes forget that, in distinguishing analytically between the moral and the political, we defend ourselves from acknowledging their inescapable affiliation. The political can at best defend us from the moral rhetorically.

One retired general told me that twice a year he travels some five hundred kilometers to visit a Harki who had been under his command and was now living in a home for disabled veterans. He had saved the general's life and, in so doing, had lost both his legs. As the general talked, it became clear that there was a sadness in these visits that surpassed the sadness, the inevitable guilt, of seeing a man who had suffered all his life on his account. Yes, they were deeply implicated in each other's lives, and that implication could be acknowledged only in silence, primordially, as copresence. But that silence, that copresence, was wrenched, not only by their different life trajectories, but also by the gap that lay between their respective understandings of the world. What finally could they say to each other, the general living in the center of Paris and the Berber, far removed from his *douar* in Kabylia, from which he was taken before he could have experienced it in full or even had an inkling of the fullness of that life. As the general spoke, I realized the pain of duty he felt. I asked him, perhaps indiscreetly, what they said to each other when they met; his silence was his answer. It was with some relief—but also regret—that he said that, at the conclusion of the war, he was back in France, in a hospital recovering from the wounds he had received at the time the Harki saved his life. I had asked him whether he had been ordered to send the Harkis back to their village at the end of the war.

FOUR

The War's Aftermath

Nous ne devons pas nous laisser envahir par la manoeuvre algérienne, qu'elle se fasse passer ou non pour des Harkis! Si nous n'y prenions garde, tous les Algériens viendraient s'installer en France.

We must not let ourselves be invaded by the Algerian maneuver that would get them to pass or not for Harkis. If we are not careful, all the Algerians will come to settle in France.

—Charles de Gaulle

"Then they—the Harkis—were told that they should return home," Mabrouk told me. "They were abandoned. The French had abandoned us." He continued:

If it wasn't the Algerian army who attacked you, then it was the people. If you were not too well-known, and if you fell into the hands of the ALN, they would take you to their garrison prison and question and torture you. If you had managed not to fall into the clutches of the ALN, when you got to your village, it was the same thing. But this time it was the villagers. They were immoral. I saw people beheaded. I still remember a man who had been in the SAS, he was beheaded in front of everyone. First, they made him work—work the earth—and then the people came and threw rocks at him. They spat on him. It was horrible. They cut his head off with a scythe. They said they had decapitated him as an example. But it was only because the people had chased him. It was extraordinary. He had rank in the SAS. He was a sergeant. So it was necessary to kill him. There was no trial—no judgment. People had only to say, "Oh, that one, he did bad things." Then they would slice him up. They cut pouches—*boutonnières*, they called them—under the skin of those they attacked and filled them with salt. They did this to a villager named Lhacen. They did it in front of all the villagers. We were just kids, but they made us leave school to watch and go around singing, "Vive l'Algérie." Sometimes, they even attacked Harki children. They threw the heads into garbage bins.[1]

My mother, sister, and I had been staying in the country with our family. My father had to stay in the casern. It was too dangerous for him to leave. He was a lance sergeant in the French army. He had gone to France to work. You see, in Algeria it was difficult to get work—only little jobs that paid nothing. My father worked as a laborer in Paris. He would come back once or twice a year. Then, with the *événements*, he decided to stay in Algeria and joined the army.

It was getting more and more dangerous for us to remain in our village. So we managed to escape to family in the mountains. Men in the family came for us and said we were leaving for a day or two. We didn't say we are leaving forever. Our neighbors always had their eyes on us. We didn't go to the family who had come for us but to another one because we knew they would come after us. They did come and were told that we had gone to Algiers. So we had to escape again. We, and another couple, traveled forty-seven kilometers through the mountains to take refuge at the garrison. I remember that walk. It was terrible because we couldn't go by road. We had to go across fields. For me it was a horrible night.

We were led by a man whom we had to pay. My father was in the casern, but he had contacts and was able to arrange this. There were Algerians who simply wanted to earn money. Our guide [*passeur*] was a distant relative on my mother's side of the family. He was also a cousin of my paternal uncle's brother-in-law. He paid the FLN off. The guides would be stopped by soldiers and had to pay up. There were some guides whom you paid, and then they disappeared with the money. Or left you with the FLN. It was horrible. Because our guide was a member of the family, he did not betray us. But he had cheated others. All that mattered was money.

The Harkis—it's true, they had a little money because, at independence, they sold everything they owned. Even a door. They didn't get much. The door may have cost them three hundred francs, but they had to sell it to a neighbor for twenty-five hundred old francs [i.e., twenty-five new francs]. Neighbors would come to our house and say, "Sell me that." [Mabrouk implies through gesture that the Harkis were threatened.] You sold things for nothing. Little sums—to be able to escape.

Mabrouk was seven or eight at the time of the events he describes. Today, he seems considerably older than his fifty-odd years. He works as a paramedic. Of medium height and build, he has notably high cheekbones and a thick moustache that he twirls from time to time. At his suggestion, we met in the lobby of a hotel where we were able to drink tea as we talked. "Here we can speak without being disturbed," he explained as he apologized for not meeting at his home. He is a soft-spoken man whose quiet manner belies the horror he experienced. *C'était horrible* punctuates his story. As his father served in the French army, he is, strictly speaking, not a Harki, but he identifies with the Harkis and participates in their rallies and protests. I was referred to him by several Harki children who insisted that I hear his story. For them it was exemplary. Though fluent, especially when he spoke of France's mistreatment of the Harkis, he often became confused as he recounted his early experiences. This was surprising since his tone of voice suggested that he had often spoken of these experiences.

Mabrouk begins his story by telling me how the Harkis had been abandoned by France. Usually conjoined with betrayal by the French, abandonment is an insistent leitmotif that runs through his and most other Harkis' portrayal of themselves. It contains and focuses the Harkis' rage against the French who did, by any standard, abandon them. It also buffers, in complex ways, the subjacent theme of betrayal. They trusted the French, and the French breached that trust as they themselves were accused of doing. (It should be remembered that some Harkis betrayed the French by secretly abetting the FLN.) Accusations of their betrayal supported and excused the violence directed at the Harkis by the Algerians at large and, as I have noted, by at least some French. The Harkis themselves were, and are, not immune to the force of such accusations. It would, however, be a mistake to understand their insistence on having been betrayed and abandoned as simply a displacement of their own sense of having betrayed their countrymen. Aside from the reality of their abandonment by the French, they live and have lived in a world saturated with accusations of treachery and the pernicious doubt cast on the purity of their motivations that arises in such a world.

It can also be argued that, as products of colonial paternalism as well as the paternalism fostered by the military, the Harkis found themselves particularly dependent on the French and, therefore, suffered their abandonment and betrayal with exceptional intensity. As they described how they had been sent back to their villages unarmed, with a small bonus and the assurance that they had nothing to fear, they could barely contain their rage and give adequate expression to their disillusionment. Most of the Harkis refused to describe to me, as they had refused their children, the horrors they had witnessed and the fears they undoubtedly felt. As one of them put it, "I don't want my children to know what I can't forget."

The Harki's silence is, perhaps, the one token of masculinity they would not lose. Silence before hardship is a masculine virtue among traditional Algerians. It is one of the characteristics of *sabr*—one their most important values. *Sabr* is usually translated as *patience, perseverance, forbearance,* or *endurance,* but can also mean "resignation," "submission," and even "renunciation." It has been associated with the Stoic *ataraxia*—a disengaged tranquility of mind—and tenacity in a holy war (jihad). But, unlike *ataraxia,* it entails for the Muslim trust in God—even when everything appears to be going wrong: "And be steadfast in patience, for verily Allah will not suffer the reward of the righteous to perish" (Quran 11:115). As silence in suffering the blows of fate, *sabr* is a preeminent value among the old Harkis and relates, I believe, less to an abstract sense of destiny than to a more situated sense of being caught up in a grand sweep of history that defies human understanding.

I remember hours spent on cold, dark March evenings in front of a stand on the outskirts of a city in the south of France, near a *cité,* or subsidized housing project, constructed for Harkis, that sold cola, snacks, cigarettes, beer, and, if the owner knew you, hard liquor. Here, I met old Harkis who came to drink whenever they had the money. When they found out who I was and what I was doing, they would recite, often in a drunken slur, their litanies of betrayal and abandonment by the French and France. Though I always asked about their experiences in the war, they rarely said more than that they had been sent on missions to ambush the FLN or that they themselves had been caught in an ambush. "*C'était dur*" (It was hard), they would say, echoing one another, and then repeat again and again how they had been abandoned. They could or would say little more. If they were not too drunk, they would sometimes tell me how the French had reneged on their promises to compensate them for the losses they had suffered in Algeria or their experiences in the camps. Usually, they turned to the owner of the stand, the son of a Harki, who was an important activist, for confirmation. With his confirmation, they appeared satisfied. So broken were they, it seemed to me, that they no longer had faith in their own words.

At times, to extricate myself from their litanies, I would simply say, as I had learned to do on other occasions, "Mekhtub" (It's written). And they would repeat, "Mekhtub. It's the will of Allah." To recast their experiences, the fatality of their nondecision, their decision, in terms of destiny (*qadar*) and of God's inscrutable will, gave them, perhaps, momentary respite.[2] At some level, even in their drunken state, they knew that they had been caught, unwittingly, in a transcending drama they would never be able to comprehend. We call it *history* (Ger. *Geschichte*) and find solace in the explanatory narratives we construct, usually forgetting that it is we who have constructed those causes, those narratives.[3] Sometimes, as I reflected on those drunken Harkis and many others whom I encountered in less disheartening circumstances, I found myself thinking that their acceptance of the incomprehensibility of contingency took more courage—was, at any rate, more realistic—than our denial of the artifice of the histories (*Historie*) we construct, the sociological explanations we offer ourselves. Destiny, it seems to me, negates history, but it, too, can be a crutch.

Mabrouk states simply that the Harkis "were told" that they should return home. Like many other Harki children, he does not say what his father specifically had been told to do. Rather, he generalizes. His—more generally, the Harki children's—generalizations may, at times, be deflections of what was specifically known but too painful to admit. Or they may reflect discretion—an unwillingness to reveal what is deeply personal to a stranger. But, most often, they seem to have been the result of ignorance of what, in fact, happened. It seems likely that Mabrouk never really knew what his father was ordered to do as the war came to an end. His father did not talk about his past in Algeria, and, at seven or eight years old, Mabrouk probably had little understanding of what had occurred. I will discuss the role of this ignorance in the construction and maintenance of Harki identity in chapter 7. Here, I want to note only that many Harki children compensate for their ignorance of particulars by personally assuming the Harkis' history.

It was, I believe, the breach of trust, their having been duped, that distressed the Harkis the most. Dupery and the pain, the embarrassment, the shame, and the dishonor it entailed took on, at times, disproportionate significance. *Le nondupe erre* haunted them. "The little guy became smaller"—more vulnerable and, thus more, inflammable, more prone, perhaps, to violence. Their society was traditionally, at least ideally, a society of the word.[4] In giving your word, in making a promise, you were under an unbreakable obligation to carry through on that word, to fulfill that promise. Were your enemy to ask for hospitality, you would be obliged to give it for a determinate time, usually three days. To fail to do so was not just to dishonor yourself before God but to elicit opprobrium and risk ostracism. Of course, there were often breaches of promise—local histories are filled with them. Not only did these histories justify enmity and feuding, but they often also served as moral lessons. They also seeded a cynicism that arises from the contradiction between trust and mistrust in the word—in the promise. With colonization, the force of obligation was, no doubt, diminished. Breaches were prevalent. Mistrust, which always hovers behind obligation, increased, especially with respect to the *colons*, who were as often misunderstood by as they misunderstood the Algerians. With the breakdown of trust, with the weakening of obligation, manipulation, which was never absent, increased dramatically and, with it, a justificatory rhetoric that rested on greater ends: freedom, fraternity, equality, independence, and nationhood.

As the war was winding down, there was considerable confusion about the status and future of the Harkis and other auxiliary troops as well as of Algerians enlisted in the French army. As the number of desertions increased, the army began to disarm the auxiliaries in order to prevent the flow of arms to the ALN. Despite the known risk of retaliation, progressive demobilization was begun in 1961, starting with the least trustworthy of the auxiliaries. Between July 1961 and March 1962, the GAD, the least dependable of them, was reduced by nearly 75 percent; the number of Harkis dropped from 59,000 to 42,100; the number of *moghaznis* remained relatively constant; and there was a slight increased in the number of men serving in the GMS (Faivre 1995, 252).[5] It was not, however, until March 20, 1962, several days after the signing of the Treaty of Evian, that the conditions for the demobilization of the Harkis were fixed; hence, roughly 17,000 Harkis who had already been released from duty (not to mention thousands more whose terms of service had ended earlier in the war) were uncertain as to what benefits, if any, they had.

The order of March 20 gave the auxiliaries three choices. (1) The Harkis could enlist in the French army, not at the rank they had achieved as an auxiliary, but at a beginning one and serve in France for a minimum of nine months regardless of the amount of time they had served as auxiliary troops. Their families would receive no support and would not be provided with transportation to France or Germany, where they would be stationed. (2) They could return to civilian life with a bonus of from five hundred to two thousand francs, depending on the length of time they had served. (3) They could ask for a *délai de réflexion* (a delay for reflection) of six months during which they would receive their salary and work as nonarmed auxiliaries. About fifteen hundred auxiliaries opted for the first choice. Several Harkis told me that, although they opted to go to France, they were never able to obtain papers and finally had to take refuge in a garrison to avoid being killed by the FLN (see also Jordi and Hamoumou 1999, 34). The vast majority took the second option, which they were often encouraged to do by their officers. In some instances, they were promised aid for constructing or reconstructing their homes and for clothing, food, and seeds as well as loans for the purchase of land for grazing sheep and priority for work on government construction sites (Roux 1991, 187–88). Personally, I never met or even heard of a Harki who received this aid.

The majority of Harkis I talked to said either that they were not given a choice but were simply ordered home or that they had not understood the choices given them (Boulhaïs 2002, 273). They described the confusion in their ranks. Rumors were rife. Fear was in the air. Uncertainty. They were exhausted and missed their homes and villages, which, no doubt like all soldiers, they idealized. Some said they expected trouble on their return but never anything as atrocious as the slaughters they were soon to witness. Others were sure that they would be welcomed back. Many of those who at first said that they had not been given a choice later acknowledged that they had made a choice without, however, admitting that they had made the wrong choice. One man in particular shook his head in such utter disgust at his own naïveté that I shall never forget his tortured expression. Others spoke with saddened gratitude of officers who not only explained the choices but also encouraged them not to return to their villages. Still others expressed disappointment in their officers, especially those who had befriended them. But, for the most part, they were simply enraged. That they were sent home without their weapons became a symbol of their betrayal.

"While he served, my father always carried his rifle, his bayonet, and some grenades," Hacène Arfi, who is one of the most quoted Harki activists, told me as we began talking about his father's return to his village at the end of the war.[6] He spoke softly, coldly, and, though he was very much in control of his words, I could feel the anger that lay behind them. Like the rage of so many Harki children I talked to, Hacène's was tempered by a personalized hurt that somehow gave his victimhood an empowering yet disabling self-sacrificial quality. "One week before he was arrested by the ALN, the French took back his weapons. He had nothing. He had been told to return his weapons because he would be issued more sophisticated ones. Once he had given them back, he and the other Harkis in his attachment were told that the war was over, the Treaty of Evian signed, that they—we— would be protected." Hacène's throat constricted. He could barely talk. "It was dramatic, dramatic. A man who had helped the French was told to go back to his village—unarmed—to find his family. Some of the Harkis were sacrificed as soon as they entered the village."[7]

The Treaty of Evian does not guaranty the auxiliaries specific protection. Article 2 stipulates: "No one will be made the object of police or judiciary measures, of disciplinary sanctions, or any discrimination resulting from—opinions issued during the events that took place before the vote for self-determination [or] acts committed at the time of these same events before the day the cease-fire was declared. No Algerian can be forced to leave or prevented from leaving Algerian territory."[8] There was, in fact, no way that this stipulation could be enforced—either practically (given the lack of preparation for, and the confusion during, the transition to independence) or legally—since it is by no means certain that the FLN signatories of the treaty had the authority either to make such a commitment or to enforce it. A split between two factions of the National Council of the Algerian Revolution was already in evidence in the council's meeting in Tripoli at the end of May and the beginning of June. Ben Bella, the FLN, and staff headquarters argued against the signatories of the treaty that the treaty was "a neocolonialist platform and an obstacle to the Revolution" (Faivre 1994, 181). Mabrouk ended the interview by repeating several times that the FLN negotiators did not represent the Algerian people.

There were French critics of the treaty who argued that, as the Algerian signatories were not representatives of a legitimately constituted government, only France was bound to the agreement—that a future Algerian government could repudiate it at any time. They further argued that, inasmuch as the French were required by the treaty to reduce their military presence to eighty thousand within a year and to withdraw completely within three years, and given that the military could not intervene in the event of infringements, France could not hold Algeria to the agreement.[9] De Gaulle himself was said to have told his cabinet that the application of the treaty would at best be capricious (*aléatoire*) (Horne 1987, 523). Yet he was adamant that the French military should not interfere in abuses for fear of retriggering the war.

The French failure to protect the auxiliaries from the violence directed at them has produced a defensive rationalization, not only among those who were in some way responsible for this failure, but also among those who had no responsibility. As I have already noted, the French responded to my interest in the Harkis in one of two principal ways. Either they simply said, usually in a detached manner, that, yes, they had treated the Harkis shamelessly. It was tragic. It was a stain on France. If they elaborated, they usually blamed de Gaulle, Louis Joxe, Pierre Messmer, Roger Frey, or some other well-known political or military figure. The most open referred, abstractly, to French racism. Or they would attempt to justify the treatment of the Harkis in terms of the confusion at the end of the war, the violence in the Algerian quarters of Paris, Lyon, and Marseilles, the flight of the *pieds-noirs* to France, the fear that the Harkis would aid the OAS. "You have no idea how close France was to a civil war," I was told, but, when I suggested that it was more likely that the *pieds-noirs* would support the OAS, if they were not already members, than the Harkis, my words were greeted with a dismissive shrug. The most bigoted claimed that cultural differences (read: race) were simply too great to permit their integration: "Look, at the Algerians who have been in France since before the war. Have they become French? Impossible. They lock up their women; they don't work; they drain our welfare system. Go to one of the hospitals. Then you'll understand."[10] No one I talked to mentioned the ten thousand Frenchmen and -women who were murdered or lynched in kangaroo courts by their fellow citizens in the aftermath of the World War II (Gross 2000, 29).

Even as objective a scholar as Tom Charbit, who has written extensively about the Harkis, writes somewhat defensively about their abandonment. At times, his objective stance serves this purpose. Take, for example, the following passage from his book *Les Harkis*. As his defensiveness is carried by his style, I quote him in French:

> La démobilisation précoce des troupes tranche, certes, avec le peu d'empressement dont font preuve les pouvoirs publics pour rapatrier les supplétifs et leur famille. A posteriori, le licenciement massif des troupes et leur démobilisation souvent expéditive apparaissent comme le preuve que l'armée a cherché à se débarrasser sciemment de ces hommes qu'elle savait pourtant menacé, tout en récupérant, bien évidement, leurs armes. En réalité, les circonstances confuses de la fin du conflit rendent la situation beaucoup moins lisible que ce qu'un regard rétrospectif laisse croire. Les déclarations rassurantes du FLN, la période de calme qui succède à la signature des accords d'Evian, la représentation que font alors les Harkis de leur engagement du côté français: l'espoir d'un dénouement pacifique du conflit est, durant quelques sémaines, encore permis. (Charbit 2006, 48)[11]

In quoting Charbit, I mean neither to single him out nor to impugn his scholarship but to demonstrate how the stain of betrayal and abandonment and the constellations of emotions associated with it can insinuate themselves into reasonably objective accounts by those whose only responsibility, if, indeed, it can be considered responsibility, arises from sharing a national identity. Charbit's twisted phraseology, as in "In reality, the confused circumstances at the end of the conflict [!] renders the situation less readable [!] than a retrospective view leads one to believe," is clearly defensive. Although the army's grasp of the situation was, no doubt, less than clear, it seems difficult to imagine that it would accept the assurances of the FLN after seven years of fighting, in which the FLN acted, or was believed to have acted, treacherously. The calm after the signing of the treaty was not without outbreaks of violence that suggested more violence to come. It should be noted that, several pages later, Charbit (2006 51) does cite a

June 1962 report to the Ministry for the Repatriated that, in April, the army estimated that four thousand auxiliaries (i.e., ninety-five hundred, including their families) were threatened, but he qualifies this number as limited ("d'ailleurs limitées").[12] No doubt, that "the hope of a peaceful conclusion to the conflict was during several weeks still permitted" had its effect on the judgment of an exhausted and disappointed military, but, as every soldier knows, however good for morale, hope is a realistic strategy's worst enemy.

Charbit's account relies heavily on French documentation, and, though he recognizes how highly politicized, and self-justificatory, military reports and historical accounts are, he gives them factual priority as he ignores—in a move that, no doubt inadvertently, echoes a colonial perspective—the Harkis' own versions of what transpired. He refers his readers, without citing any accounts of the massacres, to General Abd-el-Azziz Méliani's book *Le drame des Harkis* (1993), in which testimonies by the auxiliaries are collected.

Charbit (2006, 50–52) himself depends on a description by the subprefect of the district of Akbou in the department of Sétif that is cited in nearly all French accounts of the massacres. From March 19 to July 27, 1962, the subprefect reports a surprising calm in his district: "The most compromised Harkis lived together in the villages with members of the ALN, who sometimes invited them to drink tea in their company." But then suddenly, for no accountable reason, violent reprisal, which lasted until around September 15, broke out. The ALN killed seventy auxiliaries and civilians in the most remote villages of the district. Seven hundred fifty were arrested and sent to interrogation centers, from which you could hear from afar the screams of the tortured. Half the detained were killed, at a rate of from five to ten each night. Seven days later, on the first of August, a *conseiller général*, who had been asked by the ALN to act as mayor in one village, was buried alive, along with several other detainees, in front of 350 of the arrested. His head, above ground, was plastered with honey. "His agony, his face eaten by bees and flies, lasted five hours." The subprefect goes on to describe other tortures, including men who were dressed as women, their noses, ears, and lips cut off, castrated, buried alive in lime or cement, or burned alive. Others, in a neighboring district, were crucified on doors, whipped as they were forced to pull a plow, or had their muscles ripped apart with pliers.

Accounts reported by Méliani as well as those I heard, including Mabrouk's, confirm the torture, mutilation, and executions exacted by the ALN and the Algerian population at large. I myself heard stories of Harkis whose throats were cut in front of their wives and children, and there have been reports of others who were impaled or roasted alive or even forced to eat chunks of their own flesh (Benamou 2003, 221). Among the cruelest of the perpetrators, I was told again and again, were the *marsiens*—those Algerians who had not supported the FLN during the war but who in March (*mars*), when it became clear that the FLN would rule Algeria, suddenly claimed that they had supported the FLN and "to prove their loyalty," Mabrouk among others told me, "turned on us with horrible cruelty." "They were opportunists," Mabrouk said with complete contempt.

The subprefect's report, which was submitted in May 1963, was classified confidential and had limited circulation. But not only was the French government aware of violent reprisals from the beginning of April; they were reported in the press months before the subprefect submitted his report (Jordi and Hamoumou 1999, 40). In November 1962, Pierre Vidal-Naquet and Jean Lacouture reported in *Le monde* the tortures and executions, numbering, they estimated, around ten thousand. The press dismissed a twenty-five-page report describing the massacres—some sixty thousand—that was presented to them on December 18. In March 1963, the Economic and Social Council reported that at least twenty-five thousand had died between independence and October 1962 (Jordi and Hamoumou 1999, 40 n. 13).

Unlike Charbit, other historians, such as Jean-Jacques Jordi and Mohand Hamoumou (1999, 35ff.), who rely on Harki accounts as well as the archives, describe the ever-increasing anxiety—the near panic—of the Harkis in the months following the signing of the treaty.

The French police and military discovered FLN directives that, as cited in the last chapter, encouraged reprisals. The OAS continued attacking Muslims and French alike in their attempt to destabilize the country until a truce with the FLN was finally signed on June 17.[13] By the end of April, Jordi and Hamoumou (1999, 40) report, threats became clearer and brawls more frequent. "And then began the executions, usually preceded by abuse and torture." Though the authors do not specify when the executions began, General Faivre (1995, 157) noted that, already on March 19, a clash between Harkis and villagers at Saint Denis du Sig in which four Harkis were killed ended in the death of twelve. In June, the monthly bulletin of the army corps of Algiers reported: "The fate of Muslims enlisted on our side is tragic." In spite of promises of amnesty (*pardon*) by the FLN, the abduction of men, women, and children, summary executions, quarantining, and forced labor in ALN camps made them pariahs.

It is impossible to calculate how many Harkis were murdered after the war. Estimates have varied enormously. The journalist Jean Lacouture (1962) gave a figure, based on official French sources, of ten thousand. Lacouture's figures were immediately contested. The Harkis and those in sympathy with them claimed that there were 150,000 victims. This figure is generally considered too high. Other estimates range from 60,00 to 150,000. After reviewing various estimates, Hamoumou (1993, 248) came up with a figure of 100,000. Surprisingly, the Algerians who have ignored, if not denied, the massacres now suggest a figure of between 75,000 and 100,00 (*Quotidien d'Oran*, October 4, 2001, cited in Cohen 2006, 168). As the historian Guy Pervillé (1991, 123) has observed, "The true number of victims is unknown, but the horror of their death is disproportionate to [any] number."[14]

As I review the accounts of the brutality I recorded and those reported by Méliani and nearly every other author who has written about the Harkis, I am reminded of the violent rage directed at traitors and those assumed to be traitors at the end of a war. I think, too, of punishments meted out to sinners in Dante's *Inferno*. So many of them were, or could have been, carried out in the aftermath of the Algerian War. Dante placed traitors in the lowest, coldest, darkest, most dreary circle of hell. It is they who have breached the essential bonds of humanity, love and trust, *amor* and *fede*:

> Per l'altro modo quell'amor s'oblia
> che fa natura, e quel ch'è poi aggiunto,
> di che la fede spezïal si cria;
> onde nel cerchio minore, ov'è 'l punto
> de l'universo in su che Dite siede,
> qualunque trade in etterno è consunto.
> (Dante 1970, canto 11, lines 61–66)

By the other way both that love which Nature makes is forgotten, and that also which is added to it and which creates a special trust; therefore, in the smallest circle, at the center of the universe and the seat of Dis [Satan], every traitor is consumed eternally.

The breach of trust (I dare not say *love*) seems to perturb the innermost recesses of our psyches—the personal matrix of our sociality. It calls attention to the fragility of our communality, of our dependency on others, and of the physical contact, however conventionally constrained, that nurtures our relationship with those around us. It calls up the terror of isolation and loneliness. And, as I have already suggested, it produces the rage—the outrage—of having been deceived and the powerlessness to undo that deception.[15]

It is, perhaps, easiest for us to understand the violence that follows treachery in terms of rage and a sense of powerlessness that spurs that rage. It fits our culture-specific psychomechanic understanding of motivation. Accepting, for a moment, this mode of explanation, we must differentiate between generalized rage and rage directed at a specific betrayer; given our propensity to compress associated experiences in our response to others and their acts, particularly in moments of heightened emotion, the betrayer and the betrayal are prone to elicit an excessive response. They become scapegoats (Kara 1997, 120ff.). They come to symbolize a far larger, less graspable sense of prevailing treachery, as any reader of Jacobean tragedy will immediately recognize. Under such circumstances, if I may continue this line of argument, the rage intensifies as it incorporates the ungraspable and the sense of deficiency that the ungraspable evokes.

Though this explanation has some validity, it does not seem especially satisfying in either its generalization or its view of the violence produced by treachery. Each expression of violence reflects, not only particular biographical factors, but also the temporal, spatial, and social position in which the enraged finds himself or herself. It is also determined by the image of—and response to—the object of rage. Rage, like anger, always demands recognition and some sort of reciprocation. It is one thing to initiate violence; it is another to be caught up in collective violence. "The violence of the mob is contagious," we say, and seem satisfied with this observation, forgetting that we are making use of a metaphor that cannot do justice to experience. True, by evoking disease, it offers an implicit evaluation of such violence and our inability to resist it, but it gives no explanation for that violence. We know neither why some people are immune to the contagion and others are not nor why it breaks out and continues in one place and at one time rather than another.

I am particularly troubled by the timing of violent outbursts. The subprefect was surprised that several peaceful weeks went by before the villagers turned on the Harkis. Many accounts of violence, including Mabrouk's—the village in which his family took refuge was calm for some time—report either a delay in its onset or sporadic incidents that did not flare up immediately. Fazia, the daughter of a Harki, told me that, when the war ended and her father and other Harkis returned to their village in Kabylia, the villagers organized a huge feast—I am tempted to say of reconciliation—in which supporters of the FLN, the Harkis, and the politically disengaged shared couscous. Ideally, this should have placed them under an obligation to maintain peaceful relations, but, a few weeks later, the FLN, supported, it seems, by some of those same villagers, arrested and imprisoned Fazia's grandfather, who had served in the French army in Morocco and had been sympathetic to the Harki cause. His son was forced to flee to France, leaving his family behind. (Eventually, thanks to the intervention of the Red Cross, Fazia's grandfather was released, and the rest of the family escaped to France.)

We do not know the specific circumstances that triggered these outbursts of violence. Sylvie Thénault (2008, 82–85) argues quite rightly that one must look at each *wilaya* and each area where the massacres occurred in order to determine their causes and timing, but the research has yet to be done. Many French and some Algerian observers claim that, just as the decision to become a Harki or join the FLN often reflected age-old family feuds, so did the outbursts that followed the war. Speaking from the Harki point of view, Fazia observed that it was the FLN that forced the Harkis to make the decision to join the French, and she holds them entirely responsible for the postindependence massacres. Several French officers said that the villagers held off until they were sure that neither the French nor the ALN would interfere. A secret document concerned with ALN conduct from March 19 to independence from the Provisional Command of the Algerian Revolution, recovered from an ALN lieutenant after the cease-fire, does offer some support to this argument. It orders the ALN to treat the Harkis in a way that will not produce a French reaction and notes ominously that it is after independence, when the French army is unable to act or intervene, that "we will effectively occupy ourselves with the Harkis." In light of this future operation, it orders that lists of all Harkis be drawn up, that the maximum amount of information about them and their families be gathered, and that their movements be followed in a very precise manner (Faivre 1994, 181–82).

Though the argument that the ALN delayed violent retribution until the French could no longer interfere may apply to some of the massacres they effected, it cannot account for the more spontaneous ones carried out by civilians. Such outbursts were not planned and usually occurred in the first months after independence. (Many of those carried out or triggered by the ALN or FLN occurred later, in the fall of 1962.) These slaughters were not orchestrated the way, say, the massacre by the FLN at Philippeville had been. The Harkis with whom I spoke could give no explanation. For the most part, they simply shrugged their shoulders. What good would an explanation do? What could one expect of villagers who had been led astray by the FLN? It happened; that's what's important, not when. The trajectory of violence was, for the most part, reduced to *the* violence—a timeless icon of itself that precluded elaboration. In many of the accounts I heard, a single act—a particularly intense memory, abraded by constant recall—stood for all the violence experienced directly or by hearsay.

As I reread several cantos of the *Inferno*, I thought to myself that, there, the violence was represented in literary form, while, in Algeria, it was enacted. Dante names most of those whose punishments he describes, but there is always a background of nameless shades who suffer similar punishments. Mabrouk names only one man, Lhacen, who was tortured and killed, though he identifies others who worked with the SAS. Dante's figures reside in another, phantasmatic world; they are allegorical in a vast allegory. Mabrouk's and those of other Harkis with whom I spoke are—or were—people living in the real world and the actual subjects of Mabrouk's and others' experience. They were not allegorical, though they could be allegorized. In the immediacy of Mabrouk's account, Lhacen and the SAS workers, as well as the unidentified he refers to, are simply there—concrete, in their meaningless facticity, as Jean-Paul Sartre would, no doubt, have characterized that concrete presence, that suffering, that demise. I understand them, as they occur in many Harki accounts, as signs that turn in on themselves—signs that resist, but never succeed in resisting, the split in signification (between signifier and signified).

But who were the Harkis for the FLN, ALN, the *marsiens*, and the Algerians at large? Although I have talked to many Algerians, some of whom fought for independence, I have no reliable evidence regarding what they thought of them at the time other than that they were the enemy and, worse than the enemy, the *collabos*. One Algerian woman, who had been in the resistance and became an important Algerian diplomat after the war, stressed the blind rage that the word *traitre*—"traitor," *gheddar*—produced. She argued that it was important to remember that the majority of Algerians, especially the peasantry, were uneducated (*inculte*) and, as such, reacted without reflection. She cited the massacres that occurred in the Oranais, where she came from, and noted that they reflected century-long feuds. She added that, like other Mediterranean peoples, the Italians, for example, the Algerians were particularly excitable. Others were less sympathetic, arguing that "the *collabos* got what they deserved."

It could be argued that, as Algerians who fought against the creation of an independent Algeria, the Harkis symbolized a division in the idea of Algerian nationhood, the fragility of that idea—division and fragility that had to be denied. But I doubt that an awareness of the vulnerability of the Algerian nation fired their rage. Indeed, any number of observers claim that most rural Algerians had only the vaguest idea of a nation; for them, social reality was framed by lineage, clan, and tribe. I am by no means convinced by such clichés, and, in any case, I suspect that the expression of rage was far too immediate to have been inspired by a vacuous nationalism.[16] Its aim, at least one of its aims, as with all rages, was the desire to obliterate the object of one's rage: to expunge what cannot be expunged, given that it has already occurred. Though we cannot rid ourselves of the past, even through forgetfulness or repression, we are sometimes able to obliterate the real or fancied perpetrator who has become a reminder of what occurred.[17] One could argue that the impossibility of ever obliterating the past intensifies the rage, for, at some level of consciousness, its failure must be acknowledged. Deflections and symbols are never fully satisfactory. Lacan (1966, 626ff.) would argue that they are the products of desires, which, insofar as they are formulated in language (discours), can never reach their real object.

"The basic aim of a nation at war in establishing an image of the enemy is to distinguish as sharply as possible the act of killing from the act of murder by making the former into one deserving of all honor and praise," the philosopher J. Glenn Gray (1959, 131–32) observes in his philosophical meditation on war. One way in which this is done is to create an abstract image of the enemy, one that casts the enemy "as sufficiently evil to inspire hatred and repugnance" (133). In his exploration of the modes of abstracting the enemy, Gray notes that, on the field of battle, the soldier personalizes the enemy; they become "my enemy." But, even in their personalization, they remain abstract: "No one should underestimate the cruelty and the delight in cruelty when a soldier—or a civilian—is impelled by such personal abstract hatred. For this reason, civil wars are usually replete with refinements of personal torture and are commonly more terrible than international wars" (140).

Gray (1959, 141) goes on to note a paradox: "Personal hatred even of this sort carries with it more possibility of humaneness than does abstract hatred where no personal injury has been suffered and where the hater is without responsibility and not in danger." In the closeness—I am tempted to write intimacy—of the battlefield, the soldier may recognize at some level the humanity of the enemy. The humanization of the enemy may appear to endanger the morale—the will to victory—of the soldier, perhaps, at times, even his ability to defend himself and his fellow soldiers, but it can also be argued, as I would, that, in war, the paradox is so intolerable that the soldier must obliterate his enemy to obliterate the paradox. Gray himself does not consider the implications of the paradoxes he describes, but I believe that they must be taken into account.

We certainly cannot deny cruelty in the Algerian War, the refined use of torture by both sides. However justified the use of torture may sometimes be said to be, as a way of obtaining information vital to survival and victory— in the event, a highly contested argument—it is from an experiential standpoint always more than a means of obtaining information. Among other things, it is, as Elaine Scarry (1985, 27–28; see also Crapanzano 2004, 88–89) observes, always a demonstration of power. It serves, as one of the French military interrogators observed in a deposition to the Algerian chief prosecutor (*procureur générale*), as a "psychological preparation" designed "to terrify [*affoler*], to paralyze, the patient [!] by proving to him his impotence by staging a scene in which the most ignoble insults, abject blackmail, and death threats play an equal role; these moral tortures are accompanied by the worst possible physical violence, which increases incrementally to assassination even" (quoted in Branche 2004, 564). Jean-Paul Sartre notes that the prisoner is often treated as an animal and is made "to feel that he does not belong to the same species" (Sartre 1958, 16). But perhaps the most important effect (goal?) of torture is to create an atmosphere of terror and rampant fear (Green 1994). Despite its secrecy, when it is, in fact, carried out secretly, torture also has a theatrical dimension. In this respect, it is, perhaps, not that far from Dante's representations of cruel punishments. What effect this representational quality of torture, even when it known to occur but not actually witnessed, has on those who are privy to it is influenced by the circumstances in which it occurs.

Torture carried out in war must be distinguished from the reactionary torture carried out after a war. Indeed, I am not even comfortable using the same word, for, in the one case, right or wrong, it is considered purposeful and is administered in a more or less systemic way by technicians under orders. Usually, it occurs behind closed doors, in small spaces; though not seen, the screams of its victims are often heard outside its confines, producing a terror that I would liken to an auditory but imageless nightmare. Witnesses have said that the torturers render "the voice of the men who are victims of torture unrecognizable" (quoted in Branche 2004, 561). Torture is demonstrative of power—the power of the state. Though it may end with the death of its victim, death is not its ostensible aim. In the second case, it is spontaneous, without system and ostensible purpose, rarely secret, and carried out publicly by a populace that is neither instructed nor under orders. Though unstated, its aim is the painful death of its victim. It may be demonstrative of power and encourage social cohesion, but it may (as is, no doubt, true of the first case) also reveal a sense of powerlessness and communal division (Gr. *stasis*). The seeking of information, if it is, in fact, sought, seems in this second mode of torture a particularly lame excuse.[18] In the torture of the Harkis, when information was sought, it was, as several Harkis told me, aimed at discovering the identity of other *collabos* or confirming their supposed acts of betrayal. Torture seemed to have been, on most of the occasions I know of, part of the humiliation, mutilation, and execution of its victim. It resonated with the torture and violence of the war, which, as we know, was carried out by both the French and the ALN with, at times, orgiastic energy.[19]

What the torture of the Harkis demonstrated in general is something I cannot say. In many respects, it appears simply to have been unreflective acting out. An act of vengeance, perhaps; a punishment, even. What seems certain is that the victims of postwar torture carried enormous symbolic weight, reflecting, on the one hand, the torturer's personal history and, on the other, that of the collectivity. Public, these acts were spectacles. They collectivized the response, and, in so doing, they depersonalized it. The torturers and their audience were swept away. They ceased to be themselves, some have said.

Both the soldier and the civilian during times of war have to preserve the prevailing image of the enemy: the distance, the abstraction, the impersonality, indeed, the dehumanization that image encourages.[20] It defends the soldier from the guilt—better, the complex of entangled emotions—that usually arises from killing another human being. But what happens when the impress of reality disturbs that image, as when one's relations with the enemy become so close that one must recognize his humanity? Were the life-threatening conditions of battle absent, such recognition could lead to a sympathetic attachment to the now human enemy and promote that sort of bond that so frequently conjoins strangers, even inimical strangers, who have lived together through life-threatening events. But the circumstances of war do not usually permit such bonding (though it has often been reported between prisoners of war and their guardians). Rather, as I have suggested, the contradiction between the two perceptions of the enemy may foster a destructive rage that leads to the obliteration of the human enemy, preserving, thereby, the socially constituted image of the enemy as hateful, evil, inhuman, bestial, possessed by satanic forces, and, more realistically, dangerous.[21]

Here, with caution, I would like to suggest that one possible effect of the torture, mutilation, and execution of those accused of collaborating with the enemy was the untenable contradiction between the human ties—those of family, friendship, and a multitude of shared experiences—that the villagers had with their victims and the image of them as the treacherous enemy. *Traitors* but poorly mediates the contradiction. Rather, the paradoxical relationship fosters the obliteration of the traitor, who must first be rendered as fully as possible *the enemy*. In Mabrouk's account, the Harki victims were dressed as women. This was an act, not just of humiliation, but of symbolic emasculation that would become real emasculation when they were, in fact, castrated. They were reduced to animals when they were made to work the fields as beasts of burden. The authority they once had as fathers or potential fathers, as adults, was reversed by their being mocked and stoned by the children (and, in other accounts that I heard, by the women) of the village. Their execution seems inevitably to follow, for otherwise—it could be argued—the victims would memorialize and perpetuate their victimization.

For the most part, the Harki victims were buried, not in village cemeteries, but in unmarked graves outside the villages. In some instances, those killed by the ALN were left without a burial (Scheele 2006, 866).[22] I would suggest that neither the dehumanizing acts nor their theatricalization—their display—could render the Harkis so fully the enemy that their ties with their fellow villagers could be expunged from memory that led, in the first instance at least, to their execution. No doubt, as torture, mutilation, and executions continued, other reasons for them became dominant. It may be that the horror of the slaughter became so great that the spectators could no longer watch but had to participate in order to inure themselves from what they had been witnessing. In the event, it seems to have taken time for the experience of the contradiction between the Harkis as fellow villager and as enemy became so intense that the villagers had to destroy them.

There was, of course, another set of witnesses who claimed that they could do nothing to prevent the massacres. I am referring to the French soldiers stationed in Algeria in the aftermath of the war. By the terms of the treaty, as I have noted, they no longer had policing authority; their relationship with Algeria was now with an independent state and had to follow diplomatic procedures. Their response varied considerably. Some ignored the slaughter; one officer I spoke to simply denied knowing anything about it. Others referred with muted sorrow and regret to their powerlessness—to the unavoidable consequences that followed France's loss of the war. I spoke to no one who took any pleasure in an I-told-you-so manner or understood the massacres in racial terms, though I am sure that there were some. Racial, ethnic, and religious stereotyping was never absent from the military's understanding of the Algerians. Some officers tried to protect their men, as we have seen, by encouraging them to enlist in the French army. A few managed to secret Harkis they had fought beside to France, but this was soon prohibited by the French government (see chapter 5).

As I listened to accounts of the massacres, I wondered to what extent they addressed the French. Were they a show of newfound power? Were they meant to taunt the French? Lacan says that desire assumes (in its possessive sense) the desire of the other in reverse. The massacres as spectacles may have been a final demand for recognition by the French, a last legacy of a colonialism that refused recognition of the subjectivity of its subjects, the colonized. Certainly, the desire for recognition by the French is a dominant theme among the Harkis and, now, among Algerian workers and their children in France. The extent to which this desire for recognition played a role in the village massacres is difficult to gauge. Most often, the massacres were carried out far from the French, who learned of them only after the fact. But presence is not required for phantasmatic address. It seems clearer that the ALN tortures were often a direct assault on French sensibility. Often they were carried out within earshot of the French.

"They stopped me on the road. I had permission to visit my kid. They threw me in a deep hole. They fed me couscous with blood in it. They put sand in it. They gave me water with salt in it." Ahmed, a soft-spoken man in his late sixties, told me that he had been captured by a group of *marsiens* on March 19, 1962, a day after the Treaty of Evian was signed, and that, after being interrogated and tortured with burning cigarette butts and electric prods, he was kept prisoner in a dry well for eleven months. He was not allowed to leave the well. He was never given a change of clothing, nor had he any way to clean the few square meters in which he was kept. "I didn't see any light, just a tiny spot, all that time." When I asked him what he had thought about, he answered, "You don't think. You are dead." At the end of eleven months, for no apparent reason, Ahmed was removed from the well, and, when he regained his sight—after months in the dark he had lost it—he was ordered to work in the garrison kitchen. A few months later, on May 29, 1963, he managed to escape by hiding in a truck that carried garbage to a dump. As soon as he could, he jumped off the truck and made for the nearby French base. "It was only fifteen meters away from the well," he said, much to my surprise. "So did the French know you were there?" I asked him. "Yes, they knew it. They knew there were other prisoners there too. Some French. But they did nothing." Ahmed's voice dropped, and he tried several times to begin his story again but could not. He stumbled on his words. Finally, he said, with little emotion, that, if he were ever to see one of the *marsiens* who held him captive, he would murder him, even in front of a police station.

Ahmed was never told why he had been taken prisoner. He thinks it was simply a bunch of *marsiens*—"des sales types"—who were trying to ingratiate themselves with the FLN. "It wasn't right. I was a prisoner of war, but they didn't care." Ahmed was correct. He had enlisted in the French army in 1957 and ought to have been treated as a prisoner of war. His father, a small landowner, had served with the French in World War I and encouraged him to enlist. The FLN had requisitioned the family's food one time too many. From what I could gather, Ahmed seems to have worked in the kitchen most of the time, except when he was sent on missions. He went on at great length about how he was received at the French garrison. He was taken to a colonel in the Deuxième bureau who questioned him and, after confirming as much of his story as he could by conferring with Ahmed's unit commander, a certain Captain Martini, sent him to his unit's base. From there he was flown to Marseilles and sent on to the camp at Rivesaltes, where he remained for two weeks before being transferred to Baden Baden, where his unit had been stationed. He served his term of duty, and, against Captain Martini's advice, he decided not to remain in the army. He was discharged in Toulouse and moved to the city in which he now lives. He worked as a janitor in a local hospital and married a repatriated Algerian woman with whom he had five children. As he was describing his children to me, he mentioned a son whose mother was his first wife and who now lives nearby. I had not realized that he had been married to another women. Unexpectedly, he announced that his wife had been married to two men at the same time. "She thought I was dead," he explained without any apparent distress, "so she married another man." When I asked him how he had felt when he discovered this—the stuff of many a Hollywood movie—he simply repeated in a matter-of-fact manner, "She thought I was dead so she married another man."

Ahmed talked warmly about Captain Martini, whom he calls a friend. "He spoke Arabic like an Arab," he tells me several times during the interview. "We used to go boar hunting together." He never asked the captain why the army had not looked for him. He seems so beholden to the army that he never criticized it. It seems likely that Martini assumed he had deserted. I asked him what he thought the *marsiens* thought about what they had done. With more emotion than he had yet expressed, he said that they don't think about it. "They don't give a damn." Ahmed told me he doesn't think about his captivity. "I think about the difficulties I have now." As Ahmed was growing tired, I asked him one last question. Did he ever think about going back to Algeria? "I would go back to Algeria. No, no, no. Personally, even if it were possible, I wouldn't go back. I have good memories of Algeria." The interview did not end on that note. As so many Harkis I had spoken to concluded our meeting, Ahmed went on telling me how the Harkis had been abandoned by the French. How they had not been adequately compensated for the farms they had lost. How they had been deceived. How they were given mortgages at special rates for their homes and then the rates increased and the term of payment was extended. Like many of the Harkis I talked to, Ahmed was especially proud of his house: a large, rather attractive one in the *pavillon* style of the Côte d'Azur, furnished with comfortable leather armchairs and a couch facing a large television. It was impeccably clean and neat. I could not help thinking that any American worker would be envious. His litany of complaints, like that of so many Harkis, had been repeated countless times. It was, it seemed to me, a mode of escape, yes, from painful memories, but also from a persistent sense of powerlessness. The litany founded—ritually, I am tempted to write—a set of complaints some of which could be remedied through political action. Ahmed had often told his story at political rallies and commemorative gatherings. It had become testimony.

What is puzzling about Ahmed's account is that the French army, aware of the prisoners taken by the *marsiens*, did nothing. While it is true that, after the treaty was ratified, the French could no longer maintain order in Algeria, but Ahmed was arrested on March 19, 1962, more than three months before ratification, during which time the French still had policing authority. It seems clear that the French were reluctant to intervene. They were in a delicate situation, not only because the peace was still fragile—the new Algerian government was not even established—but also because the country was threatened by the terrorist acts of the OAS. In July, France's first ambassador to Algeria, Jean-Marcel Jeannency, expressed his country's concern about the violence directed at the auxiliary troops by the provisional government. Ben Bella told him dismissively that the Algerian people are "sage et juste—en la circonstance" (wise and just, given the circumstances) (Morelle 2004, 117).

One French businessman with important government connections (who has asked to remain anonymous) told me that the French government had been reluctant to interfere in Algeria's "internal affairs" on behalf of the Harkis because, for economic reasons, i.e., France's interest in the Saharan oil fields, it did not want to offend the new government.[23] It is also clear that, having lost the war, the French were dispirited and exhausted. Military discipline notwithstanding, officers and soldiers alike tended to retreat into a *je-m'en-fou* attitude. Some were disgusted by the orders they had received to send the Harkis back to their villages to be slaughtered. Their warnings had been ignored. Others were simply anxious to return home as soon as possible whatever the consequences. They had had it. They had witnessed, had participated in, atrocities they had never imagined possible. Many soldiers I talked to over the years were rendered speechless when I asked them about their personal experiences in the war. Without wishing to generalize, I found their attitude very different from that of those who had fought in World War II. They felt morally corrupted by a war many of them did not believe in, and even those who did believe resented, as did many American soldiers in Vietnam, the lack of support from their countrymen. It was the opponents of the war who were in the news. They were confronted—to use the existentialist idiom of the time—less with absurdity or contingent existence than with the futility of war, the lies that justified it, the sheer meaninglessness—the ultimate folly—of human engagement, of simply being human. Of course, there were exceptions: those who flourished in war.

Given the near-chaotic conditions in much of Algeria at the time, the military had more than enough to do in reducing its presence and, at the same time, ensuring that the *pieds-noirs* were able to leave. Although the French had anticipated the flight of some *pieds-noirs* (and even some Harkis), they were unprepared for the number of *pieds-noirs* who did flee Algeria within the space of a few months. They were given, without question, priority over the Harkis.[24] The French government had by no means been unaware of the threats that the Harkis faced. More than a year before the treaty was signed, the minister of state for Algerian affairs had received several reports concerning the future of the Harkis (Morelle 2004, 100). The French hoped that the Algerian government would abide by the protections stipulated in Article 2 of the treaty.[25] They did recognize that they would have to receive those few auxiliaries whose lives were endangered. At the end of May, they more than doubled the number of auxiliaries who would be offered refuge in France, from thirty-five to seventy-three hundred. But, though they were realistically concerned about the cost and the economic impact of the arrival of tens of thousands of Harkis, race and cultural nationalism no doubt played an even greater role in their policy. Justifying the neglect of the Harkis, Colonel George Buis, then director of the military cabinet of the French High Commission in Algeria, wrote in 1991: "You had to live through those dramatic moments when thousands and thousands of French, their repatriation pending, waited in the worst of conditions for a plane or boat" (Charbit 2006, 60). He added that, as a whole, the Harkis were not in any danger at the time of independence "since they always had more or less a foot in the rebellion" (Roux 1991, 213). Ahmed was by no means the only Algerian to suffer from this state of affairs.

In the months preceding the ratification, as the repatriation of auxiliaries whose lives were threatened was postponed by one bureaucratic obstacle after another, a number of French officers arranged privately for the transfer of some Harkis in their command to France.[26] In May 1962, some of them, particularly former SAS officers, founded the Association des anciens des affaires algériennes (AAAA), which organized the repatriations. But these were almost immediately brought to a halt by the French government.[27] On May 16, the minister of state, Louis Joxe, sent a top secret telegram to his high commissioner, reminding him that all individual initiatives to relocate French Muslims were strictly forbidden. He noted that auxiliaries who arrived in France under nongovernment auspices would be sent back to Algeria.[28] He added: "I am not unaware that [as] this turning back can be interpreted by propagandists of the insurrection [*propagandistes de la sédition*] as a refusal to assure the future of those who remained faithful to us, it is thus advisable to avoid the least publicity for this measure; but it is especially necessary to guaranty that the government is no longer led to make such a decision" (Azni 2002, 86).[29] Joxe's order was confirmed the following day by Roger Frey, the minister of the interior, under whose ministry Algeria fell. On May 24, Joxe told the Council of Ministers that "the Harkis want to leave en masse" and that "it was necessary to fight an infiltration, which under charitable pretext [*sous prétexte de bienfaissance*] would have the effect of our welcoming undesirable elements" (Jordi and Hamoumou 1999, 38). No doubt by *undesirable elements* Joxe was referring to, among others, auxiliaries who were attached to the OAS. Both *Le figaro* and *Le monde* had published articles at the time arguing that, once in France, the Harkis would support the OAS's aim to overthrow the French government (Roux 1991, 220). Clearly, other factors—race, ethnicity, cultural difference—were also at play since, if the OAS were to find support in France, it would surely have been from among the *pieds-noirs*.[30]

As the probable result of a scandal triggered by press reports on May 23 of the prohibition, about ten thousand pro-French Algerian personnel (including in that number their families)[31] were shipped to France and housed in military camps. But, on July 15, Joxe went further, ordering "the searching of the army as well as the administration for instigators and accomplices in the repatriation of Harkis and applying the appropriate sanctions" (Jordi and Hamoumou 1999, 38–39). Despite the intensification of massacres of the auxiliaries, Joxe suspended all repatriations. It was not until September 19, after the fiercest of reprisals, that repatriation was resumed by the order of the Prime Minister Georges Pompidou. It is, as we might expect, nearly impossible to determine accurately how many auxiliaries managed to get to France. After reviewing various estimates, Michel Roux (1991, 223–31) concluded that roughly 140,000 Algerian refugees made it to France, mostly between 1962 and 1968. Of these, 85,000 were auxiliaries and their families. The remaining 55,000 were the families of privileged Algerians: municipal elites, general councilors, deputies and senators, bureaucrats, *caids*, *aghas*, *bachagas*, career soldiers and officers in the French army, doctors, lawyers, and other professionals.

Just as it is impossible to number the Harkis who were massacred or who made it to France on their own, it is equally impossible to number those who remained in Algeria. (Some Algerians claim that there are more Harkis and their children living in Algeria than in France.) Many Harkis managed to survive the massacres. Some were imprisoned;[32] some were protected by their families; others disappeared into anonymity in towns, cities, and the *bled* (countryside) where they were unknown; and still others spent years in hiding before they finally made it to France, if, in fact, they did. I heard harrowing stories of Harkis who could settle nowhere, lived in caves, traveled at night, always in danger, not knowing what had happened to their families, and never having enough to eat. The fragmentary nature of these accounts attests to an episodic time that, having no cohesion, resists narrative formulation. Some who, like Ahmed, had spent years in prison were finally deported, thanks in part to the intervention of the International Red Cross. Between 1965 and 1970, over eleven hundred arrived in France. They were first sent to the Algerian Department of Anthropometry (Service algérien de l'anthropométrie) to be photographed and fingerprinted. They were made to sign a form in which they agreed to be *expulsés algériens* who were prohibited from ever returning to Algerian soil. Their names were sent to immigration authorities and the air police. If they tried to return, as several of the Harkis I interviewed tried to do, they were refused entry and sent back to France (see chapter 7).

Those Harkis who managed to remain in Algeria and were eventually recognized as such found themselves exiles in their own country. They were not treated as Algerian citizens. They were ineligible for passports, and they were not allowed to register at the Algerian National Office of Labor and were, thus, unable to find work. They were, in effect, condemned to lives of misery (Heinis 1977). Though some Harkis have managed to return to Algeria to visit their families, many of the ones I talked to reported that they or someone they knew was not permitted entry. The situation for Harki children is contradictory. Some, particularly women, have been granted entry;

others have been refused for no discernible reason. Still others were able to enter by bribing accommodating immigration officers. What is certain is that, whatever the actual circumstances of the Harkis in France or Algeria, they have figured and continue to figure in the political rhetoric of the Algerian government as enemies of the state.

FIVE

The Camps

Mabrouk continued his story:

It was a terrible winter—the winter of '62. In the morning we were left at the gate to the garrison. There were women waiting there. Finally they led us to a room and asked for our IDs. "Who are you?" they asked. "Who is your husband?" Then they did an investigation. They didn't keep you in the casern. It was only a *lieu d'accueil*. . . . We were taken to a camp near the sea, Zeralda,[1] where there was more room. We were hidden in between boxes because the Algerian army could stop and search the trucks. They had all the power. The French had to cooperate. They sent us in freight trucks or with the Red Cross. It was horrible. It was hard. While my father—he was a lance sergeant—was in the garrison, my mother, sister, and I lived in Zeralda. My father could not leave the garrison to visit us because it had become too dangerous after March 19. We were kept in Zeralda for several months. When there were enough of us, maybe a thousand, at least a thousand, they sent us to France. When we got to France, trucks were waiting there for us. We were surprised. We didn't imagine France was like this. Well, they squeezed us into the trucks like potatoes. When we arrived at the camp [Rivesaltes, near Perpignon], we were taken to a hangar. There was a maximum of fifteen square meters for two or three families. A soldier came and brought us a couple of blankets and some cigarettes. They fed us a porridge. I remember well.

We stayed there for a couple of months, and then we were scattered across France. For example, some worked in Perpignon, others up north. The handicapped were sent to Bias. There was an order given at the time not to let the families remain together.[2] They'd even separate brothers. They'd send them to different camps. They'd try to find them jobs. They'd keep them in one of these camps for maybe four to six months, and then they'd send them to forestry hamlets that were far from each other. They were never kept in the same area.[3]

    We saw this—the tearing apart of families. What could we do? We couldn't leave. There was barbed wire and guards. It was horrible. Finally we—my father—decided to escape back to Algeria. It had to be better than this. Oh, we fled in the night. We thought we would be able to get to Algeria somehow, but we ended up in a settlement on the outskirts of Perpignon.

Mabrouk goes on to describe a shantytown where gypsies now have a camp. There were about two hundred families there. The mayor had tried to hide the slum from de Gaulle when he came to visit Perpignon by placing billboards along the road in front of it, but, according to Mabrouk, de Gaulle saw it anyway. Without finishing his thought, Mabrouk loses himself in memory. Finally, I ask him how he had felt at the time:

> It was horrible. We lived there from '63 to '67. We had very little money, but there was enormous solidarity. As we were French citizens, the government couldn't force us to leave. You had, of course, to find work on your own. I went to school in Perpignon. We never told anyone we were Harkis. It was better that way.
>
>   You see, when we arrived in France, we had to go before the administration. We were asked, "Do you want to be French?" "Yes, I want to keep my French citizenship," we would answer and then sign a paper. They gave us ID cards. It was the only way people could leave the camps.[4]

After a long, painful pause, Mabrouk went on:

> What I can't understand is why, after all these years, the French state has not recognized what we did for France and give us compensation and jobs for the children, for example. Those who were the enemy are now treated better than we are. To have joined the French army is a handicap. To be a Harki is a handicap.

Mabrouk's last observation was at one time or another made by most of the Harkis with whom I spoke. Almost all of them described angrily being asked by a judge whether they wanted to be a French citizen. They assumed they were. Mabrouk's description of his and his family's departure for France is less developed than that of many other Harkis. This can be accounted for in part by Mabrouk's age at the time, but even the more elaborated descriptions, particularly by the Harkis themselves, were nearly always truncated. Like Mabrouk's, their stories began with their flight, dangerous and at night, to a garrison where, terrified, they found the gates closed and hundreds of people, mostly women and children, waiting. They go on to describe a meeting with a French officer who checks their identities. They do not, however, speak of their anxiety as they waited for the officer's decision. They discuss their departure from Algeria, their being stuffed into the holds of transport ships, and their arrival in one of the camps. Most of them told me that they were disappointed in France from the time they landed there. It was not the country they had imagined. Their image was, as Anne Heinis (1977) described it, near mythic and ambivalent.[5] All the Harkis stress the miserable conditions in which they were made to live, the tight quarters that, at least at the beginning of their incarceration, they had to share with other families whom they did not know, who were of a different ethnic group, who spoke a language they did not understand, the military discipline to which they were subjected, and, often enough, the corruption of the camp commanders.

Mabrouk's family's flight from the camp is, however, unusual. Most of the Harkis remained in the camps until they found work through personal contacts or the French administration.

As in Mabrouk's description, the Harki men tended to generalize their stories, alternating between *we, one,* and *I.* This oscillation reflects, I suspect, an instability in their narrative position, an instability that reflects tension between their individual identity and their membership in a group—the Harkis—and the insistent identity their being a Harki imposes and is imposed on them (Whitol de Wenden 1991; Fabbiano 2008a). It also suggests a split between what they know from experience and what they have learned by indirection. It is at this point that the men's stories begin to differ from the women's. The men showed far less emotion. They depersonalized their stories by generalization or by stressing procedure, as Mabrouk did when he explained that they had to wait until there were enough of them, a thousand or more, before they would be transported to France. The Harkis did not describe how they felt or what they were thinking about at the time. Like Mabrouk, they noted how they were crammed into trucks and barracks. Some complained about the food they were given. Most did not refer to being herded about without explanation. Almost all expressed the shock they felt when they arrived in France and were sent to a transition camp.

Hacène Arfi's account is exceptional in this respect. I had asked him whether he remembered the circumstances that led to his family's flight to France:

> I will remember that forever. To remember such things when you were four
> or five. [Hacène was born in 1957 in Orba, a quarter in Algiers.] After March
> 19, the ALN entered the camp where we were living and seized the Harkis and
> took them away in trucks. They burst into houses and kicked the Harkis and
> hit them with wooden clubs.

As he often did, Hacène used an impersonal form to refer to what had
happened to his father. But, on another occasion, he told me that the FLN
forced his father one night to destroy a road and electric poles. In the morning, the French army ordered him to repair the road and electric poles. They
did not know that he had destroyed them. When the FLN saw what he was
doing, they stabbed him fifteen times and left him in a pool of blood. "I
shall never forget the sight of him as long as I live. I thought he was dead."
Somehow he survived.[6] Though Hacène did not say when his father was
attacked, given the fact that the FLN and the French army were both active,
it must have occurred between the signing and the ratification of the Treaty
of Evian.

Hacène went on:

> We clung to our mother. She was crying. She was in tears. She was scratching
> her face. They took my father. We fled to my grandparents'. They dug a sort
> of cave outside the house, where they stored the grain, to hide us. The FLN
> had taken charge of the entire community. There was no protection for any
> Harkis—fathers, mothers, children. There were no distinctions. We lived in
> that cave for a long time. I have memories. I remember the roots of the trees
> scratching my face.

Hacène had become very anxious. In an interview in *L'express* (May 15,
1997), he remembers his mother covering his mouth with her hand to keep
him quiet and the odor of rotting corpses: Harkis, tortured, mutilated, castrated, burned alive, were kept in a wooden cage in the village square for
all to see:

> The fear cut off your breath. I am speaking of the fear. The fear. It never leaves
> you. We thought our father was dead, right away. Afterward, we learned that
> he had escaped from the place where they had brought all the Harkis and was
> now in a recruitment camp ready to go to France. He sent for us; I remember
> my mother and us leaving the cave. They led us into my grandfather's house.
> They washed us and gave us new clothes, a burnoose. We thought we were go-
> ing to a wedding. My mother told us we were going to such and such a village.

You should sing and dance. It was a celebration for independence. Women were ululating. We were scared. We weren't even sure my father was alive. I remember one woman whose throat was slashed.

Apparently, Hacène's family was meeting another family in a neighboring village who were to accompany them to the recruiting camp. When they got to the family's house, they discovered that the entire family had been killed:

I tripped over a dead dog at the door that had a gaping hole in its throat. There was a dead child on the table. It had had its throat cut. Its head was hanging off the side of the table—the void.

Before his mother could hide him behind her robe, Hacène saw it all:

We walked on to a gathering place where the French army loaded us on a truck and hid us under a tarpaulin. We were stopped at a roadblock mounted by the FLN. My mother—we—were the only survivors in our truck. She pleaded, and they let her go. The other women and children were forced to get out of the trucks. We went on, leaving them. One or two kilometers before the recruitment camp, we were told to get out of the truck. "You have to cross the field. You'll see the camp." My mother was carrying a baby. We three children were six, five, and three years old. "When you cross the field, you'll see the gate to the camp," my mother told us. "Run to it. Run. Even if I fall down, run, run, run to see your father." We crossed the field. Other families who had just arrived were running behind us. Those who had been forced out of the trucks had all been massacred. There was only a boy who survived. All alone.

Hacène fell silent. Finally, after a long pause, I asked him whether he remembered the recruitment camp:

We entered the camp. There were hundreds and hundreds and hundreds of tents. In some tents there were as many as six families. You were given a mess kit. It was dramatic. Some people were crying because they knew their families had not been allowed in when the trucks arrived at the camp. When the trucks arrived, everyone crowded around to see whether any of their relatives were there. We were lucky. My mother had taken certain military documents with her. If she hadn't, we wouldn't have been let in. I remember seeing the people who were not let in just standing there, crying, crying. When my father arrived, we jumped on him. There was a guy next to us—I remember my mother telling me that his mother and children had all been killed.

After a time, we were shipped to France. We were in the hold, stuffed like cattle. The women cried, scratched their faces, pulled their hair out. I remember how my mother tied us together. The men said nothing. My father never said a word. He was blocked by all that had happened to him. I think it was caused by his deracination. He had talked about going to France, but, when we got to Rivesaltes, he fell into a state of shock. He was crazy. Everything was finished.

They wanted to send him to Bias because he had been wounded, but he refused. He said he wanted to work right away. "I won't leave one camp to go to another," he told them. We stayed in the camp for a week until my father came to get us. We went by train to a farm near Bordeaux. My father worked there for three years. Then he discovered that his sister was at Saint-Maurice-l'Ardoise. We went to the camp.

Hacène's father decided to stay in the camp:

My father had been having work problems. He couldn't find a place big enough for all of us. We were all alone there. We were the only Harkis in the village—completely isolated. I think something had gone wrong in my father's head.

I asked Hacène how his father had felt on returning to a camp. He thought at first I was asking whether his father regretted having been a Harki:

I don't think my father had any regrets. . . . He was proud of what he had done. But in the village we were called *bougnoles*.[7] We didn't understand what was going on. My father was beaten up. But little by little we found our place in the village. I was at school. We went to the baker's. My father bought a rifle because we were threatened by the Algerians living around there.

At the end of the war, a number of Harkis were attacked by Algerians working in France. Most of them were FLN sympathizers. Many Harkis I talked to described the brutality of these fights. Flare-ups between Algerians and Harkis continued for many years. I heard of fights that had occurred that, whatever their cause, were described as between Algerians and Harkis:

He was also threatened by some of the French who thought he was with the FLN. When the mayor told him that a Madame Arfi was in Saint-Maurice, he had to go. He also knew people there: men who had been in his unit. In the village, our living quarters were too small. About thirty people living in sixty-nine square meters. So we moved into the camp.

"Your father must have been exhausted by all that had happened to him," I said. Hacène replied:

He was of the first generation. They were all fucked over. He was disappointed, lost . . .

Women often stressed the fact that they were taken into an office with a desk and chairs; it was the first time most of them had ever been in an office. Both the men and the women were impressed by those officers who spoke Arabic. It humanized their situation, as did the food they were given. Some did complain that they had to wait for hours for something to eat. They spoke of the crush of people who waited, sometimes for weeks, as Mabrouk had, for transportation to France. They also referred to how dirty the straw mattresses were, how they smelled of urine, and how they had to wash them as best they could. (They would make the same complaint about the camps they were sent to.) They did not recall or want to speak of how they felt waiting.

When I did ask them how they felt as they were taken to the ship, many of the women burst into tears, describing their fears of leaving their villages and families. Most of them had never seen the sea. One woman I spoke to described how frightened she was when she and the others were being shuffled into what I presume was the hold of a cargo ship. "It was like an enormous mouth that was going to eat us up." She went on to describe how sick she—everyone—was. "The stench was terrible. There was no air. We didn't know where we were going. We didn't know how long we'd be on the ship. We couldn't see anything." As they huddled in the hold or wherever they had been told to go, many of them wept and tore at their faces, with the desperation of mourning, until their faces were covered with blood. (Children I spoke to remember how terrified they were by the sight.) Though many said that they did not expect to be gone for long, they indicated by indirection—by a nod of the head, a flicker of the eyes, or a sinking of the shoulders—that even then they had known that they were not coming back. I asked one couple how they felt when they saw Algeria disappearing on the horizon. The husband said (with the force of absolute negation) that he felt nothing. His wife just cried. Finally, she said she remembered seeing the white buildings disappear. "We thought we would be coming back soon." Neither of them could recall how they felt as they saw the French coast.

Yamina, the rather dramatic daughter of an army sergeant, whom I met at a Harki protest in Paris, told me that, as their boat approached France, her father saluted and said in French, "Adieu, Algérie." "He knew he would never see Algeria again." Yamina went on to tell me that, before they ate, her father always said, "Eat today, and worry about tomorrow, tomorrow. You never know what God has in store for you." He had lost one of his eyes fighting in Indochina.

Listening to these descriptions of departure, deadened for the men, emotionally deadening for the women, I came to realize that the failure to recall and elaborate was less a failure of narrative capacity than a dramatic loss of the future. Terrified, thrust into situations they could not grasp, overwhelmed by both the silence of other refugees and the wild rumors that spread among them—rumors that could not be controlled, especially by the women, because they fell out of all experience—they were shunted from camp to ship with barely any explanation, several told me, other than "we are shipping out to France." They had no idea what lay ahead. One of Jordi and Hamoumou's (1999, 42) informants remembers one woman asking whether there would be sun in France. They had lost, I believe, the imaginative capacity to envision anything beyond the immediate, if even the immediate. They had neither expectation nor hope nor their loss. Some few reported praying or at least uttering an appeal to God—*bismillah*—but I had the impression that the transcendent offered them at the time neither perspective nor solace. I could empathize with them, but it was a strange sort of empathy, intense but empty, since I had neither the experience nor the capacity to imagine the immediate loss of future.

The repatriated French Muslims (FMR) fall into two principal categories: (1) those who arrived in France on their own or with private and sometimes clandestine help and (2) those for whom the French military provided the means. It is impossible to know how many were in the first category and what happened to most of them. Those in the second were sent to transition camps, where they remained until they found work or were sent to the industrial north to work in factories in Beauvais, Lille, Roubaix, and the environs of Paris. Most of the 3,132 applicants for work in March 1963 at Rivesaltes, Saint-Maurice-l'Ardoise, and La Rye–Le Vigeant were builders, laborers, farmers, masons, barbers, ironworkers, and carpenters (Moumen 2008, 139). Fourteen thousand were relocated to one of the seventy-five forestry hamlets that the French government had established in an enormous reforestation project. Another twelve thousand—the most *evolués*—were installed in subsidized housing in twenty *cités*, or residences, fifteen of which were in the industrial north. For the most part, these *cité* dwellers were in-corporated, if not integrated, into the North African immigrant populations that lived in similar or even the same housing projects (Charbit 2006, 78). By 1965, according to a government report, 13,001 family heads, that is, a pop-ulation of 41,342, were—to use the term current at the time—reclassified: 7,053, or 54.2 percent, had entered industry; 2,189, or 16.8 percent, forestry services; and 1,634, or 12.6 percent, the agricultural sector. The remain-ing 2,125, or 16.2 percent, had miscellaneous occupations (Charbit 2006, 75–76).

The first group of repatriated French Muslims—those who came privately—can be further divided into the elites—elected officials, high-ranking bureaucrats, officers in the French army, professionals, those with a French spouse, and the wealthy, often with connections in France—and more than ten thousand auxiliaries, some claim, who came to France on their own or were brought to France by officers under whom they served until this was prohibited (and even then) or who had family members or fellow villagers already in France.

Though a few of the elite spent a short time in the transition camps, most of them quickly found their way into French society. Many did not identify with other repatriated elites or with the auxiliaries. I did meet several officers who fell into this group. One, now long retired, returned to the army and spent much of the time he talked to me proudly discussing his reception at a local officers club. It became clear, as he went on, that the other officers had, in fact, distanced themselves from him or treated him with condescension. Another, a noncommissioned officer, was flown to Paris and, after being discharged, went to work for the American army stationed near Versailles. He told me that it was the happiest period in his life, that he was simply accepted as he was. (He also told me that he had preferred to serve under foreign officers in the French army for the same reason.)And still another, whose father, I was told, had been a Harki, simply denied it and refused to talk to me. He insisted that he was a French citizen, *point final.*

Boussad, whose father had been a Harki noncommissioned officer and was brought to France by one of the officers under whom he had served, reveals the ambivalent nature of his attachment to France and, no doubt, that of many other auxiliaries. A man in his thirties who owns what must certainly be the best fruit and vegetable shop in one of the more fashionable villages in the Gard, between Nîmes and Avignon, is not much interested in Harki politics. Though he readily admits that he is a son of Harki, he is not burdened by that identity: "It's the past. It was shameful the way the French treated the Harkis, but that happened a long time ago. What has it to do with my life today? I've got my work, my shop, my children. Perhaps I'm lucky. But we can't live in the past."

Boussad explained that it is different for his father and his paternal uncle. They suffered. When I asked him whether I could meet his father, he said protectively and with what seemed to me to be embarrassed concern that his father would not speak to me. He speaks to no one. He just sits at home and stares into space. Boussad thought his uncle might talk to me, but, when he asked him, if, in fact, he did, he also refused, saying, as I had heard so many times, What's the use? The past is the past. Clearly, the pastness of his past was different from Boussad's, but I could not help thinking that Boussad's position was defensive. His father's silent presence and that of his uncle, whom, I learned, was often drunk, had to be an insistent reminder of the reach of the wounds they suffered over decades—three of which Boussad had lived through.

Boussad told me that he had not known his father was a Harki until he was eighteen, when, watching the Harki protests in 1991 on television (I'll come back to them in the next chapter), his father was apparently so moved by them that he suddenly told him that he had been a Harki. As Boussad tells it, the officer under whom his father had served arranged for his father and mother to be flown on a military plane to an airport in the Vaucluse. They remained in an army camp nearby for only a couple of weeks until the officer found Boussad's father work, as a mason's assistant, and a home in a small farming village in the Louberon in which his family was the only North African one. The family was accepted by the village, and Boussad felt no discrimination at school.

After his father explained who the Harkis were, Boussad went by motorcycle to the barricades at Saint-Laurent-des-Arbres, where many former detainees had settled when the camp was finally closed in 1978. Boussad remained on the barricades for about six weeks. It was there that he met the Harki woman with whom he has lived ever since and who is the mother of his children. Like many French couples, neither Boussad nor his wife see any reason to get married. When I asked him how he felt when he was protesting, he said, much to my surprise, "It was on the barricades that I discovered that I was really French."

The best-known group of Harkis to arrive in France by private means were the Beni-Boudouane, whom the *bachaga* Saïd Boualam had organized into a *harka*. Through his connections in France—he was the vice president of the French National Assembly at the time of independence—he was able to fly the Harkis under his tutelage to France and settle them, again with the help of the military and, later, the government, in the Camargue near Arles.[8] (Extravagantly, the *bachaga* [Boualam 1962, 206] claimed to have forced the French government to repatriate thirty thousand Harkis and their families.) Until his death in 1982, the *bachaga* ruled the camp with an iron but protective hand. One of the Harki sons told Giulia Fabbiano (2006, 143) that the *bachaga* was "a real chief": "He did everything for the community. He was the father of us all. He regulated all sorts of problems—an end-of-the-year prize. He was always there with the teachers, and, once, I didn't get a prize. I had done nothing that year. How he chewed me out. . . . If there was a problem [dispute, presumably bureaucratic], he took care of everything, and, if he wasn't aware of it, it was the end, he picked up the telephone—he was the only one who had one—and dialed the number with his fingers." Another reported that the *bachaga* told his followers whom to vote for, and so they did.

To this day, many of the "*bachaga*'s Harkis" and their families live in and around his farm in a sort of involuted isolation that preserves their collective identity.[9] And, though the *bachaga* is dead, the older Harkis are still loyal to and dependent on his sons, one of whom works for the municipality in Arles, while the other, who lives on the farm, breeds race horses. Though I spent only a short time in Mas Thibert, I found the Harki community there—fewer than five hundred people—to be particularly spiritless. I wondered whether this was the result of their dependency on the *bachaga*'s family. Many of the children have left the community, most for government-subsidized housing in Arles, where many North African immigrant workers live. According to Fabbiano (2006, 146), the Harki grandchildren, especially those living in Arles, are beginning to identify with other North Africans and are less insistent on their Harki identity. For them, Mas Thibert has become "a symbolic space of burial, especially of the youngest, whose parents have preferred not to choose to repatriate their bodies to Algeria."[10] One of the first things they did when I met them was to take me to see the *bachaga* Boualam's grave.

Michel Roux (1991, 250–54) describes several other communities that were founded by repatriated French Muslims who arrived in France on their own or with the aid of a French officer.[11] They either aided members of their extended family or village to come to France and settle in their area, or they found lodging and work for those who had been sent to one of the transition camps. In one instance, an Algerian staff sergeant in the French army was brought to a village in the Auvergne in 1962 by one of his officers. Once the sergeant had been settled in an abandoned house, the officer returned to Algeria to bring the sergeant's wife and his two daughters to France. (His son decided to remain in Algeria.) The officer, who was clearly devoted to his sergeant, then arranged for the sergeant's nephew, a mason, to be released from one of the transition camps to aid his uncle in restoring the house. By the beginning of the 1980s, more than a hundred of the sergeant's fellow villagers had been settled in the area.

General Faivre (1994) has written one of the most detailed descriptions of the (re)formation of a Harki community—from the Ouled Berd in the Bobor Massif in Little Kayblia. The general had been stationed in the area during the war and knew many of the Harkis who finally settled in France. Men from the villages, some of whom had already worked in France, managed to make it to France on their own and found work in the outskirts of Paris before settling in Choisy-le-Roi and Dreux. The brother of one of the Harkis who lived in France was able to arrange for many of their families to join them. They were finally settled in an HLM, reconstituting, as Faivre observed, a sort of residential *harka*. Isolated from the Drouais, they formed a sort of community *à part*. Many were able to buy their own homes during the decades following the war's end when there was considerable work in the area, but, by 1994, after many factories in the area had closed, unemployment, especially among the young, rose dramatically. Among twenty-one- to twenty-five-year-olds, it reached 30 percent at a time when the average for the area was 15 percent. The solidarity of the community has gradually decreased as many of the Harki children and grandchildren, especially those born after 1955, about 76 percent, have married outside the community. Family size has decreased significantly, and the level of education, especially among girls, has improved. Faivre reported that, in 1994, about 24 percent of the *lycéens* went on to institutions of higher education. At the time, there were few Islamists among the young people, though I have heard that these have increased in recent years.[12]

What is striking about these stories is that the researcher never bothers to question the person responsible for the arrival of the Harkis. In many cases, it may not have been possible, but, in others, it surely was. While, in large part, this reflects the researcher's own interests, it may also reflect many Harkis' desire to keep their story to themselves, even when it involves outsiders like the French. In several instances, when I asked one of the Harki children to arrange a meeting—or at least give me the address of—a French teacher or administrator who had played a significant role in their lives and lived nearby, he or she either sidestepped my request or agreed to it but never followed through.

Though I do not want to generalize from a single example, I did find a very hostile attitude (expressed by Harkis who had passed through the camps) toward a farmer who had arranged to bring five Harki families to France to work on his farm. This was in southwestern France, at the first showing of a film made by a Harki, to which Harkis from all over France had come. In the discussion that followed, there was no mention of the French who had tried to save them. At long last, the farmer spoke, noting quietly that there had, in fact, been such French. He was immediately shouted down, almost hysterically, by several Harki daughters. Finally, one of the organizers of the screening reminded the audience of what the farmer had done for the Harkis. The protestors quieted down and sulked until the discussion was adjourned. The farmer left immediately. During the reception that followed, I asked several Harkis I knew, as well as one of the women who had protested, why they were so angry at the farmer. Even though they knew nothing about the farmer and what he had done, they simply accused him of exploiting—the woman said, "enslaving"—the Harkis. I discovered later that the farmer had treated his Harki workers fairly and was generally admired by them and their children.

Roux argues that these cases of auxiliaries who had arrived privately and founded communities demonstrate that Harki settlements in France were not started just by Harkis who had settled near the camps where they had been incarcerated. In fact, as Mabrouk reported, there were attempts to break up families. I also heard this from several other Harkis. It is not clear whether this was deliberate policy, the result of confusion at the transition camps, or simply rumor, which was rampant in the camps. It is certainly true, especially when the transition centers closed, that those judged to be incapable of adjusting to French life—widows, the sick, the mutilated, and the insane—were often separated from their families and sent to two specialized camps: Bias (officially named CARA, for Centre d'accueil des rapatriés dí Algérie), in the Lot-et-Garonne, and Saint-Maurice-l'Ardoise, in the Gard.

French policy toward the auxiliaries was divided between those who advocated an assimilationist policy and, in consequence, the settlement of Harki families throughout France and a segregationist one in which the auxiliaries were to be isolated. This divide is already reflected in a planning note issued in September 1962 by the minister for repatriation:

> The camp has to respond to double goals: Temporary lodging for families waiting to be sent out to a final destination. The sorting out [*triage*] of the newly landed pending their being transported to other places. . . .
>
> Experience demonstrates that the problem with this dispersion was a function of the planning at the transit centers and the psychological condition

that resulted. One must therefore limit oneself to doing work that will assure community life (in barrack rooms) to the exclusion of all planning directed to creating family lodgings. (cited in Roux 1991, 244)

In September 1962, Roger Frey, the minister of the interior, took, as one might have expected, a distinctly segregationist position. He noted the dangers to a policy of integrating the Harkis into the French economy posed by the Fédération de France du FLN and, closely associated with it, the Amicale des Algériens en France. He argued that these organizations would try to recruit the auxiliaries or force them to quit their jobs by violent means. "It is necessary to assure the protection of these French citizens," he wrote. He stressed the need for "vigilant surveillance" of the areas where the Harkis had found work and argued that the administration preferred to settle them in forestry hamlets that it could organize and control (see chapter 7). Two years later, a government report noted that, however strong their desire to be assimilated into "western civilization," the Harkis were becoming closer to the Algerian immigrants and would gradually use "the same groceries, butchers, and even cafés," thereby renewing their relations with the people of their village (Moumen 2008, 139–40).

Most Harkis spent at least some time in one of the six transition centers urgently but inadequately refurbished in the summer of 1962 to receive the auxiliaries. During the month of June, over fifty-five hundred Harkis were shipped by the military from Bône (Annaba), Algiers, and the Nemours (Ghazaouet) littoral, near the Moroccan border, to Cap Janet, the most isolated port in the harbor of Marseilles. In fact, they landed at night in a less isolated port and were secreted to a hanger at Port Janet, where they were kept until daybreak, when they were crammed into a train bound for an old military camp at Larzac–La Cavalerie near Millau in the Aveyron.[13] Were a boat to arrive during the day, according to Jordi and Hamoumou (1999, 42), it was ordered to turn around and wait in Toulon until nightfall before landing. The Harkis were destined, it seems, to invisibility from the moment they arrived in France.

By September, over twelve thousand auxiliaries had arrived at Larzac, which was meant to house around two hundred people (Roux 1991, 240). Eight hundred army tents were erected in long, impersonal rows. Each tent housed from one to three families, that is, between eight and fifteen children and adults, in twenty square meters. The confusion was enormous. Conditions were appalling. Illness was rampant. Tensions were high. Even the strict military discipline did not prevent fights. Food was distributed daily and was cooked over wood fires outside each tent. Harkis who were sent there remember how shocked and embarrassed they were to have to share a tent with families, especially with women they did not know. They remember the rain, the mud, and the cold; the camp was over three thousand feet above sea level. As winter approached, it became clear that the auxiliaries had to be moved. By October, they and the inmates of another camp, Bourg-Lastic near Clermont-Ferrand in Puy-de-Dôme, which had been opened that summer to house the overflow from Larzac, were sent south to Camp Maréchal Joffre in Rivesaltes, near Perpignon, in the Pyrénnées-Orientales; Saint-Maurice-l'Ardoise-Lascour near Avignon in the Gard; Bias near Villeneuve-sur-Lot in the Lot et Garonne; and La Rye–Le Vigeant in the Vienne, which specialized in preprofessional training.

The camp at Rivesaltes, about 165 acres, was located on an unsheltered, arid, windy plain with little vegetation, almost no trees, and, therefore, no shade.[14] In the winter the winds were glacial, in the summer torrid. The winter of 1962 was particularly harsh, as Mabrouk mentioned, and all the Harkis I talked to, whether or not they had spent that winter at Rivesaltes, mentioned the freezing cold in the unheated tents. It is part of their story.

The camp had been constructed at the end of the 1930s to house Spaniards fleeing Franco's Spain. At its height, in 1939, it housed over 100,000 refugees. (Nearly a half million republicans had fled to the Catalan coast.) During World War II, between August 11 and October 20, 1942, more than twenty-three hundred Jews and gypsies were collected there to be sent to Drancy in Paris and then on to the German death camps. During the Algerian War, FLN prisoners were imprisoned there. Ben Bella himself was held in a nearby house.

Azzedine and Belkacem, two Harki sons, took me to visit Rivesaltes, which is deserted today. It was closed in December 1964; the auxiliaries who had not found jobs or had not been sent to a forestry hamlet and the infirm were sent to Saint-Maurice-l'Ardoise or Bias. Others were settled in the nearby *cité* of Réart. Only a few of the buildings, now in ruins, still stand; otherwise, there are only the remnants of the buildings that had been razed, chunks of concrete, dried wooden lathes, strands of rusty barbed wire, and tufts of scrub that grow here and there amid the rubble. The Harki camp was opened in June 1962, at first for French Muslims serving in the army, and then, in September, for auxiliaries. By December, it housed 12,000 in more than eight hundred tents. By the end of March 1963, the number had been reduced to 6,784, more than half of whom were children, as some of the Harkis had found work or been sent to other camps, to the forestry hamlets, or to the industrial north to work in factories.[15] With the rapid transition of large numbers of Harkis, the confusion must have been great, no doubt terrifying to the Harkis, but few of them talked to me about the effect on them of rapid and seemingly arbitrary arrivals and departures. Each departure must surely have raised the question of their own future.

As I walked through the ruins, the two Harkis pointed out where they had lived, telling me the barrack number, as if it could have any meaning for me; where the showers had been (they were allowed one shower a week in the best of times); where the latrines were that were so dirty and smelled so badly that they preferred to go in the fields; where the clinic had been, the school, and the barber shop that one of the Harkis had opened in his tent; where the commandant's headquarters was (they mumbled his name to each other); where they had played; and where the watchtowers were and the main gate, through which they could pass only if they had permission. At one point, the two men stopped and, looking across an empty field, told me in outrage that, during the first year of their parents' incarceration there, the camp authorities had hurriedly buried the scores of babies who had died in the harsh winter conditions in unmarked graves in the camp itself.

Of course, I could see nothing, but they could. They had their memories. Though they were anxious to show me the camp, I felt like an intruder in their shared memory space. Their trip was at once a memory trip and a pilgrimage to an absolutely negative space, the very opposite of what the French historian Pierre Nora calls *lieu de mémoire*—a memory space that celebrates French history. I was to have similar experiences, usually at the Harkis' insistence, in other camps and forestry hamlets. The emptiness evoked memories whose referents were destroyed and, no doubt, the threat of forgetting.

After visiting the camp, we went to a nearby café for coffee. It was there that Azzedine and Belkacem described in greater detail life in the camp: how scared they had been; how their eyes filled with tears from the smoke of wet wood and brambles they and their fathers collected; how they had moved from the tents to barracks that were infested with cockroaches and other vermin; how in the cold winter the tents and sometimes the barrack roofs of corrugated iron were blown down; how they were always muddy and dirty and were disinfected; how they learned nothing at school . . .

The Ministry of Education had opened forty-four classes for thirteen hundred pupils in 1963. Among the fifty-odd teachers were army conscripts with little or no teaching experience. Neither Azzedine nor Belkacem had had any schooling before they arrived at the camp. "We just made trouble," they remembered. Fatima Besnaci-Lancou (2003, 80), who had spent a year at Rivesaltes, writes in her memoirs that she learned nothing at the school but old French military songs. To keep order, the soldier who taught them made them sing all day long. Nearly every Harki who had lived in a camp complained about the schools. What amazed me was how many of them managed to get an education.

Belkacem and Azzedine went on to describe the fights, usually between Berbers and Arabs or men from different parts of Algeria, that they had seen. (Several of the officers I talked to claimed that the division of the camp into "villages," according to *douar* of origin, encouraged the violence. Others said that it discouraged it.) The two men mentioned the suicides they witnessed. Azzedine, who was psychologically more sensitive than Belkacem, who was more political in his outlook, referred to the psychoses, apathy, and alcoholism among the men. Many of them lost all initiative, he told me. They were afraid of what was outside the camp. They had lost their courage and their dignity. They were empty. Many months later, Azzedine and I were to discuss the emasculation of the Harkis and the effect it had on their families and children.

Besnaci-Lancou writes about the suicides, the depressions, and the images of violence and torture that haunted her. (Her mother had counted twenty-eight tortures that had led to the death of family members and close friends [Besnaci-Lancou 2003, 37]). She herself was "possessed" by the image of her grandfather, who had disappeared without a trace at the war's end:

> I fought with all the force of a little girl to reject the atrocious images that kept coming up in my mind. Sometimes a white turban, a silhouette, the timbre of a voice reminded me of the warmth of his affection. Then I would run until I knocked my head against the barbed wire that surrounded the casern separating it from the camp. My eyes remained dry. No tears came to appease my pain. I forced myself to look up at the sky and waited until the knot in my throat that was strangling me came undone. (Besnaci-Lancou 2003, 75–76)

In her quest to reconstruct her parent's life trajectory, the writer Dalila Kerchouche (2003b, 54–68) describes the feelings she had visiting Rivesaltes for the first time. Her parents had been interned there; she was born after they had left the camp. In her account, she stands at attention in front of a small monument to the Spaniards, Jews, and Harkis who had been interned there. As she looks at the desolation, she feels sickness, a malaise, grow in her. She asks herself why they housed the Harkis in such rough and isolated places: "In surveying these sordid and uninhabited places, I felt how undesirable the Harkis were. France, this country where I was born and that I loved, didn't want my parents. They were shunted to the side, knowingly relegated to inhospitable areas. Deep in me, I began to doubt: if this land had rejected those close to me, why would it want me?" (54). Kerchouche's experience was, of course, mediated by her mother's words. Self-dramatizing, her language yet echoes the impassioned ambivalence of many of the Harkis with whom I had talked.

Later, in the chapter on Rivesaltes, Kerchouche recounts her mother's description of the first Christmas there: "A Christian holiday for Muslims. A ludicrous idea . . . as nothing had been prepared for the 'Id al-Kabir and as they had not been allowed to build a mosque. To believe that the administration totally misunderstood the customs of this population and its religious celebrations." Reading her description of the celebration, I realized how far apart the two populations were. In ignorance—and despite their smug self-satisfaction at having thought to organize that celebration—the French were trying to share their experience of Christmas. In the morning, they gave toys to the children (four thousand of them, according to Kerchouche), perfume to the women, and cigarettes to the men. Amid military fanfare, they prepared an enormous mechoui and a huge couscous. In the afternoon, a plane dropped little yellow packages at the feet of thousands of overexcited children, who chased them wildly. A soldier disguised as Father Christmas parachuted from the plane and gave out gifts. "Snacks were then served around Christmas trees," Kerchouche (2003, 63) reports coldly, "under the eyes of satisfied officials."

Saint-Maurice-l'Ardoise, a military camp a few miles outside the village of Saint-Laurent-des-Arbres, which the Harkis liked to call Saint-Laurent-des-Arabes, is set among vineyards that produce Lirac wines. Before the Harkis, it had housed Spanish republicans, German prisoners of war, Russians, Poles, Malagasies, members of the FLN, Messali's MNA, and the OAS. It was completely razed after being closed at the end of 1976 and is now only a vast and abandoned field surrounded by barbed wire. A sign prohibits entry. I went there by myself one evening as the sun was setting, casting extraordinarily beautiful light over the vineyards, but to me the light on the campsite seemed dulled, absorbed, as it were, by scrub, weeds, and dried earth.

Saint-Maurice was soon so overcrowded that the commandant had to requisition the fifteenth-century Chateau de Lascours three kilometers away, where he installed a kitchen for the distribution of food twice a day to family heads, an infirmary, and administrative headquarters.[16] With the help of the Harkis, he had prefabricated barracks installed and others of light brick constructed. The camp of approximately fifteen hectares was divided according to ethnic origin into five "villages," each of which developed its own character. Here, as in other camps, the separation of Berbers,

Arabs, and Chaouia encouraged tensions and fighting between the different groups. The camp, run like a military post, was apparently better organized than Rivesaltes, but, still, confusion prevailed in the early years of the Harkis' incarceration, especially given the continual change of the population. Conditions were miserable. "The barracks were abominable, dirty and cold. Tents and barracks floated in a sea of mud when it rains or the snow melts," the head pediatrician at Sainte-Marthe Hospital in Avignon reported. He was particularly critical of the head camp doctor's neglect. He noted that there was only one thermometer for the entire camp and one spare tire for its two ambulances and that unit doctors had to use a candle to do throat examinations. The doctors had to struggle to get the seriously ill to hospitals in Nîmes and Avignon, "the camp commander not wanting to encumber them." This resulted in many deaths, including those of infants who arrived dying because their transfer was hindered by the camp administration. (The milk allowance for children under two was a box every other day.) Once camp conditions were publicized, the army improved medical facilities.

At the end of 1964, Saint-Maurice's designation was changed, from a transition center to a welcome residence (cité d'accueil et d'hébergement). Now it, like the camp at Bias, was to house those Harkis thought incapable of working. They were divided into two groups, living in separate quarters: the irredeemable (irrécupérable), that is, the physically and mentally handicapped and widows, and those with feeble resources (Moumen 2008, 141). Until 1975, when it was finally closed, the center housed about eight hundred people (140–150 families). The birth rate, was exceptionally high: on the average, between thirty and forty births per year. In the camp's last four years, two-thirds of its population was under twenty-one (Heinis 1977). Chateau Lascours, which remained a transition center, was closed in 1970.

The interned describe life in the camp as a little hell. As in all the Harki descriptions of camp life I heard, they stress their sense of having been imprisoned. They refer to the strict military discipline, the barbed wire, the watchtowers, the ten o'clock curfew, and the need for a permit to leave the camp, and, when they do tell me, they often remind me, with bitter irony, that France is the land of freedom, equality, and fraternity. Yet, despite these conditions, some of them managed to create little gardens, start small craft enterprises, including those for rug weaving, and open barbershops. Several even began building mechtas, or traditional houses with little interior courts.[17] The desire for privacy, for a home, must have been very great. Over time, conditions did improve. A soccer field was constructed, a food cooperative organized, and a resident center, which also served as a meeting room, built with a game room, a café, and, in 1967, a television set. In 1969, a movie theater and a center for teaching women to sew, cook, and learn to read opened. Finally, in 1974, a year before Saint-Maurice was closed, a workshop for the handicapped was started.

As in the descriptions of life in other camps and, in particular, the forestry hamlets, those who were interned there refer to the corrupt administration, or at least corrupt administrators. I was told that, at Saint-Maurice, residents were made to pay for clothes that had been donated by the Red Cross. Their corrugated iron barracks, latrines, and showers were without heat. They had to pay to use public showers, which not only infuriated them but also offended their sense of modesty. Hacène Arfi referred to it as a "psychiatric asylum but with children." As did all the Harkis and their children I talked to, Hacène assured me that, as bad as conditions were at Saint-Maurice, they were even worse at Bias.[18] Troublemakers were often sent to psychiatric asylums where, as several Harki children told me, they were given drugs so strong that, when they returned to the camps, if they did, they were "vacant souls in an emaciated body."[19]

Anne Heinis, who worked as a social welfare inspector with the Harkis from 1962 to 1975, frequently visited Saint-Maurice. In her 1977 doctoral thesis for the University of Montpelier, she assumes a bureaucratic but sympathetic attitude toward the Harkis. She is quite critical of the way in which the camp was run. She notes that, as the salaries of the administrators were very low, they took charge of the Harkis' allowances, which they thought were too high. The Harkis were less polite than Heinis, accusing them of simply stealing their allowances. Heinis reports that most of the administrators and social workers were badly trained, often unsympathetic, and isolated, particularly those who lived in the camps. They felt that their careers had been dead-ended. She stresses the clash of cultures and, in a manner reminiscent of Lévi-Bruhl's theory of the primitive mind, the symbolic-associative thought of the Algerian peasant.[20] She insists on the men's idleness without taking into account the effect of their war and postwar experiences and attributes it to the public charity (*aumône publique*) they received.[21] She argues that living on the dole destroyed their sense of responsibility to themselves and their families. Women, however, worked hard, attending to their ever-expanding families on limited budgets that they managed themselves. This situation, Heinis argues, destroyed the family equilibrium and had a negative effect on the children, particularly the boys.

One of the most serious problems in Saint-Maurice was mental illness, the frequency of which, according to some specialists, was eleven times that of the French population as a whole. Heinis stresses the violence, particularly of drunks, several of whom attacked their wives and neighbors. She refers to one man who killed his wife, leaving seven children who probably witnessed the murder. Several of the Harkis, including Hacène, also told me about this crime and the shock it sent through the camp. He said, however, that the father had shot his children as well as his wife. "He used to make them stand at attention at five each morning in front of the barracks in which they lived."

Another source of violence and vandalism was a gang, which the children referred to as *les grands*. Heinis suggests that young men who returned to the camp angered and dispirited after leaving school or failing to find work encouraged the gang's vandalism. Apparently, children could get away with what the young men could not. When Saint-Maurice became a *cité d'accueil*, its police station was closed despite the continued violence and disorder. Heinis observes that the closing created a paradoxical situation in which "a difficult population, poorly adapted to our way of life and its exigencies, was infinitely less surveyed than a normal population."

Harki families complained about the violence too, and, in a roundabout way, Heinis suggests that the absence of a camp *gendarmerie* allowed administrators to act with impunity. From 1964 to 1974, there were, among other reported crimes, 3 homicides, 3 attempted homicides, 98 knifings, 14 brawls (which Heinis likens to the Algerian *nefra*, a fight in which members of a fighter's clan or tribe are obliged to support him), 114 drunken disorders, 10 rapes, 33 robberies or attempted robberies, and 10 cases of swindling, mostly related to unpaid bills owed local merchants who had encouraged the Harkis to buy things they could not afford. In December 1975, the merchants accused the Harki youth of extortion and vandalizing shops, especially those owned by Algerians. They claimed that some of them were armed with hunting rifles (Choi 2007, 233). Undoubtedly, there were more unreported crimes.

Heinis does claim that the medical service was well equipped—in fact, better equipped than those for the general public in the area—and suggests that many of the Harkis went to the infirmary because it was more comfortable than their lodgings. Presumably, she is referring to the period following the medical reforms. A camp nurse I interviewed confirmed the Harkis' picture of camp life, though she gave the Harkis more responsibility for their situation than they themselves were prepared to admit. She talked about the problems of controlling contagious diseases; the never-ending lines of lice-ridden children, many undernourished, with colds, diarrhea, impetigo, anemia, and rickets; the number of deliveries she performed because the clinic was understaffed; and how difficult it was to teach mothers to nourish their children (they had never used the bottle). She stressed the women's refusal to change their ways—their confusion. She told me about patients who died because there were no resident doctors. She seemed most troubled by the frequency of wife beating, about how often she had to treat seriously wounded women. She attributed the beatings to the husbands' frustration, their (sense of) impotence.[22] Though the nurse often spoke in stereotypes about the Algerians, about how embedded they were in tradition, how simple their *mentalités*, their mode of thinking was, she was genuinely sympathetic. Though her Harki neighbors described her with unusual affection, they did not visit her, she said, but still always greeted her warmly.

Children had very little contact with the outside world because their school was in the camp. It was only when they reached the sixth form (roughly the seventh grade) and were sent to schools outside the camp, many to boarding schools, that they discovered the outer world. They returned home with new values and modes of thinking that conflicted with those of their parents, further destabilizing the families.

Several Harki children described the shock on their first day of school outside the camp, how strange everything seemed, how alienated and marginalized they felt. Almost all of them said that they were ignored by the teachers, arbitrarily punished, and falsely accused of causing trouble. The boys seemed to have a rougher time than the girls. Heinis reports that girls were generally better students than the boys. (Yahiaoui [1990, 48–49] observed the same thing for urban Harkis in the 1980s and I for both rural and urban Harkis in my interviews.) Some Harki daughters described the freedom they felt once they got used to the school and also the difficulties they had with their parents, particularly their fathers, who frequently called them *whores* (*putes*) and beat them because of the "corrupt ways" they learned there. Several told me that they stopped talking, sometimes for several years, to their mothers, with whom they had always talked in Arabic or Berber. They said they were ashamed.

Heinis notes that, though most Harki children married among themselves or with other repatriated French Muslims, many of the girls expressed the desire to marry a European.[23] Ideally, and paradoxically, they seemed also to want to remain in the camp near their parents. Those who were successful in school were particularly motivated to find jobs, despite their parents' disapproval. Boys were generally less motivated and more embittered.[24] Many returned to the camp on graduation and simply hung around like their fathers. In February 1974, a protest organized by the young men denounced the "administration *presque militaire*," and, in December of the same year, a violent altercation between the young men and the head of the camp led to the 1975 protests and the final closing the camp.

Harki boys who had attended schools, particularly in the transition camps and reformatories, recounted the harsh, at times sadistic, punishments they were made to endure. Some of these reminded me of the torture they may have witnessed in Algeria if they were old enough. Teachers threw objects at them, beat them, attached electrodes to the soles of their feet, made them crawl naked in front of the class. Noura, a cleaning woman at a school in the Harki *cité* on the outskirts of Narbonne, told me that, when she went to clean classrooms one Saturday morning, she discovered a little boy tied to a chair with barbed wire. The teacher had apparently forgotten to release him. On the following Monday, she went to the principal of the school to tell him what had happened. He told her it was none of her business, threatening her job if she pursued the matter.[25] If schoolboys were particularly violent, they would be sent to "correction homes," where they were locked up and beaten until they were "submissive" enough to be sent back to their camp. Azzedine recalls the beatings he received and the angry humiliation he felt at a "special" school in Ongles in the Alpes de Haute-Province where he was sent because he was, apparently, a troublemaker.

I could go on listing abuses—I heard many more—but I would be reproducing the Harki litany. However true the stories are (and I have no reason to doubt that they are), they have become part of a politicized litany. As such, they are caught between personal experience and political rhetoric. It is for this reason, perhaps, that witnessing, *témoignage*, is so important to the Harkis. Told by those who experienced the now-storied events, the stories served to refire collective pain, shared memories, and political engagement, which, as time goes on, dissipate. Reproduced again and again, witnessing loses its force. To put it as strongly as I can, it dies with the witnesses. What is left, what will be left, are the litanies composed of narrative shards detached from their lived contexts.

There is one feature of some of the accounts of camp life, particularly those by Harki daughters, that interrupts this list of abuses. They recall the support—the care—they received from one of their teachers, an administrator, a nurse, a social worker (*monitrice*), or farmer living near the camp. The narrator of Dalila Kerchouche's novel *Leïla: Avoir dix-sept ans dans un camp de Harkis* (2006, 71 and passim), which, however sentimental, is a fairly accurate extrapolation of camp life, describes her relationship with a peasant woman, Juliette, who lived near the camp where she and her parents were housed: "For the first time in my life a Frenchwoman treated me as a human being." Not only does Juliette befriend her, but, mirabile dictu, she finds a way for the family to leave the camp and settle in a nearby farm.[26] Boussad Azni (2002, 113), one of the most inflammatory of the Harki activists, recalls in his polemic, *Harkis, crime d'état: Généalogie d'un abandon*, one of his teachers at Bias, "the only human in the camp," who was not only "pure kindness" but also proud of the accomplishments of the players, including Azni, in the camp's football (soccer) club. Yamina also mentions both a teacher and a village doctor who made house calls and always welcomed her and her sisters if they fell down and hurt themselves. Azzedine did not remember anyone French who had a positive effect on him, but he vowed to show the care he never had to the delinquent boys with whom he now works. It was this support, as the Harkis tell it, that had a transformative effect on them and on their future. The attention that they received not only humanized the caregiver; it removed them from the distant, impersonal and impersonalizing administrative identity that they were given. It gave them a sense of their individual worth and possibility.

One of the most dramatic examples of these encounters with kindness is that of Celestine Rolland. Celestine is a passionately articulate activist and feminist. With the help of the Red Cross, she and her family came to France in 1967, after her stepfather was released from prison in Algeria. When she was nine, she and her family were billeted in a camp in Jouques, a village near Aix-en-Province. Unlike most other Harki children of her generation, Celestine attended the lycée. Today, she is married to a former soldier, a quiet man, who is proud of her activism. Unlike most Harkis, Celestine was able to visit Algeria in the 1980s.

Celestine took an immediate interest in my research. Our first interview lasted more than four hours. I asked few questions. Celestine spent the first twenty minutes describing how she came to have a French name. (I had not asked her.) Her mother, an orphan, was raised by her paternal uncle and aunt, who married her off to an older man when she was thirteen. At the age of fourteen, she gave birth to Celestine. "My mother did not want to stay with him," Celestine explained, because she was traumatized. "She told me that, for days, she lay on the floor weeping. Though she had lived in misery at her aunt's house, she wanted to be with her family. She told her husband, 'I want to be with my relatives, or I'll kill myself.'" He was not an abusive man; he never beat her. He gave her her freedom. He must, in fact, have been an exceptional man, for, though by Muslim law he had the right to keep the baby, he let her keep Celestine. Two months later, Celestine's mother was married again, this time to an older cousin who drank and beat her. It is this man Celestine calls father. He had been a Harki courier, "not a fighter or torturer." After independence, he was arrested by the Algerians, tortured, and imprisoned for five years until the International Red Cross managed to get him released and sent, with his family, to France. Celestine stressed her mother's suffering. She had also been a courier and was continually insulted during the years of her husband's imprisonment. "People would spit at her," Celestine said angrily.

When Celestine was sixteen, she was informed that her papers were not in order and that, if they were not regulated within six weeks, she would be deported. She was terrified. "Where will they send me?" she asked the gendarme who had brought the order. "To Algeria," he said. "But where in Algeria? It's a big place. I have no family there." "That's not my affair," he said. Celestine was virtually reenacting the occasion. And then, dramatically, she switched emotional registers as she went on mechanically to describe in excessive detail the bureaucratic entanglement she found herself in. It turned out that, when her stepfather came to France, he neglected to include her among his children. Thus, as she bore the name of her real father, she had no legal status as a Harki child and no right to remain in France. She cried as she told me this. She was panicked; her family was panicked. "The arrival of gendarmes always terrifies us." Finally, a camp administrator and his wife intervened and arranged for her naturalization. ("I thought I was already French, but they had to make me French again—what I was to begin with.") As the camp administrator prepared the papers, he told Celestine that she could change her name if she wanted to. "It hurt me not to have the same name as my brothers and sisters. You are nothing, you are not configured, you are not part of the family, you have no bonds [attaches]. For a little girl, you don't know who you are."

Celestine was despairing and quickly changed the direction of her story, announcing that she did not know who had paid for her naturalization. Calm again, she went on: "I revolted. Why me? I should have the same name as my father. I suffered enormously from the difference. My father had made it clear from the time I was two or three that he didn't want me to call him 'father.' Still, I wanted to be accepted, to be treated as family. I said, 'Yes. I'll change my name.' I'll change my name because I'm no one's daughter. I want to be someone." Celestine took the most French name she could think of. "After all, I'm in France; it's my land [ma terre]." I could sense her anguished, embarrassed ambivalence. Though a Harki activist, she had chosen a French name.[27]

Unlike Celestine, who voluntarily took a French name, a large number of Harki children, especially those born in the camps in the mid-1960s, were simply given French first names, often without the consent of their parents, by French authorities. (Some parents, encouraged by social workers holding assimilationist views, also gave their children French names.) Roux (1991, 22), quoting two brothers, one called Edouard and the other Saïd, reported that, as children, each wanted to change his name, Eduard to an Arab one and Saïd to a French one. But neither ever bothered to do so. I did, however, meet several Harkis who either changed their name officially or just used an Arab one in their daily life. Like other Harkis, they were outraged by the French presumption. One Harki with a French name told me that, whenever he arrived for a job interview, having made an appointment by phone, he would be told the job was filled as soon as the person saw his face (*"ma gueule arabe"*). Still, he did find what was by most standards a good job.

When I asked Celestine about the administrator, she immediately referred to him and his wife. In fact, it seemed that it was his wife who had been the more sympathetic. The couple lived in the *cité* with the Harkis. They gave her an identity, she implied, but (perhaps because of her activist stance) she could not admit it directly. She went on to tell me that the couple now lived nearby. She runs into them sometimes when she is shopping. "We say hello and embrace," she says, quickly and dismissively. Her response undermines their importance to her.

During the summer of 1962, forest fires ravaged southern France, calling attention to the need to protect and extend the forests. The AAAA, which was active in repatriating auxiliaries, urged the government to employ repatriated Muslims in what was to become the largest reforestation project in French history.[28] As I noted, seventy-five forestry hamlets scattered across the south of France were established, the earliest in September 1962.[29] Aside from rebuilding the forests and fire lanes, the hamlets were purportedly designed to protect the auxiliaries by isolating them from the FLN, which continued its pursuit of the auxiliaries in France at the war's end, and, ostensibly, to integrate a large number of Harkis into French society (Moumen 2003b, 66). This dual mission reflects the tension in French policy between the assimilationists and the isolationists.[30] Put another way, it reflects the challenge that the Harkis and other repatriated French Muslims posed to French republicanism. The assimilationists wanted to make them French; the isolationists wanted them to disappear. No doubt, some of the hamlets did facilitate Harki integration, at least as the French understood *integration*, but others, perhaps the majority, had the opposite effect. Isolated, they created enclaves of Harkis who had little, if any, contact with French society (Jordi and Hamoumou 1999, 97).

Belkacem, a builder in his late forties, an astute, if at times overly passionate, activist, took me to the abandoned forestry hamlet Pujol-le-Bosc in the

Montagne Noire, north of Carcassonne, where, along with his mother and sisters, he had spent five years of his childhood. The camp lies in a densely forested valley, which, judging from the age of the trees, must have been barren when the first Harkis arrived in the early 1960s.[31] Until it was finally closed in 1978, it housed between thirty and forty-five families. (Generally, only families were moved to the hamlets.) About seven kilometers from the nearest village, with a population of a couple of hundred, it was certainly the most isolated place I had ever seen in France, a country I know well. Several kilometers before arriving at the camp, Belkacem pointed out where a guardhouse had stood—to prevent escapes and unauthorized visitors.[32] "When they sent us here, they claimed it was to integrate us into French society," he told me bitterly as we rounded a bend and saw the hamlet for the first time. It consisted of stone huts that reminded me of pigsties above which stood a robin's-egg-blue block house where the commandant and his wife had lived. As at many other forestry camps, they were *pieds-noirs* "because they were supposed to know the Arab mentality." The couple was notorious for their abusive discipline and their robbing the Harkis of the pittance they earned. "It's now the commandant's hunting lodge," Belkacem observed cynically. "When they shut down the camp in 1978, he was able to buy it for six thousand francs." With the exception of a few Germans who had converted the larger of the stone huts into vacation homes and some hippie squatters, who knew nothing about its history, the village was deserted when I saw it in 2005. Today, it is advertised as an ideal holiday spot known for its tranquility. No mention of its past history is made.

Shaking his head sadly, Belkacem looked at the abandoned cars, the stacks of old tires that lay at the entrance to the hamlet, and an incongruous city telephone booth. With tears in his eyes, he showed me the hut where he had lived, the one well (the Germans' houses are now fed water by bright yellow hoses that snake their way through the village), the field where he played soccer, and the school he attended. It is a long rectangular ruin. "I didn't learn anything there; the teacher was interested only in disciplining us." Nearby are the remains of a much better camp school where French children from Carcassonne came for country weekends. "No, we didn't play with them. They were kept apart." I was overcome by an image of Belkacem and the other Harki children watching the French children, dressed in clothes they could never have, eating more food than they had ever eaten, and ignoring them—the "traitors'" children.

The conditions must have been terrible. The houses had dirt floors and poor, if any, caulking and were heated in the winter by a fireplace or a charcoal stove that "smoked so badly that we always had tears in our eyes."

Once a week, a traveling grocer arrived in his truck. A baker came more often. "The commandant's wife advanced us money on our salaries. She kept the records. Oddly, we never had any money left at the end of the month."

At lunch, Belkacem explained that his mother had been sent to the forestry camp as a punishment because, as she spoke French, she had interceded on behalf of the other Harkis at Bias, where, as a widow, she had been sent. "What could a widow and three small children do in a forestry village?" Belkacem asked. Belkacem's mother is an extraordinary woman. In 1968, she managed to leave Pujol. After working as a maid in Narbonne, she found a job as a cook in one of the better hotels. She taught herself to read and write French. She sent her three children to school in Narbonne, and even Belkacem had to admit that he learned something there. He received a diploma at a vocational school and started a construction company, but, after seven successful years, it went belly-up. He attributes his failure to French racism. "Now I only do small jobs—*bricolage*—but it pays the bills." He tells me that he had built a big house for his mother but that she made him sell it and build her the smaller one where she now lives.

After a long pause, Belkacem said that one of his sisters had nearly died from an operation. The surgeon had made a mistake. His mother found her half dead on a gurney in a hospital corridor. She forced the hospital authorities to fly her daughter to the university hospital in Toulouse, where she was saved. Despite all the obstacles the local hospital put up, she succeeded in taking the surgeon to court, where it was discovered that he had made over forty errors while operating in the hospital. He lost his license and now works as a pharmacist in the hospital. He told one of the surgical assistants, "We don't have to worry. She's a Muslim, and they don't let us perform autopsies." After another pause, Belkacem said admiringly, "When they tried to stop her—to humiliate her—she explained that, though she was a Harki, she was also French and wanted to save French lives. 'Under the knife we're all the same,' she said."

Before being sent to Bias, his mother, her two daughters, and Belkacem had spent nearly a year at Rivesaltes. Belkacem told me that, between March and June 1962, the FLN had decapitated fifteen Harki villagers, seven of whom were members of his mother's family; later, twenty-two more were killed when the FLN attacked a train in which they were fleeing. He went on to tell me that the FLN had slit his father's throat in front of his mother. Without ever saying that he had also seen his father's throat slit—he would have been three or four at the time—he said he could never forget it.

On the long drive back, Belkacem, who had been drinking heavily at lunch, sat silently, ruminating. Finally, he said, "I make this trip twice a year. It is my memory, my pain. Were it not for my mother, I would kill myself. She is a strong woman who says we always have to look ahead. I can't do that to her. But she is old. I don't know what I'd do . . ." He stopped himself. Later, after receiving a business call on his cell phone, he told me about a protest he was helping organize, and, forgetting that he had already told me about them, he went on to tell me about other protests he had been in. This seemed to relieve the depression into which he had fallen.

Not all the camps were as isolated as Pujol-le-Bosc.[33] In the Vaucluse, for example, they were attached to small communities—Sault, Apte, Pertuis, and Cucuron—and it was hoped that their presence would not only provide workers for various communal projects but also contribute to the local economies, which, before the onslaught of *estivants* later in the decade, were moribund. Still, there was considerable opposition at both the departmental and the local levels to the implantation of an alien, "savage, and dangerous population." Jean Escande, the prefect of the Vaucluse, wrote to one of the ministers in charge of the creation of the hamlets:

> I ask that the Harkis not be assigned to forestry work in my department. I call your attention, Mr. Minister, to the fact that the Department of the Vaucluse is apparently among those that have, with respect to the importance of its population, the largest group of repatriated inhabitants (for 310,000 inhabitants there are about 30,000 repatriated). Furthermore, earlier important arrests in the last weeks and those that are anticipated for the following weeks demonstrate that the activity of the OAS in the Vaucluse is increasing. I recall that since the beginning of the year my department has had, deplorably, forty-seven bomb attacks. These facts lead me to think that the presence of the Harkis in the Vaucluse is apt to create new incidents. (Quoted in Moumen 2003b, 67)

Local opposition (Moumen 2003b, 68–78) argued that there would be no work for the Harkis, that their settlement would change the political composition of the municipality, that there was no land for a camp, that the nearest police station was too far away, that the presence of the Harkis would discourage tourism, that they would put a financial burden on the community, and that they could have no future in the area.[34] Nevertheless, the camps were established, and the first Harkis, most of them from Saint-Maurice, were welcomed by the towns' notables, offered food, and, later, provided with clothes by many of the townspeople, even those who had initially opposed their arrival.

Each forestry village in the Vaucluse was constructed according to the same plan. There were seven poorly insulated prefabricated buildings, six of which were divided into four small apartments of about thirty-four square meters each. The seventh was for a classroom and offices for a social assistant and the head of the hamlet, both of whom were always French. As in other forestry camps around the country, the head of the hamlet—the *commandant*, as Belkacem called him—had very considerable power in the way in which the camp under his charge was run. Particularly in the more isolated camps, like Pujol-le-Bosc, where oversight was weak, the camp heads tended to be petty despots, exacting rigid and, at times, abusive discipline. Noting that they were often former military officers, Abdelkrim Kletch, one of the most articulate and influential of the activists, said that the forestry camps, like all the other camps, were a perpetuation of colonialism in France.[35]

Although some of the Harkis and their children recalled with gratitude, if not affection, the social assistants, or *monitrices de promotion sociale*, critics, like Kletch, stressed their paternalistic attitude and the dependency, indeed, the sense of inferiority, the attitude fostered and encouraged. Their function was essentially educational—to teach the camp dwellers, particularly the women, French values and conduct. Aside from helping the auxiliaries with bureaucratic matters, with arrivals and departures, births, deaths, and hospitalizations, they taught the women how to keep house, raise children, shop, cook, dress, knit, brighten the camp with flowers, garden, and encourage school attendance and learning French. They often inspected the Harkis' homes. Although they were assumed to be familiar with Islam and Algerian manners and customs, many, even the most committed, offended the camp dwellers by their high-handedness.

The camps were not meant to be permanent, and many of them had been closed because of their deteriorated conditions before the 1975 protests. Their population was often transient, for many of the auxiliaries soon found jobs elsewhere. When a camp did close, the Harki residents were transferred to other camps, attached to fire brigades in forest areas in the south, or housed in HLM built especially for them. Protests by the French living in villages near the camps were at times so forceful that some of the HLM, in the Var, for example, were never built (Jordi and Hamoumou 1999, 100). Those Harkis who found work outside the camps or stopped working for whatever reason had to leave the camp immediately. Inadvertently, this policy produced another problem: when a boy reached eighteen and, thus, was old enough to work, he had to leave the camp even if he did not have a job. Some of the Harkis regarded this policy as a means of breaking up their families.

It should be said that, with the exception of those living in camps like Pujol, many Harkis were thankful to escape from the transition camps. The hamlets were smaller and more personal. Even Dalila Kerchouche (2003b, 72) writes positively of her parents' reaction when they arrived at a camp, La Loubière, in the Mende: "My parents discovered a hamlet of human proportion without barbed wire or wire fencing where a few soldiers were busy." Despite the cold, they were "agreeably surprised" and settled into lodgings, next to a laburnum tree, that had already been prepared, as had the school and the infirmary. The camp was in the middle of a forest of Austrian black pines.

Kletch took me to the camp at Jouques, the Logis d'Anne, where he had spent part of his childhood. He and his family had arrived in France in 1963, when he was nine years old. They were sent to Rivesaltes and, then, to Jouques. Kletch, who suffered from asthma, was sent from Rivesaltes to an army hospital near Perpignan and, later, to a sanitarium in the Massif Central where he spent eighteen months. His family then moved to Narbonne. The Logis d'Anne was the camp where Celestine Roland had grown up, though the two had not met there. It was located in a pine forest over a hill from the small Provençal town of Jouques. The site was chosen in 1963 because the French electric company (EDF) had already built by then vacant barracks for workers on a hydroelectric project. Agricultural work, as well as work at a nuclear energy plant in the nearby town of Cadarache, was available (Jordi and Hamoumou 1991, 102). One hundred and ten families were installed in barracks that were divided according to ethnic group. Kletch told me that there were frequent, at times bloody, fights between the different groups, especially between Berbers and Arabs. The Harkis' complaints were similar to those at other camps. They were particularly angered by the poor quality of education and by their rejection by French teachers and students. In 1994, the camp was finally closed.

As Azzedine and Belkacem had at Rivesaltes, Kletch pointed out where the barracks had stood, how the Harkis had to go through a forest and across a mountain to get to the town of Jouques, if they did not take the far longer route along the road, and where some of the children had been killed crossing a highway to go swimming in the Durance on the other side.

I had a much different reaction to Kletch's description of the camp than I did to Azzedine's and Belkacem's descriptions of Rivesaltes. Kletch was older, more sophisticated, and a more experienced activist than Azzedine or Belkacem. He was canny, shrewd, and outraged, at times calm, forbearing, and ironic.[36] The first time I met him, I felt that he had an almost saintly, certainly an exceptionally patient, perspective on all that the Harkis had endured. Speaking about the camp, he conveyed a disturbing nostalgia—disturbing because I had always assumed that nostalgia grew out of a positive desire, a desire for something positive, absent to be sure. There was nothing perverse, nothing masochistic, about Kletch's nostalgia.[37] Had he so reconciled himself to his past that he could overcome the pain and humiliation he had suffered in the camp? Was his nostalgia simply that of an adult for the past? Or had his particular style of protest freed him to experience the kind of nostalgic sentiments that were prohibited to the majority of Harkis and their children?

After visiting the camp, Kletch and I drove to the town of Jouques, which, as its tourist office describes it, is "a typical Provençal village," "peaceful and serene," with "a rich rural heritage." We sat in an outdoor café owned by one of Kletch's friends and were soon joined by French residents of the town who knew him. They seemed pleased to see him and could joke about his latest protests, his proverbial hunger strikes. He could laugh. Other townspeople, I should add, walked angrily by, shaking their heads. The French people who joined us reminisced with him. One, who worked for the municipality, recalled the protests at the camp; he seemed to admire Kletch's role in leading them. Another—an engineer—made fun of an administration that could start to refurbish the camp and then, with the work nearly completed and tens of thousands of francs spent, destroy in a couple of days what had taken months to negotiate and build. He himself had been paid for work he was unable to complete and for tearing down something he had just built.[38] Kletch enjoyed the irony.

After the Frenchmen left, an old Harki whom Kletch knew stopped at the table. We offered him a coffee, and Kletch questioned the man—as if he were interviewing him for me. I do not recall much of what he said, but I do remember that he lived in a house on the outskirts of the town that he had built and that he had shared with his wife until she died. Now he lived alone and spent much of the day tending the garden that she had loved. It was a sort of memorial to her. Kletch asked him at one point whether he had any desire to return to Algeria. "No," he said defiantly. "I don't know anyone there any more. I'd be a stranger. I belong here now. I'll be buried in the cemetery near my wife." Kletch turned to me and said, "You see." I said yes, but I am not sure what he had wanted me to see.

As soon as it was feasible, those Harki families judged to be the most "evolved and prepared for life in an urban setting" were moved from the camps into *cités* in industrial zones, particularly in the north of France (Amiens, Beauvais, Dreux, Lille, Roubaix, etc.), where there was work (Charbit 2006, 78, quoting Baillet [1976, 52]; see also Yahiaoui 1990).[39]

Two thousand families were given apartments in HLM, similar to those that Sonacotra (the Société nationale de construction de logements pour les travailleurs) built for immigrant laborers on the outskirts of major cities. Often, as in the Cité de la Briquetterie in Amiens, the cheaply constructed buildings deteriorated quickly. In the case of La Briquetterie, which had been built primarily for Harkis, those houses that were not too dilapidated were renovated in the 1980s and sold at favorable rates to their occupants. Harkis whose houses had to be torn down resisted moving, even when they were offered better housing. As Yahiaoui (1990, 47) notes, they had found a haven and did not want to have to adjust to yet another neighborhood.

Given the high unemployment among the young people (85 percent in Amiens in 1990), the Harki and other immigrant communities became hot-beds of unrest. Theft was the principal form of delinquency in the 1970s. It was replaced in the 1980s by drugs, which continue to be a major problem among Harki (and immigrant) youths throughout urban France (Yahiaoui 1990, 46–47; Muller 1999, 23–72; Abrial 2001, 175–87). One young man living in a Harki hostel in Strasbourg observed, "Everything you were told is not a thousandth of what we suffer. Our parents will die knowing that their children have not escaped misery" (Muller 1999, 31). *Glander* (to muck about, to screw around) and *galérer* (to have a hard time) were words that punctuated my conversations with unemployed youths.

Although there have been conflicts between the Harkis and the other North Africans, particularly between those Algerians sympathetic to the FLN and the auxiliaries soon after the war, Harki children and grandchildren in these *cités* have begun to identify with the immigrant workers and have experienced much the same marginalization (Fabbiano 2006, pts. 3–4, passim). Marriages of French Muslims with Algerians and Europeans have increased significantly. It should be observed that, while an argument for the forestry hamlets had been the protection of the Harkis from the FLN, the *cité* dwellers were in a far more vulnerable position. What protection did they have? What protection did they need?

Approximately three-quarters of all the repatriated Algerians in the north of France live in the industrial town of Roubaix.[40] For the most part, they were installed in *cités* there between 1962 and 1965 and found work in the then thriving textile industry. Like their Algerian counterparts, most of them trace their origin to Bouira in Kabylia. Today, as in so many industrial cities in France, unemployment in Roubaix is high (14.3 percent, compared to 9.6 percent for France as a whole, in 2005). For young people, it ranges between 15 and 24 percent, and, for those living in "sensitive urban zones," it is probably comparable to that in similar zones in other large cities (36.2

percent for males and 40.8 percent for females). Abdelmoula Souida (1990) found that, in 1990, the Harki youths in Roubaix tended to be slightly better educated than the Algerian population, that Islam played a slightly more important role in French Muslim lives, and that, given unemployment, Harki children and grandchildren often lived under the same roof as their parents. (Sixty percent of French Muslim families own their own homes.)

Unlike the Algerian population, which voted—and votes—for the Left, mainly for the Socialist Party, the French Muslims were split in their political orientation. The older generation voted for the Right, even for the extreme Right; their children had a more nuanced political orientation; and their grandchildren tended to vote the way their Algerian counterparts of the same age did. Souida, however, found that the one significant difference between the French Muslims and the Algerians was their history. The Harkis' story serves, as we have seen, as the gravitational point around which their identity is constructed. As Souida (1990, 64) put it: "The question of the French Muslims is more in the order of the symbolic and the imaginary [than that of the Algerian workers], and its solutions lie elsewhere." By *elsewhere*, Souida meant the relations between France and Algeria. Though this relationship is still important today, it is no longer of central concern to the Harkis. I suggest that the difference between the two populations lies their expectations of the state.

On the outskirts of Narbonne, six HLM, exclusively for Harkis, were constructed soon after the war. Unlike the northern *cités*, the Cité des Oliviers was more of a camp than a subsidized housing project. The six buildings were fenced with barbed wire. The *cité* was run like a military base by a captain. Its gates were closed at eight at night, and, even during the day, you had to have a pass to leave. The Harkis were isolated, not only from the French, but also from other immigrants.

Fazia and her family arrived soon after the *cité* was built and considers herself lucky that a school had not yet been built there. She was sent to school in Narbonne, and, unlike other Harki children her age, she grew up knowing French children. "Once the school here was built, the children grew up with absolutely no contact with the French." Proud of the fact that she was one of the first Harkis to pass the *baccalauréat*, she now works with the Harkis and other residents of what has become a mixed suburb of Narbonne: Saint-Jean-Saint-Pierre. Today, some of the Harkis own their own homes next to those of Europeans, and I have been assured by those Harkis and their children that they get along. Fazia did tell me that, when Harkis vacated their apartments in the *cité*, the government filled them with Moroccans. "They wanted to avoid fights between us and the Algerians."

Though she expressed dislike of the Moroccans, she said, laughing, "Our children are growing up with Moroccan ways." When I asked her whether there were Islamists among the Harkis, she quickly answered no and then, after a pause, said, "It is possible that there are some among the Moroccans." She added that the Moroccans are responsible for the drugs, mainly hashish, that many of the young people smoke. "It's a big problem in the north." I had heard this from many other Harkis.

The watchtower in the *cité* figured importantly in all the stories I heard of life in the *camp,* as the Harkis and their children still call the project. The tower is a symbol of their humiliation, which, I imagine, was even greater than in the camps since it was in sight of the city three kilometers away. "We were visible in our invisibility, and this must have bugged the Narbonnais," a Harki's son told me. Another remembered the Narbonnais who, on their Sunday walks, looked at them through the wire fence as though they were animals in a zoo.[41] He went on to talk about how reactionary the city government was and how to this day the Harkis are in constant struggle with the municipal authorities, especially the mayor. "They begrudge us everything," he said. The Narbonnais Harkis have been among the most politically active and are known, as we shall see in the next chapter, for their protests.

SIX

After the Camps

The Harkis are kept in the position of the colonized—of little Muslims from the Algerian *départements*. This policy was carried out in a deliberate and knowing manner by successive governments. The Harkis were willingly prevented from developing, constrained by internment, and [forced to turn] in on themselves. From time to time, a little measure for improving their lot was taken. All the political parties have engaged in a game of clientelism, soliciting the Harkis at election time.

—Abdelkrim Kletch, undated press release (2006?) from the Collectif national justice pour les Harkis

"During the summer of '91, I became a spokesman for the children of the Harkis," Hacène Arfi told me as we were discussing Harki protests in the office of Coordination Harka Saint-Laurent-des-Arbres, which he had founded. The walls of the office were covered with photographs and newspaper clippings about Harki demands and protests for recognition and compensation, in many of which Hacène had participated. The office was next to a small mosque to which the old Harkis went to pray several times each day.

Hacène continued:

I helped organize the protests. We broke the wall of silence [surrounding the Harkis]. We had nothing to lose. Our lives had been fucked up. That was clear. It was thanks to this violence—unfortunately it had to be so—that after thirty years the Harkis could finally emerge from the oblivion in which they had been living. The French now had to recognize the Harki problem—their situation. The press—the international press had been alerted. We received journalists from Switzerland, Holland, Belgium, Turkey, and the Americans. It all started here.

"I thought the protests had begun in Narbonne that summer," I said. "That's what everyone told me there." "No, no," Hacène responded. "It started here and then spread to Narbonne. I have the press reports in the archives. I'll show you later."

He did show me them later. They seem to confirm his story:

> One year earlier I was focusing on the Harkis in Marseilles. I was a forestry guard. I received a letter naming me, according to the election roles, a juror for the *cours d'assizes*. Eight months later I received a second letter that said that I had to report to the Palais de Justice in Aix-en-Provence on March 19, 1990. I received the letter at noon. It was a boom in my head. March 19. The day the war ended. The day our slaughter began. How could they?
>
> The day before, as we were working, we came on an old minefield from World War II. We called the authorities, but before they came I was able to squirrel away three grenades. They were unusable because they had rusty pins. I don't know why I took them. I had to work on the afternoon I received the call to jury duty. It was as though another bomb had exploded in my head. I decided that, instead of appearing at the Palais de Justice, I, the son of a Harki, would show the French. I already had the idea of what I was going to do six months earlier. I went to the prefecture of Marseilles. I had the grenades—I had changed the pins—and a plastic revolver, a toy. I occupied the prefecture for eight hours. When I decided on this action, I was conscious of the fact—I knew that I could die there. I had two choices—to die or to be imprisoned. I opted for prison. In my head, it seemed inevitable. I could not return to society. The prefect and the public prosecutor asked me why I had taken over the prefecture. I said for this reason and that reason. A year later, the protests exploded at Saint-Laurent. The town hall was occupied for a week. I was not there but in Salon de Provence.

Hacène became evasive and jumped over what had happened to him after he was arrested. He was, in fact, released after a couple of hours.[1] By releasing him, the French had pulled the rug out from under him. As he put it: "I didn't understand what had happened." He continued:

> In my head, I had decided that I would commemorate March 19 by distributing tracts on the Harkis. Each year, I distributed them in a different *départements*: in Marseilles, in the Vaucluse, the Gard. In 1991, I was stopped. I made

a smoke bomb in front of the prefecture in Nîmes to call attention to what I was doing. There was black smoke all over. The prefect called me in, and, after I explained why I had made the smoke bomb, he released me. A month later, one of the associations for the repatriated from Algeria—it was backed by the Front national—condemned my actions, saying that I was unbalanced. They released this to the press. I was not allowed to respond. I seized a truck filled with lumber—*stères* of lumber—and drove it into the offices of the newspaper *Midi libre* in Nîmes. I was arrested.

In his interview in *L'express*, Hacène claimed that he had smashed into the *Midi libre* agency because he was outraged when he read that funds for the Harkis had been diverted. He had mentioned this in an earlier interview with me but had not related it to his protest in Nîmes. Another cause for his protest was intertwined in what he was telling me. On returning to Saint-Laurent-des-Arbres, he discovered that the association of the repatriated that had condemned him was sponsoring a mechoui there. He was so infuriated by this that he smashed into the newspaper offices. Whatever the sequence of events was, it is clear that Hacène had been so enraged that he lost control of his protests (as he was losing control of his story). The article in *L'express* mentions that, in July of the same year, he attacked a company in Carcassonne implicated in the diversion of Harki funds, declared himself an ambassador of the Harkis, and distributed identity cards:[2]

I was arrested on Friday, June 9. The following day, the Harkis here at Saint-Laurent—they were tightly knit—demanded my release. They occupied the mayor's office for eight days. That Sunday, people from Narbonne arrived for the mechoui. They discovered that the mayor's office was occupied by four Harki sons and asked to meet with them and negotiate. It turned out that I had done serious damage to the newspaper agency. It was argued that I could not be condemned because I was in revolt. If they condemned me, they would have to condemn all the people—the Harkis—who were protesting the system. They allowed us [!] to leave after eight days. It was then that the protests in Nîmes began. In July, I organized the Coordination nationale des Harkis in Carcassonne and became its representative. The protests lasted for six weeks. We took over the autoroute that goes to Spain and let everyone go through free. We said we were determined not to surrender until the government was willing to deal with us in concrete terms. We were determined at that time.

Hacène's story is confused. He was tired and, I think, caught between re-living the experiences he recounted and the dissolution of their effect in the course of their frequent public retellings. His protests had begun to merge. As he was describing them to me, I could not help but think that the details were of little importance because their object remained psychologically, if not factually, constant. Clearly, they bolstered a threatened identity. Like many Harki children who talked about their activism, Hacène personalized the protests in which he had participated, but those other accounts never seemed as emotionally invested as his. His sense of self was centered, it seemed to me, on the protests he had initiated. His father had been the last to leave their camp. It had become his turf, and, no doubt, his attitude toward the camp and the nearby town were reflected in their importance for Hacène. However degrading the camp was, it was home. Hacène often said, not without a touch of pride, that he had spent his childhood there. One of the driving forces of his protest spree in the early 1990s was a rumor that the army was going to sell the land for a symbolic franc. "How could they? Children were buried there. It should be a center of pilgrimage—a memorial." Death, burial, and home, indignity, rage, and protest, and above all a sense of injustice, knotted as they were, gave to his activism a self-sacrificial dimension.[3]

Whether the protests in the summer of 1991 began in Saint-Laurent-des-Arbres, as Hacène suggests, or in Narbonne, as the Narbonnais insist, they have become one of the most significant events in what Hacène has called "the Harkis' emergence from oblivion." The first protests—perhaps the most effective—began in 1975 at Bias and spread to Saint-Maurice-l'Ardoise and to some of the forestry villages. In fact, the protests were so effective that the government was forced to close the two remaining camps and push forward the closure of the forestry hamlets. They were mentioned in nearly all the interviews I had, but no one I spoke to had actively participated in them. Hacène was no exception. His father had ordered him and his brothers—they were still children—to stay away from them. "He worked in the camp administration," Hacène said, "and didn't want any problems." Hacène remembered little of them. He simply called attention to fragmentary episodes that were generally known, concluding excitedly that it was the protests that finally enabled the Harkis to enter France, thirteen years after they had arrived.

On April 22, 1975, M'hamed Laradji, an elite Algerian who had taken up the Harki cause, started the protests in Bias.[4] Two years earlier, Laradji had founded one of the first associations organized by an Algerian for the benefit of repatriated Muslims: the Confédération des Français-Musulmans rapatriés d'Algérie et leurs amis (CFMRAA). Until then, as the historian Mohand Hamoumou (quoted in Roux 1991, 340) observes, there were only associations for repatriated French Muslims, like the Association nationale des Français de l'Afrique du Nord, d'Outre-Mer et de leurs amis and the Comité Parodi, that were neither organized and nor staffed by the repatriated themselves. The following year, Laradji started a hunger strike in Evreux. It spread to Lille, Longwy, and Saint-Étienne and ended at the Madeleine in Paris, with considerable publicity, after the chef de cabinet of the French president, Valéry Giscard d'Estaing, arrived "to confirm the personal interest that the president takes in French Muslims." Expressions of "personal interest" were to become a leitmotif in the Harkis relationship with the French government.

At Bias, Laradji and his companions were assisted by a mysterious man, referred to as Monsieur Christophe, who had been an officer in the French army, an OAS militant, an exile in Canada, and, on his return to France, a *nostalgique*. (The *nostalgiques* were *pieds-noirs* who had begun supporting the Harki cause, less out of sentiment for a lost Algeria than as a way of gaining political support for their demands for indemnification for lost property.) Throughout the month of May, Harkis blocked access to the camp, occupied administrative headquarters, and encouraged strikes. When the protests ended, after the CRS occupied the camp, the local prefect formed a committee to investigate camp conditions, and Michel Poniatowski, the minister of the interior, created a special commission to oversee the camps. The commission was, as Roux (1991, 346; see also Langelier 2009) observes, one of the interminable commissions concerned with the Harkis; they have continued to this day.

Protests had spread to Saint-Maurice-l'Ardoise after Laradji and Christophe visited the camp on May 19. A month later, armed protestors invaded the municipality at Saint-André-des-Arbres, kept the mayor hostage overnight, and threatened to continue the occupation until their demands were met.[5] These included closing down the camp. On the same day, in an article in *France-soir*, Mourad Kaoua, an ex-deputy from Algeria and a member of the CFMRAA, took responsibility for the event, noting that the Harkis still did not have the same rights as the Algerian immigrants, including the right of free movement. He also claimed that all the initiatives to find work for the Harkis had been private (Choi 2007, 331).[6] It is certainly true that, during the first five years after the war, Algerian immigrants continued to receive many of the same benefits, including housing allowances, that they had had during the colonial era. The Harkis were either ineligible or discouraged from applying for them. During those same years, the government did attempt to find jobs for those Harkis who qualified, but their efforts often failed because employers preferred the immigrant workers, who were, for the most part, more experienced than the Harkis. They complained about the cost of having to train unskilled workers.[7]

In July, protests began in some of the forestry hamlets. At Joucques, Harki delegations met with local authorities to complain about the lack of employment, which they attributed to racism, the lack of communal equipment, such as a telephone to call for help in case of an emergency, and the camp administration. They demanded the improved housing that they had been promised in 1972, the removal of the military, and compensation for their losses in Algeria. The litany of complaints was largely ignored, although in November new housing was begun.[8]

Protests continued sporadically until the end of August. The most dramatic was the seizure of four Algerian factory workers at Bagnols-sur-Cèze on August 5 by six Harki sons. They vowed to hold the workers hostage until the Algerian government released the seven-year-old son of a well-known Harki who had been detained on petty bureaucratic grounds when he and his mother had visited Algeria. Three days later, the boy was returned to France, and the hostages were released. The young protesters were given a choice of jail or being sent to other regions of France. Most moved to the Paris suburbs, but Laradji, who was not given to compromise, chose prison, where he was held for several months (Azni 2002, 129).[9]

Though most of the demands raised by the Harkis in the summer of 1975 were not met, Bias and Saint-Maurice-l'Ardoise were finally closed in 1976.[10] The protests marked a dramatic change in the Harkis. They taught them the power of collective action, the efficacy of protest, and the value of politically active associations. Their sense of empowerment gave them a sense of possibility, albeit one limited by the wounds they had suffered and the realism fostered by their past. But the protests also intensified the Harkis' frustration, outrage, and—despite their sense of empowerment—feelings of powerlessness.

"I spent my entire youth in the camp," Hacène said, not without a touch of nostalgia:

We were the last family to leave the camp, in November 1976. My father worked in the administration there. He was an employee. He did a little bit of everything. At the end, he became an ambulance driver. . . . When someone was seriously ill or had an accident, they would send for my father. Because of the curfew, he would have to go to the commandant for keys to the gate and the ambulance. I saw people burned and wives who were beaten by their husbands or stabbed with a knife. They agonized. There was no help for them.

A month before we left, the last family left. They are still living in Saint-André. We lived in the camp for a year without water, without electricity. The well was stopped up. My father had to travel for seven kilometers to get water. We were surrounded by empty barracks, in ruins. It was as though there had been an earthquake.

There were Harki families who lived with us in town after they left the camp. They spent the next twenty years hiding, hiding from the revolution—the changes we wanted to bring about. They had left the camp, but they were still living behind barbed wire. . . . The mother of one of these families began taking pills—drugs. Her sons lived in paradox. They lived alone with their father in an apartment in the village. They had suffered so badly that they couldn't resist alcohol. The father fought with his eldest son for work. A year later he murdered him. . . .

My father had a future because he had been in the administration. We were sent to Miramas, in the Bouche du Rhone, near Salon de Provence. But he had to work in Nîmes. He had to commute 160 kilometers a day. He had problems finding a car. He earned next to nothing. Early one morning, after having written letters to Giscard d'Estaing, without ever receiving an answer, he stuffed us in a car. He was in a crazy state. He wanted to leave France—to go to Italy. We were stopped at the border. But then he was able to get a job in the Miramas town hall. It had taken him three years.

Apparently, Hacène's father's attempt to flee France alerted the mayor of Miramas to his desperation, and he offered him a job, which he kept until he retired.

"We took all sorts of jobs," Hacène remembered. "I worked on cars, on heating, picking grapes. Anything." He stopped, caught up in his memories. I asked him how his mother had reacted to village life after so many years in a camp. He had trouble answering. He appeared never to have thought about it:

Well, in the camps she had had a life. There was a life for women. You had to have permission to leave the camp. The men would get wine or beer and sit under a tree playing cards or dominoes. The women left their homes to meet three or four of their friends and gossiped.

"But wasn't she depressed?" I asked. "At first there was depression," he replied. "But in the camps there was no future. You were in prison. There was no reason to work. We couldn't even buy a bit of land. There was nothing."

The camp at Bias was officially closed on December 31, 1976. State support was stopped, and the building and land were sold to the local town and renamed—for the second time—the Hameau d'Astor. About half the six hundred occupants left the camp between August 1975 and October 1976 and, for the most part, settled in the region.[11] Families had been promised a million old francs (roughly $2,000), three years of rent-free lodgings, and work (Roux 1991, 353).[12] The remaining three hundred occupants—the severely handicapped and their children—were to be lodged in subsidized housing on the campsite. They would have the same benefits as the Harkis who had left the camp, but, until the new housing was built, they would remain in the rapidly deteriorating barracks in which they had been living. The mayor of the town, who hoped the new housing would eventually serve the local middle class, was reported to have said, "You don't expect us to maintain buildings that are to be destroyed," and to have added, "In any case, if the lodgings are filthy [*infectes*], it's because those kind of people live like that" (*Libération*, February 11, 1985, quoted in Roux 1991, 354). Once lodged in the new housing, the Harkis, who had not understood the terms of occupancy, were soon in deep debt.

The openness of the mayor's position is exceptional, but it is illustrative of the racism that has regularly undergirded French policy concerning Harkis (Pierret 2008). This is not the place to discuss the history of French racism. It has been the subject of countless newspaper and magazine articles, books, government studies, conferences, workshops, and films and is considered a "hot subject" by the media.[13] In the course of my research, I met French racists who actively slur the Harkis as they do Arabs in general, the Jews, and other foreigners (including Americans), but such overt racism is generally condemned by the French public. Its covert form is, almost by definition, more insidious.

I remember a long conversation I had in the 1990s with an elderly Algerian taxi driver who had immigrated to France in the late 1940s after being discharged from the army. He was settled in France, spoke fluent French, had a *petit pavillon* in one of lower-middle-class Paris suburbs, and considered himself and his family to be French. He told me that his two sons had passed the "bac" and had good jobs. Neither he nor they had had any intention of returning to Algeria. And then, to my surprise, he said that he was sending his daughter and youngest son back. When I asked him why, he told me that he did not want them exposed to the racism that had become prevalent in France. *Racisme voilé*, he called it, "veiled racism." "It was better for us during the [Algerian] war. Then you knew who you were—the enemy. It was dangerous. You were always liable to be beaten up. You were stopped by the police whenever they felt like it, and, if they didn't like your face [*gueule*], they'd slug you. I know, Monsieur, I lived through it all. But I tell you it was better that way. Today it's veiled, and I don't want my children to grow up with it." When I pointed out that it would be dangerous for his children—Algeria was in the middle of a civil war—he became sullen. "It's better that way."

Talking to Harkis about discrimination, I often thought about that conversation. I have no idea what motivated the driver's decision. He was not an Islamist. We had joked about a *bon coup de rouge*. His observations about the debilitating power of veiled racism were nothing new: it produces a double bind in its victims. They are assured that there is no racism at the same time as they experience the racism that lies behind that assurance. One of the most insidious expressions of this racism has to do with being cast as a problem that requires a solution. Just as the general charged with the education of Harki children in the camps saw his task as simply a problem to be solved, so did many of the bureaucrats I met who had to "deal" with Harki affairs.

Some of the bureaucrats acted in good faith and did their best to help the Harkis. Some joked about their protests but with a certain affection. Those who knew Abdelkrim Kletch respected his diligent activism, though they thought he carried his hunger strikes—in 1997 and 2000—too far. Their relations with Hacène were quite different. They worried about the state of his health. "He's taken on all the pain of the Harkis," one of them said. "Who can bear that?" Of course, there were bureaucrats who, if they were not dismissive, responded to the Harkis' requests in an impatient and impersonal fashion. Although, in my observation, they treated the Harkis the way they treated other peoples (particularly foreigners, including me at times), the Harkis felt slighted. What was different about the bureaucrats' response was their stereotyping the Harkis as a group whose demands they (already) knew and, therefore, whether or not they acknowledged it, already knowing how they would respond to their requests. It could be argued—as several of the Harki activists did—that, in their stereotypic objectification of Harkis, the bureaucrats were replicating colonial attitudes. I am not certain. This may well have been the case in the years immediately following the war, when many *pieds-noirs* were charged in one capacity or another with the administration of Harki affairs.

Stereotypic objectification—that "knowledge"—though a prerequisite for racism, is not the same as racism. The Harkis are sometimes trapped by their interpretation of that objectification as racist. It identifies them with precisely the group with which they do not want to be identified—Algerian immigrant workers. They tend to sidestep this entrapment, when it becomes too evident, by restricting the object of racism to themselves. I have often heard Harkis describe the substandard council housing (HLM) in which many of them live with North African neighbors as a sign of French racism. But, if they are unable to find housing in one of the cités, they will accuse the French in racist terms of favoring the immigrants and will support their accusations by listing similar cases and reciting the wrongs they have suffered.

Racists tend to lump the Harkis together with other North Africans, except when it suits their purpose to distinguish them. This is particularly true of the Front national and other extreme-right groups, which, as they promote a racially based anti-immigration policy, solicit the Harkis' vote by distinguishing them from other North Africans, stressing the fact that the Harkis are French, proclaiming the sacrifices they made for France, condemning their shoddy treatment, and promising to support their cause.[14] Most of the Harkis I talked to were skeptical, and some even laughed at the transparency of the gesture.

Other right-wing groups unable to forget what they consider to be de Gaulle's treachery in surrendering Algeria to "a bunch of thugs"—who have demonstrated over and over again that they cannot rule a country—have taken up the Harki cause. Some of these groups, such as the Association pour la défence des anciens prisonniers et exilés de l'Algérie française, are made up of pieds-noirs, particularly those who had supported the OAS, and their children, or veterans who firmly believe that France had won the war militarily but lost it politically. There are others who idealize the Harkis as they condemn the Algerians on racist grounds. Foremost among them are writers, mostly right-wing veterans of the war, who produce popular war novels, memoirs, and short stories that extol the Harkis with a tough-minded but sentimental realism. They do describe how the Harkis were used during the war. Among them are young professionals with distinct fascist leanings who seem unable to come to terms with France's loss of military glory (rather more than its loss of empire) and see France's abandonment of the Harkis as a symptom of political and military degeneracy.[15] When several of them learned that I was writing about the Harkis, they contacted me spontaneously. When I asked whether they could introduce me to any of the Harkis they knew, they told me that they had never met or even thought to meet a Harki. The symbol was enough.

It is by now a cliché that empowered racists force their opponents to argue in the terms they are combating. Certainly, the Harkis, like other immigrant populations in France, are caught in this predicament, and many of them know it. What escapes their attention is that they have been led to argue their cause as a "problem." This is particularly true of the Harkis who have administrative posts in the municipalities or in the repatriation centers that give advice to and keep track of the rights of the *pieds-noirs*, the North African Jews—who were also forced to flee Algeria—and the Harkis. Some of the larger of these have research centers with archives and libraries. I spent an afternoon in one of the centers listening to Harki administrators describe "the Harki problem" quite impersonally. "One of the Harkis' major problems is that they cannot forget that they are Harkis," one of them said. "They blame everything that goes wrong in their lives on their being Harkis. They can't move on." Earlier in the conversation, he described how difficult being a journalist had been for him. He was never assigned important stories, only those about Harkis. A young artist, something of a hustler, who had stopped by immediately began to tell me about the problems of Harki youths—mainly their use of drugs "because they had no opportunities." He was soon so excited that he lost his objectifying stance and told me about the problems he was having as a Harki artist. He went on to recite the Harki story in an increasingly self-distancing manner as he calmed down. When he left, after insisting that I visit his studio, the former correspondent smiled. "You see the problem," he said.

Kletch is one of the few Harkis I met who is aware of the way in which the Harkis have been led to see themselves as a problem. He arrived in France in 1962, at the age of nine, and was sent with his family to Rivesaltes and, then, to Jouques. He has told me that, as power is corrupting, he has resisted getting involved in politics (a point contested by many of his Harki critics). He delights in outwitting the French. His talk, particularly when he is outraged, is punctuated by a nervous, ironic laughter that calls attention—as he no doubt recognizes—to the absurdity of whatever he is describing. No one I met better understood French bureaucracy.

Kletch often casts himself—parodically—as a nuisance in his own protests, marches, and hunger strikes, which are often so long that he loses consciousness and must be hospitalized. He told me that as he has got to know the CRS guards—who keep watch over him during his protests—they greet him with an "ah, you're at it again" attitude. He was one of the first to join the famous Marche des Beurs (officially the Marche pour l'égalité et contre le racisme) in 1983 as well as a later march across France for the Harkis.[16] He once lay across the tracks in front of the TGV in Marseilles and, thereby, shut down the entire high-speed train network in France. His protests are carefully selected to maximize their impact, but, like other Harkis, he is often carried away by slights to the Harkis' dignity and honor. He showed little interest in Benyoucef's *Name of the Father*. I am not sure whether he dismissed the affair because he thought of it as a literary matter and of little consequence or because of his relations with AJIR.

Kletch is careful to warn Harki activists not to protest events organized by those state or local authorities who favored the Harkis because such protests would not only damage the Harkis' reputation but also confirm the government's negative attitude toward them: "Look, we offer them what they want, and they go on protesting." Though he is far too realistic to assume that the Harkis will ever achieve satisfaction, he has, nevertheless, devoted his life to their cause and has done it with some success. He reminds me of those figures—the French lawyer Jacques Vergès, for example—who, through trickery, defy the hegemonic rationality of a bureaucratic state, thus exposing its artifice and presumption (Crapanzano 2008). Like all good tricksters, Kletch knows that he cannot play tricks on others without tricking himself. He seems aware of the human comedy, its seriousness, its cruelty, its absurdity, and its contorted joyfulness.

Celestine Rolland is Kletch's opposite. She is a passionate woman, outraged and hurt, as we have seen, and ever ready to promote the Harki cause. She believes that the suffering of the Harki women has not received the attention it deserves. The first time I met her, she told me that there were a lot of Harki women who risked their lives for France and have been ignored. While she herself is self-dramatizing, she finds Kletch to be far too self-involved. "He works for himself," she says. "He is too political." She is not as reflective as Kletch and frequently refers to the Harki problem without appreciating how *problem* frames the Harkis. She recognizes that the activists were "sold a bit at the beginning " by politicians. Though she is involved in local politics, she trusts politicians of neither the Right nor the Left. "They're out for their own good." She herself stresses the Harkis' rights as French citizens. "We want to be treated like everyone else. We want to be represented in parliament. I want the right to address those who represent me."

On December 16, 2004, while Kletch was camped in front of the Senate protesting a proposed law concerning the recognition of—and compensation for—the suffering and sacrifices endured by repatriated French, Celestine spent the day in the Senate.[17] Kletch had been camped there since October 7. Like other Harkis, he was angered by the fact that the proposed compensation was only for the Harkis and their wives, not for their children, even those who had grown up in the camps. He was equally angered by what he considered to be the government's delaying tactics. Forty-three years had passed since the Harkis arrived in France, he told Philippe Bernard of *Le monde*. "We have five deaths a month. . . . They're trying to gain time, to economize on our backs." He stressed the exceptionally high unemployment and suicide rates among Harkis. "The high-flown phrases of recognition" (*les phrases ronflantes de reconnaissance*) no longer satisfy him or the other Harkis, he said.

Celestine was disgusted but not surprised by the Senate proceedings that day. The morning session was well attended, but, by the time the Harki question came up in the afternoon, there were, according to her, only four senators present (in fact, there were more) and a lot of Harkis in the audience. "We were there to witness the farce. We were not allowed to speak," Celestine said with disgust. The senators spent all their time discussing and rejecting one amendment after another favoring the Harkis. Some of these concerned the wording of the law, whether, for example, *événements* (events) should be replaced by *guerres et combat* (wars and combat) or whether Harki children should receive the same compensation (twenty thousand euros) as their parents. Compensation was rejected on financial grounds and because, it was claimed, the children had already received some compensation as well as educational and employment benefits. The rhetoric was high, pretentious, and politically partisan.[18]

"Finally I couldn't stand it any more. I had to put an end to this masquerade," Celestine said angrily toward the end of a long interview in which she talked nonstop about the abuses the Harkis had suffered. As she went on talking about the session and her role in it, she was transported to the scene she was describing, reliving it, and, no doubt, exaggerating it and her role. I paraphrase, using Celestine's words:

> My heart was crying. It was clear that force majeure was required. I jumped up, interrupting the session. I shouted very loudly, very loudly, very loudly, "Mr. President. Senators. I am ashamed of you. You represent the Republic. You represent the law. You are talking about veterans—soldiers of France who saved your lives. While my father was fighting for France against the Germans, you were in your cribs. If it weren't for men like him, France would be German today [*germanizée aujourd'hui*]. You don't have the right to insult my father. I defend my father because he was a soldier of France. You are ridiculing, you are fucking over veterans [*Vous êtes en train de se foutre de la gueule des anciens combatants*]." I shouted very loudly, very loudly. "You show no respect for those veterans who were for the most part mutilated by the war. Thanks to them, they made this country what it is today, and yet they are still living in camps. You are fucking over the history of the Harkis." I was told to shut up. I began to sing the *Marseillaise*. "Allons les enfants de la patrie." One of the guards asked my name. "You ask my name. You don't do your work.

You should know my name. You should consult the intelligence services [*ren-seignements généraux*]. They know my name. They know my age. They know what I ate last night. Why would I give you my name?" "Because you are a leader" [the guard said]. "We are all leaders. Why should I go with you?"

According to Celestine, once she began singing the *Marseillaise* and was joined by the other Harkis in the audience, there was pandemonium in the hall. People were getting up and leaving. Some were screaming. Harkis were crying. Celestine had told the old Harkis in Arabic to join hands and form a chain and sing. When a guard ordered her to follow him out, she said, "Why should I follow you? Why should we talk? I won't follow you. I know the music. If you touch me, you touch a citizen of the Republic." She continued after catching her breath, "The Gardes republicains would not touch me. When they tried to, I asked them, 'How will you be able to sleep at night? You are wearing the uniform of France. What will you tell your children? That you led the Harkis, who sacrificed themselves for France, out of the Senate?'" The guard in question apparently gave up and assured her that he and his men would not touch her. Finally, the CRS were called in, and, after resisting for a while, Celestine and the Harkis left the hall holding hands and singing. They continued singing in front of the Senate, and, though the CRS tried to stop them, they refused. "'We have a right to be here. It's a public street,' I told them. 'We are citizens of France.'"

Other Harkis also protested the law, but in a calmer and more subtle fashion, by publicizing their criticism in the press and on the Internet. Among the most determined is Fatima Besnaci-Lancou, who has written or edited, among other works, her memoirs of life in the camps (Besnaci-Lancou 2003), collections of Harkis' testimonies (Besnaci-Lancou 2006a, 2006b, 2010), and a history of the Harkis (Besnaci-Lancou and Manceron 2008; see also Besnaci-Lancou and Moumen 2008). The Association Harkis et droits de l'homme, which she heads, is one of the most active of the associations. Aside from scrupulously monitoring Harki affairs, Besnaci-Lancou has organized scholarly conferences and workshops.[19] On October 22, 2005, she received the Françoise Seligman Prize, which is awarded people who have fought racism, for her opposition to the law of February 23, 2005 (no. 2005-158), which was based in part on the law discussed on December 16 in the Senate.[20] The award was given to Besnaci-Lancou and her association for organizing protests by the children of both Harkis and Algerian immigrants, who called for the "reappropriation of confiscated memories" because "our parents, whether by choice, chance, or necessity, found themselves in different camps during the Algerian War," and who condemned "the simplistic duality that asserts that there was a good and a bad side [in the war]."[21] Article 4 of this highly controversial law, which has been in part repealed, states: "University research programs should give to the history of the French presence overseas, notably in North Africa, the place it deserves. School programs should recognize in particular the positive role of the French presence overseas, notably in North Africa, and give to this history and the sacrifices fighters of the French army coming from these territories the preeminent place for which they have the right."[22] Other articles in the February 23 law were favorable to the Harkis. They recognized the Harkis' suffering for France and granted them, but not their children, a choice of allocations (*allocations de reconnaissance*), the maximum of which amounted to thirty thousand euros. It was on the basis of Article 5 that AJIR brought its case against *The Name of the Father*. What is, of course, exceptional about Besnaci-Lancou's opposition to the law is her inclusion of both Harkis and Algerian workers. Since receiving the prize, she has continued to fight the law, along with at least seven of the major Harki associations.[23]

At one point in my interview with Celestine, she told me that the Harkis wanted to work like all French citizens and not to be given work as a gift. I am not at all certain that most of the Harkis I met, and certainly not the unemployed, would agree with her. But the point she was making merits consideration. What impressed me most about the Harkis' expectations was that they were government centered. At first, I attributed this attitude to their history, which had created an excessive dependency on the powers that had colonized, exploited, and manipulated them—broken their will, really—a dependency that had been transferred to their children in complex ways. There is, no doubt, considerable truth in my understanding of the causes of the Harkis' dependency on the government, but it must be understood in terms of the central role the French government plays in maintaining the social welfare of its citizens.

I remember sitting with Belkacem in a café in a working-class, multicultural neighborhood in Arles and watching a young man crumble when he learned from some friends that, as the child of a Harki, he did not qualify for the compensation he had counted on to start a disco outside town. He seemed more apprehensive than disappointed. His friends were very supportive, even embracing him. I do not know what inspired his fear—financial commitments he may have made prematurely, for example—but, as far as Belkacem knew, he had made none. Much to my surprise, Belkacem described his reaction in terms, not of fear or disappointment, but of humiliation. "You will hear *humiliation* often in your research." he said. "Do you mean loss of honor, loss of pride?" I asked. "*Humiliation*," he repeated. After a short pause, Belkacem, a tough judge of character, went on to dismiss the young man's reaction as typical of many Harki children who "expect everything from the government rather than fending for themselves."

I had heard Kletch and other Harki activists criticize Harki children, indeed, the Harkis generally, for not fending for themselves. Anne Heinis (1977) attributed the lack of initiative to the dependency created by camp life. She was, of course, writing about the 1960s and early 1970s. Michel Roux (1991, 27) understood it in terms of an unpaid debt, which engenders passivity and a sense of impotence as one awaits compensation. How does this passivity, this sense of impotence, relate to humiliation? The continual failure to pay the debt certainly produces disappointment, frustration, and anger but not necessarily humiliation, unless the failure is—or is perceived as—a belittling insult. It is the personalization of the young man's response, or at least Belkacem's understanding of it, that demands explanation. Whatever biographical factors can be held accountable for the young man's reaction, I would argue that his humiliation is less a personalization than an assumption of the collective experience of the Harkis. In critical situations, the Harkis tend to subsume themselves to that experience, as they do in recounting their stories. It confirms their identity, their marginality, and their victimization. Derogation—in the case in point, refusal and consequent disappointment—promotes a stigmatized identity that offers some solace in the face of their marginalization. It is less the failure to pay the debt, which can never, in fact, be repaid, than the refusal (psychologically, the rejection), continually metaphorized as betrayal and abandonment, that promotes passivity and dependency.

But, before attributing passivity and dependency to the Harkis' unique history or to a weakness in character, we must recognize that, like other French citizens and legal immigrants in need of assistance, the Harkis immediately turn to the government since there are few other resources available to them in as centralized and, one might say, generous a state as France. By the standards of conservative Americans, and not just conservative ones, the French are spoiled, their character weakened, their ambition diminished by a social security system that is one of the most supportive in the world and whose guarantees are scrupulously monitored by their unions. As supportive as the government is, it has its limits, which seem, at times, arbitrary and encourage a political skepticism that is supported by real and imagined abuses of power and financial scandals. In my experience, strikes and protests, particularly by students, have a ritual quality, however serious the cause.[24] Their outcome is, as it were, orchestrated and surmised, if not expected, by their participants and by the public at large. Despite their skepticism, Kletch, Celestine, and Hacène are often carried away by the excitement of their protests. But, in their outrage, they can laugh cynically. There are others who find no solace in cynicism. They are among the deeply wounded.

This is not a political statement—many French critics agree with the "American" position—but a comparative and, I hope, illuminating one. Most Americans would be surprised, as I have said, by the quality of the houses that favorable subsidies and mortgages have enabled many Harkis to obtain and of which they are immensely proud.[25] (They often worked on their houses. Celestine herself was redoing her kitchen when I met her; Azzedine showed me the new wing he had built.) Yet many Harkis complained about how small their housing subventions were, how their mortgage payments increased unexpectedly, and how their mortgages had been extended without explanation. I suspect that their complaints about mortgage payments resulted from misunderstanding, though there may well have been abuses.

Since the exodus of both *pieds noirs* and the Harkis (understood broadly), the French government has granted both groups compensation for the losses they have sustained, subventions for buying and restoring housing, furniture, and, at times, food, and debt relief. Generally, it has been far more generous with the *pieds noirs* than with the Harkis and has not always acted in good faith. One of the most egregious examples was its failure to publicize, indeed, to inform, the Harkis of the subventions they, like the repatriated *pieds noirs*, were entitled to by a law promulgated after the armistice on December 26, 1961. Since then, the Harkis and their associations have kept careful track of indemnifications and subventions. Over 9,000 applications, covering approximately 42,000 individuals, were made for indemnifications offered in 1970 and 1978, the average being the franc equivalent of 1,850 euros. In 1982, there were 145,885 applications for a fixed indemnity of 1,524.50 euros for married couples, widowers, and bachelors with children and 915 euros for unmarried men and divorcees without children. In 1994, the Harkis were entitled to a subvention of 12,196 euros for the purchase of a home or 2,286 euros for home improvement. These were increased in 2005, along with a "final" grant of up to 30,000 euros for Harkis and their widows but not for their children. Aside from special subventions (school charges, debt relief, health care, death grants, etc.), the average capital grant from 1987 to 2005 was 55,916 euros. Subventions, indemnifications, and capital grants from 1995 to 2005 have cost the French government over 60 million euros.[26]

Though given the ever-increasing cost of living in France, the sum is not as great as it may seem to many readers. What irks the Harkis is the manner in which the payments have been made over the years and the need for continual oversight and constant lobbying. By doling out relatively small sums over more than forty years, not only has the French government humiliated the Harkis by what they believe is a cheap, condescending attitude, but it has also fostered the Harkis' sense of community. Given the diverse backgrounds and degrees of assimilation and integration—I would prefer adjustment and accommodation—some conservative authorities have argued that there is, and never was, a real Harki community. Tom Charbit goes so far as to call it a "fiction." Whatever one's definition of a community is, there can be little doubt that the Harkis are united by common experience, a wound that has become, at times, a near-obsessive reference point in their self-understanding—their identity. As I will argue in the next chapter, they form a community of memory.

On our way to Pujol le Bosc, Belkacem stopped to see an elderly Harki who, unlike most Harkis, was literate and spoke fluent French. Belkacem was intervening on his behalf with a government housing agency because of an error in the calculation of his monthly payments. From what I could gather, the government admitted its error but had not yet refunded Belkacem's friend's overpayments. Belkacem explained that, as his friend was old and lived far from the nearest town, where he could have filed a complaint, he had agreed to help him as he had helped many other Harkis with similar complaints. A builder, he had contacts in many municipal offices. He told me that a home was particularly important for Harkis who had lost everything, their roots even, when they fled to France. Unfortunately, many Harkis and their children were too poor to have good housing. He was especially angered by the dilapidated conditions of the subsidized housing, the HLM, in which many, particularly the unemployed, were living. He failed, however, to mention the tiny, often windowless rooms in the slums in the industrial north in which unemployed, often drug-addicted young people live.

Although Belkacem was helping his Harki friends on his own, most of the Harkis I met would go to a Harki association for advice, unless they had personal contacts in the government. I have been told that, aside from the government-sponsored *maisons de rapatriés*, there are as many as five hundred associations, no doubt an exaggeration, of which about eighty are active and a handful important. Until 1971, when the first Harki-run association was started by Jean-Claude Khiari, organizations concerned with the Harkis were founded and run by the French, most often with government support. In the 1970s, the number of Harki associations, mostly founded by families and small communities to address local concerns, increased dramatically.[27] An attempt was made in 1978 to federate them, but it had little success. Today, the most important associations are affiliated with each other in an informal and ad hoc way.

The cynical head of one of the *maisons*—the son of a Harki—told me that most of the associations were founded in order to receive a tiny subsidy. Their proliferation demonstrated the lack of unity in the Harki community (see also Hamoumou 1993, 308). "Without unity, the Harkis will never accomplish anything," he said, pointedly disgusted. He blamed the lack of unity on the separation of families and villagers in the camps and forestry hamlets as well as a tradition of feuding. (He did not mention the tension between Berbers and Arabs, which was usually mitigated by the Harkis' common experiences.) It is true that members of the most important associations often appear to be jealous of one another, though they do cooperate, as in the case of February 23, 2005, law, when they find it necessary. In my experience, many of their leaders are deeply entangled in local politics, often for their own ends. Such connections give them a sense of importance that finds its roots, I believe, in the dislocations they have suffered.

Aside from the advice they give individual Harkis and the demands they make on the government, the associations are careful to monitor any slight to the Harkis and, as we saw in the case of *The Name of the Father*, to take legal action if they think it is justified. They scrutinize the speeches of the president of Algeria, Abdelaziz Bouteflika, for derogatory references to them, and they have condemned the friendship treaty between France and Algeria, arguing that it was unidirectional, motivated by economic interests, and ignored the FLN's failure to carry out the terms of the Treaty of Evian. AJIR has brought a suit against Pierre Messmer for his failure to safeguard the lives of the Harkis.[28] This was based on a radio interview in which the former minister of the army said that he took no responsibility for the Harki massacres and had no regrets (for what he had done). AJIR was successful in legally pursing Philippe de Gaulle, who wrote, in his memoirs of his father, Charles, that the Harkis had rallied with the ALN after the signing of the peace treaty. It publicized the desecration of a monument to the Harkis in Roubaix. In May 2010, it succeeded in closing an exhibition at the Picasso Museum in Vallauris by the Franco-Algerian artist Zineb Sedira, who referred to the Harkis as collaborators in her translation of her mother's memories of the war (*L'express*, May 13–19, 2010).[29] During the 2007 French presidential election, it kept track of the (contradictory) positions of each of the candidates. Some of the Web sites showed a definite political bias, most often for Sarkozy and the Union pour un mouvement populaire. (As I am writing at the end of 2009, many of the sites have been critical of Sarkozy, arguing that he has not kept promises he made during his presidential campaign.)[30] They publicize meetings and cultural events that are of interest to the Harkis.[31]

In the late spring of 2007, I met Kletch in a little Algerian restaurant in—as the French say—*un quartier mixte* on the outskirts of Paris. I had not seen him for over a year and was anxious to catch up with him. We were joined by two of his friends, both sons of Harkis, who, like Kletch, were outraged by remarks made by Georges Frêche, the outspoken socialist president of the Languedoc-Rousillon Region and mayor of Montpellier from 1977 to 2004. Frêche, sometimes called the Socialist Baron, had called the Harkis "subhuman" in a debate on February 11, 2006, over the positive side of colonialism. (He is famous for his outspoken, often politically outrageous remarks of a racist cast.)[32] And he had lost his temper when he was heckled by two Harkis in the audience and shouted at them: "You have gone with the Gaullists. . . . They massacred your people in Algeria. . . . They cut their throats like pigs. You belong to those Harkis who have taken up the vocation of being cuckolded until the end of time. . . . You are subhumans; you are without honor. . . ."

The Harkis brought a case against Frêche in March 2006 on the grounds that, by calling them *subhuman*, he had committed the crime (*délit*) of insulting a person or group of persons because of their origin or ethnicity. Frêche was found guilty in the court of first instance and fined fifteen thousand euros. His appeal was to be heard in a few weeks. Kletch and his friends expected him to win the appeal, and, as they expected, on September 13, 2007, the court of appeals acquitted him on the grounds that his words were addressed, not to the Harki community, but to two individuals.

All three men supported the case against Frêche. It was obvious, they argued, that he was referring to all Harkis and was, therefore, guilty. Still, Kletch was troubled by the case. Though Frêche had clearly insulted all the Harkis, Kletch did not and could not support the law on which the case was based. How could he? he asked. Colonialism is indefensible. The Harkis themselves are the product of colonialism and have acted and suffered accordingly. One of his friends, who had not thought through this argument, immediately agreed with Kletch. The other, while agreeing that colonialism was indefensible, questioned Kletch's calling Harkis a product of colonialism because it demeaned them. They had come to an impasse. The contradiction, as I saw it, was clear. They were caught between the desire to maintain their fathers' autonomy and the desire to see themselves as victims of a colonialism that had given their fathers no choice but to become auxiliary troops.

It is one thing to recognize the ambiguous situation in which one finds oneself and quite another to have it confirmed by an outsider. When I pointed out the paradox—one of the many paradoxical situations in which the Harkis and their children find themselves—Kletch and his friends ignored my comment. They began talking about how the Harkis were being used politically, as hostages of one ideology or another, on the Right or the Left.[33] They were seeking the protection of the Harki story, or so, at least, it seemed to me. They concluded their conversation by telling me about their efforts to fund a case in the World Court against France for crimes against humanity.

SEVEN

Reflections

Man is the only being that makes promises.

—Attributed to Friedrich Nietzsche

Straddling several worlds, anthropologists find themselves in between. Whatever observations they make, and whatever objectivity they claim, their descriptions and interpretations must be judged in terms of the unstable position they inhabit, not only during their field research, but also in its aftermath, when they attempt to give shape to what they have learned for a projected—mixed—readership. However hard anthropologists try, the people they worked with are always a silent but insistent—a determining—audience.[1] The anthropologist is caught. At least, I was caught by the Harkis. From the start, as I have said, the Harkis and their children turned me into a witness of what they had suffered and their descriptions into testimonies. Our relationship was immediately framed legalistically, as though they were preparing a brief that I was to argue for them. They were, however, less interested in convincing me of the truth of what they recounted—that needed no proof for them—than in spreading that truth. I was both their immediate interlocutor—to be informed—and, they hoped, their *porte-parole*. I use the French *porte-parole* rather than the English *spokesman* because it lays emphasis on the *parole*—the "word"—that I was to carry forth. Yes, but it also suggests the *word* (*kelma*) that seals a contractual arrangement. The Harkis gave me their words, and, in receiving them, I was assumed to have given my word, not only to be faithful to what they confided in me, but also to do whatever I could to make their case known in the English-speaking world.[2]

I felt bullied since the Harkis were insisting that I do what, obviously, I could not do. I told them that I did not have the contacts they assumed, quite unrealistically, I had. My aim was not, in any case, to argue their cause, as moved as I was by it, but to describe, as accurately as I could, what they had gone through and how they were living with it. "The facts would speak for themselves," I said. For the most part, they accepted my position, although I am certain that several of them were sure that "the facts" would eventually turn me into an advocate. The Harkis' attempt to recruit me was clearly political, but it was also a way of affirming their identity—an identity that had been so brutally undermined that many of them were never able to find firm footing again.[3] They had become victims of a stigmatized identity that they had no choice but to accept, if only because that identity afforded them a means of claiming the recognition and the compensation that they believed, not without reason, they deserved. But it also marked their membership in a dispersed community of memory. They were caught in a paradox. To free themselves of this stigma, they had to accept it; to cease being a victim, they had to be a victim. Given the assault on their identity, they did not have the distance to play the victim. Their demands for recognition, compensation, and apology must, I believe, be seen in this light. They cannot simply be dismissed, as some French and Algerians try to do, as playing the system for only material gain. The Harkis cannot be bought, as the French government ought to have learned by now. They have been given some recognition, but they have not yet received the apology many of the younger generation believe would restore meaning to their parents' lives and, indeed, to their own.

I am rather more skeptical. For forgiveness to occur, the wrongdoers and their victims must, ideally, acknowledge the wrongdoing, appreciate each other's perspective, and recognize the role it has played in the way in which they have each configured their individual and collectives lives (as, e.g., a central trauma, an excuse for inaction, a source of rancor and resentment). And, as the philosopher Charles Griswold (2007, 174), argues, they have to "reenvision" both the offense and their sense of self. The forgiver must forswear revenge, moderate resentment, and not vindictively remind the offender of his or her wrongdoing; the offender must, of course, agree not to repeat the offense or retaliate for having had to apologize. Ideally, the offender should acknowledge the truth of what he or she has done and resist rationalization and self-justification.

Irreversible events of magnitude, like the massacre of the Harkis, always figure dramatically in the self-constitution—the identity—of both aggressors and victims. Paradoxically, forgiving and being forgiven for such tragic events can have a devastating effect on both the forgiver and the forgiven: the rug, so to speak, is pulled out from under them.[4] As Emmanuel Brillet

(2001) argues, and as I have suggested, were the French (or the Algerians) to apologize for their treatment of the Harkis, the Harkis' sense of self and community (insofar as it is centered on the French refusal to apologize) would be threatened. "All recognition, and, a fortiori, that which confers pardon, is at once comforting and a little death [*petit mort*] for a community marked by the proof of disaster," Brillet observes.

I suggested on several occasions in my conversations with the more sensitive Harki children that the only way they could be liberated was by pardoning the French, but, as they knew and I knew, this was impossible, for they had no platform from which to proclaim forgiveness. What were they to do? Stand up in front of the Elysée and say, "La France, je vous pardonne." One woman said that she had thought of this but realized how impossible it was and, in any case, was not sure it would work. Another suggested that I was being "too Christian." (I had not thought of this.) And the others could make no sense of what I was saying. Forgiveness was simply impossible. "And if the French apologized?" I asked. It would still be impossible, they insisted.

Were the Harkis confronted with the paradox that Jacques Derrida (2001, 32–33) noted in his essay "Forgiveness": that you can forgive only what is unforgivable? If you are prepared to forgive only the forgivable, Derrida argues, then the idea of forgiveness would disappear.[5] I am by no means convinced of this argument. It is important, as Derrida himself recognizes in Christian terms, to distinguish between different types of sin. I would argue that there is a difference between the conventional forgiveness of those trivial acts, however hurtful they may be, that, in one fashion or another, are taken to be remediable, dismissible, or annullable and the forgiveness of serious ones—the ones Derrida would claim to be unforgivable—which are irreversible.[6] These demand unconditional forgiveness, a forgiveness that, if I understand Derrida (2001, 44–45) correctly, must, in its purity, divorce itself from the conditional—"from what is heterogeneous to it, namely the order of conditions, repentance, transformation, as many things as allow it to inscribe itself in history, law, politics, existence itself." The two poles are absolutely heterogeneous, irreconcilable, irreducible to one another, yet indissociable if forgiveness is to become effective within concrete historical situations. Derrida's emphasis on the unconditional here is an attempt to free forgiveness from its political implications, say, reconciliation, and an economy of exchange. It is between these, the unconditional and conditional poles, within this aporetic tension, that decisions are made and responsibilities assumed.

But can forgiveness ever be removed from the political? The ethical from the political? No more, I suppose, than can unconditional forgiveness be detached from the conditional. Though Derrida (2001, 59) argues that un-conditional forgiveness requires the suspension of individual sovereignty, he fails—or nearly fails—to address those situations in which the victims of, say, colonial oppression are, as Kelly Oliver (2004) argues, deprived of psychic space for forgiveness.[7] It could be so argued for the old Harkis, but such an argument would, not only simplify the circumstances in which they found themselves, but also deny them—to use the jargon—what agency, however shattered, what illusions of agency, they still have. We cannot ig-nore those Harkis who overcame the most grueling of their plights—their forbearance, their resiliency, and their creativity.

As I thought about the Harkis' demand for an apology, I realized that, with the possible exception of Azzedine, none of the Harkis or their chil-dren ever suggested that, were the French to apologize, they would forgive them. One can, of course, accept an apology without forgiving in return. Think of the expression, "Oh, forget about it," after someone has apolo-gized for having wronged you. Does it imply forgiveness? Or is it simply an excusing, a way to get on with the business at hand? We normally think of an apology in terms of spiritual transformation (remorse, contrition), for-giving reciprocation, and, in consequence, reconciliation. It is by no means certain, however, that the apology the Harkis demand of the French requires a real change of heart. They are realists, and they know that the events for which they are asking an apology are given, irreversible, and, in the end, unforgivable. Many suspect that, were the French to apologize, their apol-ogy would be conventional and, ultimately, dismissive. They both know the power that lies in refraining from apologizing. The Harkis may see the apol-ogy as simply an occasion for sparring, for getting the better of the French by forcing them into a humiliating admission by succumbing to the Harkis' demand, for "internalized" revenge.

A number of writers (e.g., Brillet 2001) have understood forgiveness as an exchange, most often referring to Marcel Mauss's (1990) essay on the gift, in which the French anthropologist refers to the reciprocal obligations (give, receive, return) in any exchange system and the power that resides in the gift itself. It has often been noted that, etymologically, *gift* and *forgiveness* are related to each other in many Indo-European languages: *gift/forgiving, dono/perdono, Geben/Vergeben*, etc. But can a gift (*cadeau* or *présent*, as op-posed to *don*) and forgiveness be equated? Derrida would say no, if only because exchange precludes the unconditional necessary for forgiveness.[8] Paul Ricoeur (2000, 624) argues that, although both giving and forgiving are bilateral and reciprocal, their insertion in analogous circles of exchange precludes distinguishing between forgiveness (*pardon*) and payment (*rétri-bution*), which, he claims, equalizes the relationship between the two parties in the exchange. To distinguish the two, he suggests (in Christian fashion), it is necessary to turn to the "radical commandment to love one's enemy without return [without expecting anything in return, *sans retour*]." This "impossible commandment" appears to be the only one that can rise "to the height of the spirit of apology [*seul à la hauteur de l'esprit de pardon*]." "The enemy does not ask for pardon; it is necessary to love him as he is." But must all demands for forgiveness demand unconditional love? Must forgiveness be distinguished from retribution only in spiritual terms? Can it not be simply a formula for realigning the forgiver and the forgiven? Must any act of apology be inserted in a system of exchange? Or is a single exchange sufficient for forgiveness?

Ricoeur's model of exchange ignores risk. Even the most conventional-ized exchanges are dangerous. The gift (like an offense) can be conceived as a challenge demanding a response, as Pierre Bourdieu (1965) suggests in his discussion of the dialectics of honor among the Kabyles. He speculates: "Perhaps every exchange carries in itself a challenge more or less dissimu-lated, so that the logic of challenge and riposte may only be the extreme limit toward which every communication tends, especially where the ex-change of gifts is concerned." In offering a gift, the donors risk the recipi-ent's refusal. In accepting the gift, the recipients risk the donor's withdrawal of the gift. Those approaches to gift exchange that focus on tangible gifts, as do most anthropological ones, fail to recognize that the acceptance of the gift is itself a gift insofar as it relieves the donors' anxieties about the risk they have taken. By not withdrawing the gift, donors give, as it were, a dou-ble gift—a tangible gift and an intangible one—ensuring thereby their supe-rior position. Unlike the recipients, who always remain in debt, they appear to be debt free, that is, until they are forced to accept a gift—minimally, the acceptance of the gift—from the recipient.

Risk is equally at play in the pardon. Those, like the Harkis, who de-mand an apology from the wrongdoer place themselves in the inferior, vulnerable position of a petitioner, for the wrongdoer—the French—need not forgive, maintaining, thereby, the superior political position, and per-petuating the petitioner's humility. But, by refusing to ask to be forgiven, by rejecting the petitioner's demand, wrongdoers find themselves in a mor-ally compromised position, one that is intensified, in the case in point, by their ostensible (Christian) commitment to forgiveness and the change of heart it demands. Thus, they are at once in a superior and inferior position vis-à-vis the petitioners. The Harkis have a moral hold over the French. If the French were to apologize, they would surrender their political superiority and strengthen their moral superiority, but, however praiseworthy their newly acquired moral stance, it is always tarnished by the wrongdoing they have committed. The taint can be removed, if at all, only by the Harkis' acceptance of their apology. Were the Harkis to refuse to accept the apology, the risk the French had taken would be worthless. The Harkis would have gained the upper hand—revenge—by humiliating them. Would the Harkis' have surrendered their moral superiority by refusing the pardon? By French standards, yes. But do the Harkis share this standard? Is their approach to forgiveness premised on another set of presuppositions? Another etiquette of forgiveness? One correlated with revenge?

The old Harkis are enraged but cannot direct their rage at the object of that rage in any active manner. They cannot avenge themselves. One of the ways in which anger is dissipated, Aristotle observed in the *Nicomachean Ethics* (1126a), is through revenge. It has often been observed that rural Algerian society is vengeful. Its history is one of family feuds, some lasting for generations. The French were quick to seize on this stereotype in their attempt to understand why villages were often split between the FLN and the Harkis. Jean Servier did, in his analysis of the Toussaint Rouge in 1955. Many French officers, including some I spoke to, as well as some Algerians, argued that the Harkis often joined the French to avenge themselves. I have even heard French say that Algeria is a society of vengeance and France one of forgiveness. Such stereotyping is inexcusable on many grounds, including racist and supremacist ones.

I do not want to deny the Harkis the capacity to forgive or to love unconditionally, any more than I want to deny the French the possibility of revenge. I am arguing—far too mechanically—that the assumptions we make about forgiveness as an occasion for a change of heart, an expression of unconditional love, the expiation of guilt, and the extinction of shame are not necessarily universal. To argue that the Harkis' demand for pardon without reciprocation is embedded in a culture of the vendetta, in which honor is always at stake, would be to deny the Harkis and their children a transformational response to their historical experience. They would become wooden figures. But to ignore the possible effect of the values of traditional Algerian society on their response would be to deny an important dimension of that response. Nor do I want to deny the importance of revenge in the Christian understanding of forgiveness. Its preclusion merits critical reflection. The desires for forgiveness and revenge must be seen in terms of the historical conditions that inspire and formulate them. Given the historical circumstances in which the Harkis and the French found and find themselves, it would be egregious not to recognize the interpenetration of desires for forgiveness and revenge in both of them.

Hannah Arendt (1958, 237) suggests: "Without being forgiven, released from the consequences of what we have done, our capacity to act would, as it were, be confined to one single deed from which we could never recover; we would remain victims of its consequences forever, not unlike the sorcerer's apprentice who lacked the magic formula to break the spell."[9] Arendt's depiction of what would happen if forgiveness were impossible bears an uncanny resemblance to the situation in which the old Harkis find themselves. They ruminate. They are fixated on how they have been betrayed and abandoned.[10] Does this fixation spare them acknowledgment of the fact that they made the fatal decision that, ultimately, led to their being betrayed and abandoned? Or do they dwell on the decision itself, as was implied by several of the Harkis with whom I talked?

The Italian sociologist Gabriella Turnaturi (2007, 8) argues that betrayal presupposes a shared experience—"a We relationship," which, I would add, need not be symmetrical. Its artifice and fragility may be recognized or defended against by all parties to it. It may be fraught with tension and suspicion that are controlled, if they are controlled, by custom, law, or institutional (military) regulation, as it was for the Harkis and the French. Of necessity, it is intensified in combat situations where dependency on one another is a matter of life and death. But, even in such circumstances, mistrust is not infrequent. Betrayal occurs, Turnaturi argues, when the relationship is attacked from within the confines of the We (9). It always involves abandonment. One betrays not a person or a group, but a relationship, she argues (13). It is not an aggressive act directed toward the other or others but a "more or less intentional act aimed at destroying that relationship or withdrawing from it" (13). Whether or not one can separate the relationship from the person—I have my doubts about that—the betrayed personalize the act of betrayal and understand it as an aggression directed at them. (The betrayer *per contra* can depersonalize and justify the betrayal by focusing on the relationship, legalistically, pragmatically, rather than on the person.) Certainly, the Harkis personalized what they took to be a betrayal. They had no doubt that it was directed at them. Though they sometimes referred to specific officers who sent them home without arms or without explaining their choices, for the most part they depersonalized the betrayer. It was the French who betrayed them; the officers were simply following orders. It is, of course, possible that the betrayer became more and more abstract for the Harkis as time passed and as they subsumed their own experiences in *the* Harki story. As Turnaturi puts it:

Betrayal demonstrates our vulnerability. We lose our bearings, our identity, our sense of worth, and our trust in the other (not just the betrayer but, more generally, others). We are emptied—wounded. Anger, rage, and hatred are not just turned on the betrayer, now the enemy, but on ourselves. To be betrayed denotes an immediate loss of self-esteem; we feel ourselves diminished, scorned, and even guilty of having in some fashion done something to merit betrayal. We can slip into self-pity and depression; we soon develop an image of ourselves as a victim, incapable of discerning or understanding what goes on around us, as well as the other as unfaithful and wicked. (30)

We are shamed. A sense of abandonment, a seemingly inevitable consequence of being betrayed, induces a paradoxical situation: as you focus on the perpetrators, indeed, on yourself, you abandon those people in your immediate circle, in existential terms, your *Mitwelt*. They lose significance; they fade away. You fall into harrowing solitude. Depopulated, your world darkens, folds in on itself, leaving you fixated on the abandoner and the traitor—on abandonment and treachery. With the affective devaluation of your *Mitwelt*, you lose perspective, for there are no others significant enough to afford you a vantage point. If Arendt is right, with the loss of others, or, as she puts it, "plurality," forgiveness—self-forgiveness—become impossible.[11] I would add self-acknowledgment, rationalization, and self-justification. There can be, it would seem, no escape.

As the Harkis have been continually reminded of their collaboration by people around them, most notably by Algerian immigrant workers and, at times, close family members, the treachery attached to their decision or nondecision, regardless of their motives, echoes forward to being betrayed, narrowing their world even more. Betrayal is a breach of trust—of implicit, if not explicit, promise—and, with that breach, the future loses whatever certainty it may have had. It is the promise, Arendt (1958, 217) argues, that attenuates "the chaotic uncertainty of the future."[12] As such, it, too, can offer no escape from what one of the Harki children referred to as the "prison of memory."

In nearly all our conversations, the Harkis and their children mentioned June 16, 2000, when Abdelaziz Bouteflika called the Harkis *collabos* on French television, in front of Jacques Chirac. He said that the return of the Harkis to Algeria would be like asking a French member of the Résistance to touch the hand of a *collabo*. The Harkis were furious at the Algerian president and, if one can compare levels of fury, even more so at the French president for not having responded immediately to Bouteflika's insult—"an insult addressed to French citizens," several of the Harkis said. (Chirac did respond a few days later.) Chirac's failure seemed to be a replay of their abandonment by France. Bouteflika's insult was expectable, though perhaps not on an official visit to France. Since the end of the war, the Algerian government has used the Harkis as a scapegoat for its failures—as a rallying point for creating the illusion of the unity of the Algerian people during the war and its aftermath. One of its most egregious accusations was that the Harkis were active supporters of the Islamists in the 1990s—one of the objections the Harkis had to *The Name of the Father*.

As I noted earlier, none of the Harkis I spoke to asked why the Algerians massacred them. They were simply infuriated. When I asked them why, several said, What can you expect from the Algerians? Other stressed the fact that the carnage was committed or triggered by the ALN and the *marsiens*. They did not hold all the Algerians responsible. But none of their answers seemed satisfactory. They were not being evasive. They had not asked the question or preferred not to think about it at all. In the event, they too are—or were—Algerians. They certainly did not expect recognition of responsibility, recompense, or an apology from the Algerian government, although on March 4, 2006, in a declaration following a symposium on the Harkis, the participants expressed the desire that the Algerian government stop demonizing the Harkis and express regret over their massacre (Besnaci-Lancou and Manceron 2008, 209).[13] And earlier, on August 15, 2004, in an article in *Le figaro*, Yazid Sabeg, the president of the Convention laïque pour l'égalité, and Fatima Besnaci-Lancou argued that, if there were to be any reconciliation between Algeria and France, all parties involved would have to abandon polemical history, acknowledge courageously what they did, and respect their different memories. Apparently, Bouteflika has moderated his position on the Harkis. In Oran, on September 8, 2005, he said: "We have committed errors in countering the Harkis and those close to them, and we did not show proof of our wisdom. We have aroused in them feelings of hatred and rancor, prejudicing our country" (Haroun 2008, 202).

There are several Algerian and Algerian-immigrant blogs that have discussed the Harkis. Opinions vary from calling them "unforgivable *collabos*" to calling them "victims of French colonialism." One man wrote angrily in English, "In the past we used to say that the lion is the son of a lion, today we say that too but in a different way, one can say, the snake is the son of a viper." He was referring to several Harkis who had killed two *moujahidine*. Others said that the Algerians should feel sorry for the Harkis, forget what they had done, and recognize that they too are Algerians. An Algerian professor told me that he had had no idea what had happened to the Harkis until he began teaching in France. He expressed cautious shock. Like several other Algerians, including a well-known writer, he found the Harkis' understanding of themselves as victims demeaning. He was surprised by it. "Algeria is a land of a thousand heroes," he said ironically. He argued, not without sympathy, that the Harkis, especially their children, must accept the reality of their situation and get on with their lives. Others made similar observations. One highly educated Algerian woman who lived in Paris was particularly disgusted by the Harkis' self-indulgence: "The Harkis say they cannot go back to Algeria because they know that their life is better here." She ignored her husband's reminder that they would not be welcomed, even if they were permitted reentry. "They—and their children—have to recognize the harm they did to their country and bear the consequences," she insisted.

Many other Algerians working in France remain mistrustful of the Harkis and appear at times to be envious of what they consider to be the Harkis' privileges, especially those that come with French citizenship. (Their envy has been attenuated by the fact that their children born in France have the option of French citizenship.) It would be an oversimplification to reduce the object of envy to privilege alone. One could argue, as Abdelmalik Sayad (1999, 333–42) does, that Algerians, particularly those who fought for independence, consider the surrender of Algerian citizenship a betrayal of their country. Were this the case, it would add yet another dimension to the Harkis' supposed treachery. No Harkis ever mentioned feelings of having betrayed Algeria by becoming a French citizen. How could they?

Given that the Algerian government refuses to acknowledge the massacres or even its breach of the Treaty of Evian, any possibility of compensation or apology is excluded. But is this a sufficient cause? Or is it, rather, that accusations of treachery (or, indeed, a barely admissible sense that they may have betrayed their people) have determined the Harkis' response and, in complex ways, their children's? I have heard from both the French and the Algerians, as well as several American colleagues, that the Harkis cannot expect anything from the Algerians, that they cannot even blame them, because they are guilty and, accordingly, direct their rage at the French with inordinate intensity. Such answers are pat; they coordinate with our psychomechanics. And they may soothe us, at least the French and the Algerians, but they certainly do not conform to my experience of the Harkis and their children. Perhaps. I prefer to leave the question open and live with the disquiet. We are, as I have noted many times, concerned with breaches of the most fundamental requirements of consociation and the taboos buried deep within the psyche. They have, perhaps, been best articulated in mythic terms or, in the case of our anthropologies and psychologies, in metamythic terms, which, as Claude Lévi-Strauss (1969, 6) remarked, inevitably replicate their target myths.

Depth aside, the Algerians and the Harkis are entangled in a never-ending struggle for identity. On the one hand, the Algerians—their government at least—use the Harkis as an internal enemy that must be and is, in fact, external. For the Algerians, the Harkis must be Algerian in order to be traitors, and, as such, they must be cast out of the very society that requires or is made to require them. The Harkis, ostracized by the Algerians, are for the French still Algerians and, as such, only legally but not culturally French. They are forced, as it were, to be Algerians when they want to be French, and, for the Algerians, they are identified with precisely the people who reject them. They find themselves in a situation in which the negation of themselves—to be other than themselves—demanded by wanted or unwanted assimilation or identification is impossible. There can be no stability in such a situation. The Harkis, it would seem, are forced to bracket off any affiliation with—any expectation from—the Algerians in order to maintain at best an interstitial marginality in which they are at once Algerian and not Algerian and French and not French. Often identified with the immigrant by the French, though not usually by the immigrants, they see themselves as ostracized and exiled. We might ask where the treachery lies and come to appreciate the oscillating neither-nor to which their abandonment and ostracism have left them.[14]

In many respects, the Harkis' relegation to the camps continues symbolically to this day. Giorgio Agamben (1998, 174) argues that "the birth of the camp in our time appears as an event that decisively signals the political space of modernity itself." The camp is a space in which "bare life and juridical rule enter into the threshold of indistinction." It is at once in and out of society. Whether we agree or disagree with the Italian philosopher's contention that the camp is a permanent fixture of the modern nation-state, we must agree that, as a product of sovereign exception, it is "a hybrid of law and fact in which the two terms become indistinguishable" (170). As such, the camp can be a place of unconstrained abuse and extinction, as in the German death camps.[15] But, as we have seen, even in the Harki camps, where the rule of law was, in principle, in effect, unchecked abuses were not uncommon, and, if only through neglect, preventable deaths were not infrequent. The camp became, for the Harkis, not just the locus, but the symbol of abandonment, the existence of the one intensifying the force of the other. It has served as an implicit, if not always explicit, figure for the Harkis' sense of apartness, marginality, and interstitiality. As I talked to Yamina in a square not far from the National Assembly in Paris, where she was protesting, she pointed out how the bureaucrats and assemblymen who passed the protest turned away. "They can't stand to look at us," she said. Marked, the Harkis' invisibility was perpetuated.

My speculations are tangential to the Harkis' biographically invested experience of betrayal and abandonment, but they do suggest the existential dimension of the Harkis' sitting against a wall, lost in themselves, with a future deflected onto their children or without any future at all. True, but faced with death, many of the old Harkis—who, unlike their children, pray each day at the local mosques or in the quiet of their homes—do have, I believe, an otherworldly sense of the future, even if it is only a recited expectation. We must not forget the importance of the remembrance of death in even popular Islam. "Remember death abundantly, for to recall it wipes away sins and makes one abstemious in the world," Malik ibn Anas, one of the most esteemed of the early Muslim scholars, said (quoted in al-Ghazali 1989, 10). To what extent do they practice the remembrance of death and the afterlife? Who am I to tell? I can, at best, surmise.

The proliferation of paradoxes, like the ones I have just described, characterizes Harki life. Among other paradoxes is the use of the word *Harki*, which, as we have seen, has both a restricted and an extended sense. The ambiguity reflects the problem of classifying peoples living or having lived in Algeria (perhaps in all colonies) that has troubled the French since they first arrived in Algeria. The Harkis are trapped, as it were, in the politically vested identity that they have taken up—that they have been forced to take up. It perpetuates a public distinction between them and the French, a distinction that most of them, like Celestine, say they want to efface: "We want to be treated just like the French citizens we are." But, as should be evident by now, they also want to perpetuate that identity. To distinguish public and private goals here may be analytically neat, but it ignores the paradoxical interplay between the two stipulated domains—the public and the private spheres—that have been in particular fashion in the social sciences since Jürgen Habermas (1990) wrote *The Structural Transformation of the Public Sphere* in 1962. As Azzedine said one afternoon, as we were talking about the identity he would want his children to have, "The Harkis have a special perspective on society. We are always in and out at the same time. We see things ordinary Frenchmen do not. It is not always easy." When I asked him whether he would want his children to lose this perspective, he hesitated for a long time, said no, then quickly added, "It would be impossible."

The Harkis' use of the term *Harki* promotes generalization and stereotypy that ignore the diversity of the Harki population. It masks, not only differences in origin (Berber/Arab, urban/rural), generation, education, linguistic ability, profession, class, identification with and engagement in the Harki cause, and degree of assimilation and integration in one or another sectors of French society, but also the relations between these diverse groups.[16] It dehistoricizes them, denying them as individuals and as a group the possibility of change, indeed, of the changes that have occurred in their lives, values, attitudes, and desires ever since they became Harkis.[17] By this, I do not want to suggest that the Harkis and their children are unaware of the changes that surround them and the changes in themselves. Rather, I mean that they are caught, as they are in their story, in a fixed identity or, perhaps more accurately for the children, a compelling image of that identity. That image may be political, legal, indeed, rhetorical, but it dramatically influences their experience of themselves.

Generalization and stereotypy present an irresolvable problem in ethnographic writing. We want to preserve the individuality of the people we work with (perhaps, given our individualism, more than they desire) as much as we want to describe them as a group. We sometimes forget that collective identity can give people a sense of power—something the Harkis learned after their first protests in 1975. But the power of collective action is not its only benefit. Collective action also promotes a sense of community or, at least, the knowledge that what one has experienced has been experienced by others. One can also hide behind or excuse oneself through that identity. There seems to be no end of the ways in which humans can manipulate their membership in a group. In my encounters with them, many Harkis hid, at least initially, behind their Harki identity and the story that bolstered it.

I have tried, as I wrote in the introduction, to remediate generalization and stereotypy by citing individual Harkis when it seemed appropriate. The citations should give the reader an idea of the range of the Harkis' experiences, personalities, careers, and outlooks. They highlight the inevitable gap between the collective and the individual, a gap that constitutes the space in which the identities are created and re-created: the space of puzzlement, struggle, resistance, surrender, and temporary resolution. It is the space of fissure, a chiasma in which habituation, however longed for, is always in question.[18] Usually ignored, it comes to the fore in crisis, self-critical reflection, and creative turmoil. It became, at times in my research, the space in which the contradictions between the Harkis' individual and collective identities were not only discussed but also enacted, sometimes in heartrending manner, as when Kletch, Belkacem, and Hacène spoke nostalgically about their boyhood in the camps we visited at the same time that they expressed outrage at their incarceration there. It was the space in which conflicts between the Harki story and individual experience were played out. I will have more to say about this below.

Of course, the citations cannot reveal changes in the Harkis' lives as they occurred. Their past is the past of memory, a memorialization of that which was once significant and is still significant but refashioned in light of all that has happened since then and by the circumstances in which they now find themselves. Masked by a sense of certainty, revision is, nevertheless, inevitable. Given documentation that extends over the years, I have, to some extent, been able to recognize, if not actual changes, then possible ones. To give one example, which I find troubling: although I never heard a Harki child refer to his father as a *traitor*, Michel Roux (1991, 21) reports that Harki youths, especially adolescent boys, often did refer to their fathers in that way. He goes on to say that these accusations had less to do with what their fathers had done during the war than with the consequences of what they had done. It was a reproach for having led their families down the road to exile. As they themselves put it, "To have been made to be born in France [*nous avoir fait naître en France*]." The Harki children were, at some level, angry at their fathers and probably expressed that anger during their adolescence, but they rarely admitted it verbally. It was sometimes apparent in their facial expressions and gestures (see below). But, certainly, none, as I have said, accused or admitted accusing their fathers of treachery.[19] How does one explain this discrepancy? Is it a result of the different relations that Roux and I had with the Harki children? Is it an effect of his being French and my being American? Does it reflect their desire to whitewash themselves in my eyes, seeing me, as they did, as a potential *porte-parole*? Or is it a consequence of historical change? In France? In Algeria? Or in the relative distance from the events that permits greater discretion? Or an intensification of loss that interdicts the expression of animosity toward one's father? Or, finally, does it relate to levels or expectations of integration? I cannot, of course, answer any of these questions in a satisfactory way.

The citations also reveal my perspective and some of the ways in which it affected our encounters. It suggests the gap in intention, understanding, and characterization between us, as in my ethnographic commitment and their desire to enlist me as an advocate and in how we responded to each other and produced the data I am making use of in my portrayal of them. As I reflect back on my field experiences, I recall my determination to get beyond the Harki story, to the individual's story, whatever that might have been, and the resistance I encountered, despite my interlocutor's willingness to work with me. I was looking for the particular, for the depth it would reveal. Of course, they insisted on their collective story—where particularities were simply exemplifications. And, though they addressed me as their immediate interlocutor, they attempted to turn me into a "third" who would publicize that story. As a result of being cast as a *porte-parole*, I felt the loss of resonance that comes with immediate interlocution. Did they? I imagine they did. I changed my approach. Rather than interview the Harkis and their children, I entered almost immediately into conversation with them. (There were obviously exceptions, particularly among the old Harkis.) I took an active, sometimes argumentative part in the conversations, monitoring, as best I could, their reaction to my suggestions. Most of the children seemed far more comfortable in conversation than they did in formal interviews. They did not feel the same obligation to convince me of their story.

I spent several days at Azzedine's home. Azzedine is a particularly sensitive man in his late forties and far more introspective than many of the other Harki children I have met. He often refers to the pain, the wound, the Harkis and their children feel. He bears that pain—"the pain of the fathers," he called it—with rare intensity. He recalled crying, as he lay in bed at night, thinking about how his father had been humiliated that day by the camp authorities.

Azzedine had arranged for me to talk to several old Harkis whom he thought I should meet. There was something a bit staged about these meetings, but they turned out to be among the most interesting I had. Azzedine and I discussed each of the Harkis before and after my meeting with them. He saw each of them as a representative of one facet or another of the Harki experience: torture, witnessing the massacres, terrified night flight, arrival in France, camp life, and the near-impossible search for work. Though Azzedine was clearly moved by what the Harkis said, he did not engage with them, at least in my presence, in a personal manner. Their representative function seemed to override his personal interest. He had, of course, heard their stories before. No doubt, he had arranged similar meetings. He also had to maintain the respectful distance that a younger Algerian man must show his elders.

Between these meetings, Azzedine and I talked about many things, as we would have with any friend or acquaintance: my work, his work, French politics, American politics, September 11, the Iraq War, the Islamists, sports, a project for a memorial at Rivesaltes, and violence in Algeria. We also talked about women's liberation. Azzedine insisted on the equality of the sexes, thought it important for husbands to take an active role in family life, and, like most Harkis I met, opposed wearing the veil.[20] More abstractly, we talked about preserving memory and the passage of *trauma*—Azzedine's word—from generation to generation. Many of our conversations focused on childhood—Azzedine's, his wife's, and his children's. The subject of our conversation oscillated between the impersonal—repetitions of the Harki story—and the personal, mostly about the humiliation he felt at reform school and the murderous rage he experienced as a child.

As I listened to Azzedine switch from the personal to the impersonal, I felt that the impersonal deflected the pain of the personal. No doubt, there is some truth in this observation, but I think that such a psychological explanation blinds us to an important dimension of the Harki story—the responsibility it demands. The Harkis have a continual responsibility to recount their collective story, a responsibility that overrides any desire they may have to tell their own story. Their identity rests on this responsibility.[21] Harki children often talk about the responsibility they have to their fathers—to the Harkis of their father's generation.

Azzedine carries that responsibility further. He fears that the Harki experience will be forgotten with time. It is one reason why he has been active in promoting a memorial and museum at the Rivesaltes campsite. He also encourages Harki youths to learn their story and join the activists. I recall driving with him and a Harki grandson, Ali, to the showing of a film about the Harkis. It was a long drive. Azzedine spent much of it telling Ali the Harki story. He was so insistent that his narration sounded at times like an indoctrination. To my surprise, Ali, who was not yet twenty, seemed to know little of it. I could not help thinking that he would have preferred going to one of the blockbuster movies playing in town or spending the afternoon with his friends watching a soccer match on television. Ali was genuinely moved by the film and the discussion that followed it. On the drive back, he kept saying, "I didn't know, I didn't know," and asked Azzedine a lot of questions about what he had seen. Azzedine was less doctrinaire, moved, perhaps, by Ali's feelings about the film. When we dropped Ali off at his home, Azzedine invited him to attend a meeting of Harkis that was to take place in a couple of weeks. Ali promised to attend, but, as we drove off, Azzedine said, "You see, they know nothing." "But will he attend the meeting?" I asked. "Probably not," Azzedine said emptily. "You see, they know nothing," he repeated, and then, to bolster himself, he added, "That's why the memorial is so important."

I describe this occasion in some detail in order to call attention to a dimension of the protests that the Harkis rarely consider. Whatever their ostensible purpose, the protests are a way, not only to perpetuate Harki identity, but also to resist forgetting.[22] The Harkis do not want the French to forget. "We are their conscience," they say, not without a certain sadistic pleasure, and they have been doing their best over the last forty-odd years not to let the French forget. Like Azzedine, they also speak about the importance of passing their story on to their children. For the most part, they spoke about remembering, not about forgetting. They know at some level that, with time, their story will be forgotten. At best, it will be preserved in a couple of lines in a history book. But they defend themselves against acknowledging this inevitability. Forgetting destroys what meaning they have managed to give their suffering. Its inevitability intensifies, I believe, the urgency of their protests. The protests themselves become part of their story—one that extends beyond its initial subject matter to the present or immediate, experientially graspable past. Not only did activists, like Kletch, Belkacem, Hacène, and Celestine, constantly describe their protests, but other, less engaged Harkis did too.

The relationship between the Harkis and their children centers, as I have suggested, on a wound—the father's wound—that is articulated in terms of betrayal and abandonment. The children also speak of their own lives in terms of a wound. The wound of those, like Belkacem, Mabrouk, and Yamina, who spent their early life in Algeria and witnessed the massacres, and of those who grew up in the camps has concrete referents. Those like Boussad, who experienced neither the camps nor the massacres, seem less burdened by the wound. Some of them use the Harki experience as an excuse for their exclusion and failures.

Two Harki teenage sons I talked to in the central square of a little town near Saint-Maurice-l'Ardoise complained about discrimination at school, how none of the "French girls" would go out with them or even befriend them, how they were bullied by other North African students, and how, as they were identified with Algerians and Moroccans, they were not allowed in the local *discotèques*.[23] As their list of discriminations grew, we were joined by one of their Moroccan schoolmates, who confirmed their complaints, particularly about French girls. Neither of the Harki boys seemed in the least embarrassed by the presence of their Moroccan friend—they had introduced him to me as their *copain*, their "pal"—as they talked about the impossibility of ever having a North African friend. As I was about to point out the contradiction, we were joined by one of the French girls in their class, who greeted them with a kiss on each cheek and flirted with all three of them. Later, they took me to the house of one of the Harki leaders. His neighbors, including the girl's family, were French. They greeted us in an unusually friendly manner as we piled out of my car. Two more girls joined us, and they talked about their all going to a *discothèque* that weekend. When

I finally had a chance to point out the contradictions between what they said and what had just happened, they laughed. "That's the Harkis for you," the Moroccan said with mocked derision, and we all laughed.

I have witnessed similar occasions, though I must remind the reader that the bulk of my research was focused on the old Harkis and, especially, on their children who had lived in the camps. While these children were certainly wounded by their experiences in Algeria and in the camps, it would be a mistake to reduce their explicit and implicit references to the wound to what they themselves experienced. Whatever their reality, those wounds also serve a symbolic function. They represent the Harkis' wound—and the burden it imposes on them. The children, particular the men, tend to conflate their suffering and humiliation with their father's. They too are victims of the French.

In Mabrouk's account of his family's flight to France, we noted his switching back and forth from a personal to the collective narrative, from his own perspective to that provided by the generalized narrative, and from *I* (and, less frequently, *we*) to *he, they,* and sometimes, more ambiguously, *one (on)*.[24] At times, Mabrouk seemed to surrender his narrator's position and authority to those of the implicit diegetic narrator in the Harki story. Listening to Azzedine's description of his treatment at reform school as a result of betrayal and abandonment, I was not always sure whether he was talking about his own mistreatment or his parent's. His father's service as an auxiliary in the French army—the military discipline that demanded—his family's internment, and his grueling life in the reform school metaphorized one another in a self-containing and (for me, at least) exhausting way. These events all evoked the same humiliation, the same loss of dignity, honor, masculinity, and autonomy, and the same assault on their bodies, but these, too, were metaphoric: technically, synecdoches for the emotional bolus I referred to earlier, turning inward like a black hole as it affects Azzedine's existence and that of countless other Harkis of his generation and, in other ways, the old Harkis themselves. A result of the wound, whatever the wound may be, the bolus is also the living exemplification of the wound—functionally, the wound itself.

As I use the term, a *bolus* can have no clearly definable referent. Thus, any referent attributed to it, like the wound or the emotional state that arises from betrayal and abandonment, calls attention to that referent's insufficiency and further impedes the referential capture of the bolus. Nor can an event or a complex of events ever be held fully responsible for it since the attribution of a causative event presupposes such an event and its eventfulness. I have argued elsewhere (Crapanzano 2004, 89–95) that one of the characteristics of a trauma is that it can never be attributed to any single event or set of events because events (at least in mental life) slide into one another. They are never fully independent of their antecedents and consequences, but they are delimited by those presumptive antecedents and putative consequences. Technically, we can call this back-casting of an event *cataphoric indexicality*. The perseverance of trauma rests, I suggested, on the need to deny the temporal fragility—the mortality—of the traumatic event and to preserve that event in its eventfulness through repetition and reiteration. I want, not to equate bolus, wound, and trauma—there are important differences between them—but to note that they are responsive to the same failure of reference and artifice of temporal punctuation.[25] Turned in on itself, devoid of referential capacity, the bolus becomes a ruthless indexical because it cannot be referentially contained. It indexes itself and, as such, indexes its context. It cannot, to speak figuratively, be exorcised, although it may fade away with time. We know so little about how emotions end (Crapanzano 2008). What can be argued, I believe, is that, given the impossibility of reducing the bolus to a referent or a complex of referents, every attempt to do so in fact strengthens its irreducibility and, thereby, its indexical force.

There is, of course, an important difference between the wounds of the Harki children, even those who suffered in the camps and previously in Algeria, and those of the Harkis themselves. For the Harkis, the wound, whether configured by betrayal and abandonment or by some specific event, appears to be the constant object of their ruminations. It serves, one could argue, to mask the responsibility that the Harkis took on themselves when they decided to become auxiliaries. However knotted with conflicting and intolerable experiences, they know at some level what those experiences were. They can regret, they can justify, they can righteously blame the French, and, indeed, the Algerians, for what was done to them, but they cannot deny that the decision was, finally, theirs. I have never met a Harki who admitted that he had made a mistake, although, when I asked Yamina whether she thought her father regretted his decision, she reluctantly said yes. The old Harkis, however, said stubbornly that they would not hesitate to make the decision again. Most of them did add—and quickly—that they were not against Algerian independence, only against the FLN. They often referred to the bloodshed, poverty, and corruption in postindependence Algeria as proof of their hatred of the FLN. Most French would admit that their betrayal and abandonment of the Harkis were contemptible, but that admission cannot undo the Harkis' decision or in any way alleviate its effect. The Harkis may have been duped, but they fell for it, and, for this, I believe, they torture themselves.

While the Harkis themselves were not given to describing their feelings, indeed, their inner life, it would be a mistake to assume that they were not, in fact, giving expression to those feelings. This they did in what might be called an *inverted poetic manner*. The events they described, as minimal as they were, seemed to condense their experiences, their memories of those experiences, and their evaluation of them. I would liken them to what T. S. Eliot (1964, 124–25) called *objective correlatives*: "set[s] of objects, a situation, a chain of events, which shall be a formula of that particular emotion: such that when the external facts, which must terminate in a sensory experience, are given, the emotion is immediately evoked." However, unlike Eliot, I would stress the way in which the emotion so envelops the event, or, more accurately, the memory of the event, that it cannot be elaborated. Though turned inward, seeming to communicate to no one, not even to the speaker (or the silent one), these objective correlatives are, in fact, highly expressive. Evoked, the event speaks to those who have shared their experience; it draws them into the same emotionally intensive but static memory space.

I spent a lazy Sunday afternoon talking to a group of old Harkis in the shade of one of the houses in which they lived in what had once been a forestry village north of Aix-en-Provence. The Harkis had been sent there in the mid-1960s, mostly from Rivesaltes, and remained there after the hamlet had been closed in the late 1970s. Though they complained about the quality of their housing, particularly about how difficult it was to keep warm in the winter, the housing was superior to that which I had seen in other camps. Several of them, who spoke fluent French, immediately entered into conversation, and, after rehearsing their litany of suffering, they recalled their experiences in the camp since it had closed down. They focused on their efforts to improve their housing, mentioning by name, as if I would know them, local politicians who had helped or hindered them. Though they spoke of the arrival of electricity, telephone lines, municipal water, and the first television set, sometimes even arguing over dates, there was something timeless about their account. It was less historical than a series of evocations—*timeless re-presentations* might be more accurate—of memories that they shared and seemed to solder together as a community. They were old and assumed that I appreciated the events as they did.

We were surrounded by about dozen more Harkis who did not take an active part in our conversation. Many talked among themselves, mainly in Arabic. But, from time to time, when they heard a particular event mentioned, they would confirm it by repeating a word or two that the speaker had said. Some of them took a more active role when the conversation turned to the war in Iraq. They expressed neither approval nor disapproval. War was war—a given. Their participation was far more lively than I would have imagined possible when I first met them. They argued, much to my surprise, over various strategies. It was as though mention of the Iraq War resurrected, if not actual memories of the Algerian War, than its emotional tone. The conversation continued until we were joined by a man of some authority who, on entering the argument, contradicted what each of them said and, thereby, silenced them. It turned out that he had been a noncommissioned officer attached to one of the SAS units. When he went on to discuss the Algerian War, they all lost interest and left me stranded. Only occasionally did one of them interrupt and ask me something about myself. Had I been to Algeria? Had I been to Rivesaltes? Would my book be in French? They seemed content with yes or no answers. I had the feeling that they were trying either to stop the sergeant's harangue or to get him to show some interest in me—an interest that would, perhaps, authorize their view of me. He would know what to ask, but he never did.

To the outsider—to me, for example, but, I imagine, even to the Harki children—these events cannot have such evocative significance; at most, they signal an unknowable experience or set of experiences. I do not, however, recall any Harki children mentioning the effect these memory evocations had on them. As I observed earlier, if they accompanied me when I visited their fathers, many would, in fact, encourage them to recount a particular episode that they had heard before. In my experience, they never asked for elaboration, though sometimes they tried to place the event historically in their father's life or in the Algerian War as they had come to know about it. The event may have evoked moments in their own lives when they first heard it. They may have been relieved, for it broke their father's silence.

Nearly every Harki child I met and many of the Harki wives referred to the Harkis' silence and the pain it caused them. Wives seemed to accept the inevitability of this silence, but most of the children did not.[26] Their father's silence contained a plea—not to be asked. Oedipus says at Colonus, "For kindness' sake, do not open / My old wound, and my shame" (Sophocles 1959, 102 [lines 515–16]). Yet that plea, that silence, proclaimed the possibility of an answer. Many children could not live easily with the mystery that lay behind it. Many of the imaginative possibilities it suggested were, no doubt, intolerable and immediately foreclosed. None of the children ever told me that they wondered whether their father had been a torturer or had betrayed members of his family. Still, I believe, imaginative possibilities left their trace. The children had to respect their father's silence since, as I have said, silence before hardship (*sabr*) is a masculine virtue in Algerian culture. Given the Harkis' emasculation, their silence, as I have also suggested, might well be the last token of their masculinity.

A young Harki I met had tried, as part of her doctoral work, to encourage old Harkis to break their silence in group settings. She assumed that, if they were able to express the traumatic experiences they had kept inside them for so many years, they would be liberated from their effect. She had little success, for the old Harkis were not about to surrender their silence. Nor, I should add, is it clear that the Harkis repressed their traumatic experiences. It seems more likely that, if these experiences had had any traumatic effect, it arose from their persistent clarity. As Benyoucef's (2005, 9) SNP observed, "It's their past that they do not stop looking at and ruminating! Because it's their past, it is never past to them. It lies across their throats." That "it lies across their throats" does not mean that it can be given expression. The Harki politician and magistrate (*maître des requêtes au Conseil d'état*) Jeannette Bougrab[27] observed: "If even a single evocation of these facts makes my father unhappy, I prefer to know nothing. If he does not talk about them, it is perhaps because what he has experienced cannot be told [*parce que ce qu'il avait vécu n'était pas racontable*]." Silence seems to be another exemplum of the wound, all the more harrowing because it is essentially an empty exemplum.

Here, again, the children are confronted with a paradox. They want to preserve what happened without knowing exactly what happened because their fathers, many of whom also want the events documented, do remain silent. They are haunted, if not tortured, by what Ellen Fine (1988, 46, quoted in McNay 2009, 1179) has called *absent memory*. As I noted, many of the Harki novels and memoirs are quest stories, and many of the Harki children I talked to described their desire to learn what their fathers actually did in Algeria and why and how they made the decision to become auxiliaries. When it was possible—that is, when their fathers talked or their mothers—some of the children kept family archives. They usually centered on postwar experiences. Several of the Harki associations have also collected testimonies. Fatima Besnaci-Lancou (2006a, 2006b, 2010) has published several books of such testimonies, and Harki historians (e.g., Abdellatif 1984a, 1984b, 1990; Hamoumou 1993; and Moumen 2003a, 2003b) have attempted to reconstruct the history of the Harkis, also focusing on their postwar period. They reflect the ambivalence of many of the Harki children, who want and, at the same time, do not want to know what their fathers did in Algeria. Some seem to collude, unwittingly to be sure, in their father's silence—which was sometimes, I suspect, less of a silence than they are willing to admit. I have often been surprised by a Harki son describing his father's silence and later referring to some of his wartime activities. When I pointed out this contradiction, they quickly assured me that they must have learned the details from their mothers, older siblings, or former neighbors.

Unlike their fathers, the children can take no responsibility for what they inherited from the cradle. They are doubly wounded. They have suffered from the consequences of their father's decision and from the effects of their father's wounds—a silent but emotional transfer—without knowing what they were. They cannot resurrect the wounds in their particularity because they never knew them in their particularity. They cannot even repress them in their particularity, though, no doubt, they repress some of their effects. They are tortured by an absence: an unknown that they can never know but that has moved them deeply. All they have is a generalized story, one that contains, to be effective, fragments of particular stories (hence, the importance of witnessing) but is, in its generality, removed from the particular—from that which can be possessed and transmitted in its particularity. Their story can never, I believe, satisfy their desire, their curiosity, indeed, their wish to forget, for they can never *really* know what lies behind that generality—what their fathers actually did and why.[28]

Algerian immigrant children (and those living in Algeria) have also suffered their father's unwillingness to talk about their actions during the war, but, given that they have not usually been so indelibly stained, they do not have as much invested in the particular. Like the general, the particular can also conceal, but, unless it is an outright lie—and even then—it does so, indexically, by framing the account in such a way as to preclude consideration of what is concealed. It frames out, while generality simply excludes. Framing in or out depends on the intensity of the particular—its symbolic resonance. As such, it has enormous power. As an exemplum, however, the particular loses its power in the Harki story. It is rhetorically reduced and cannot energize that story. The story can only be repeated over and over again, for political purposes, to maintain an identity (as that identity is challenged by integration) and to preserve memories, which will fade with time and become second- and third-hand. All that is left is a frozen story. Paradoxically, it becomes a wound, an exemplum of a wound, as it describes that wound and the circumstances that led to it.

Clearly, the relationship between the Harki children and their fathers is fraught with contradictions. The children have to bear the burden of the hope and responsibility that their fathers have placed on them. Many have had to live with a father's arbitrary punishments, his drunkenness, his depressions, his retreat into himself, sometimes with his suicide or the suicide of a relative or friend of the father's generation, and unaccountable changes in his humor. Some have seen their fathers taken away to a psychiatric hospital and returned to them months, even years, later—suffering, as they frequently report, drug-induced stupors. Like Azzedine's, their memory is imprinted with images of their father's powerlessness and humiliation, of his failure to find work, of his losing a job because he did not understand what was expected of him or had been too ruthlessly exploited to stay. They must live with their mother's fears, her disorientation, her misunderstanding, and her inability to communicate in French—with the isolation forced on her by custom and by circumstance. Often, at a very young age, they have had to act as intermediaries between their families and the authorities. How often have I heard them describe accompanying their fathers to an administrator to serve as both a translator and a support.

The portrait I have drawn is grim. It does not do justice to the often remarkable ways in which many Harkis and their families have been able to preserve their dignity, their honor, and that *élan* that is a prerequisite for successful family and professional life. It fails to acknowledge how hard many Harkis worked—even when they were exploited by their employers—and the pride they took in that work. I recall one old Harki telling me in great detail how, after working for a pittance for several years as a gardener at a nursery, he managed to get a truck driver's license. He went on to outline the various routes he had taken across France, describing proudly how, even after a breakdown, a flat tire, or foul weather, he had still managed to make his deliveries on time. When he completed his seemingly endless account, he showed me the medals he had received for his service during the war. Nor does my portrait give credit to the mothers, particularly the widowed ones, like Belkacem's, who managed to raise their children under often grueling circumstances.[29]

Noura was thirteen in 1959 when she was married to a man more than twenty years older than she, a warrant officer (*adjutant chef*) in the French army whom the women who had recommended her to me called a Harki. (Though Noura likens her story to those of the Harkis, she does not consider herself to be a real Harki.) As she recounts her life, her mood changes dramatically. She whines and sometimes cries as she describes the hardships she experienced. She refers to them as *chagrins* and *souffrances*. At other times, she speaks with a stoic realism, punctuated by a laughter that hovers between nervousness and amusement. She is an intelligent, reflective woman who talks a lot about raising children. She refers to herself as an Arab but not a Muslim. She says she has no religion and, much to my surprise, seems at ease in referring to the Virgin Mary and other Christian figures. When I first met her, she told me that, for the French, her identity lies between the savage and the maid. Later, she tells me that, though she is a French citizen, she finds herself to be neither French nor Algerian but that she raised her children to think of themselves as French.

Noura's husband was brutal, but she was protected by her family—the family that had arranged the marriage—until she left her village near Bône (Annaba) for France. At fourteen, she had a daughter, and, at fifteen, she was pregnant again. In November 1962, her husband was transferred to France to work with the Harkis in one of the transit camps. He came home one day and said, "Put on your coat and scarf. We are going to France." She was confused. She thought she was already in France. "I was so naive." After spending three days in a barracks in Constantine, waiting for transport, she saw the sea for the first time as she boarded a boat for Marseilles. It was a military ship, and she was the only Arab woman on board. She was scared and desperately sick. "I swore I'd never take a boat again," she repeated passionately three times.

After working for three months at Rivesaltes, her husband was transferred to another camp. He locked Noura and her baby in the hotel room in which he had been billeted. "I didn't know where I was. I spoke no French. I just held my baby and walked around and around a little table where we ate at night, waiting for my husband to come home." Crazed by the way he was ordered to treat the Harkis, he began drinking, Noura says, adding that it was really after he retired that he began to drink seriously. "He was an army man [*un homme de guerre*]," she says. "He would have liked to fight until the end of his life, but there were no more wars." He had fought in World War II, in Indochina, and, of course, in Algeria. He was highly decorated, and Noura listed, with surprising pride, some of his decorations. It was about then that they moved into an isolated little house on the outskirts of a forest. There he let her out to do the gardening and the wash. By then she had given birth to her second daughter and was pregnant with the third.

Her husband's drinking got worse and worse. "He'd come home, yell at me and then beat me up," she remembered, "sometimes until I was bruised all over. I didn't know what to do. I pleaded with him not to beat me in front of the children. It would scare them. But he didn't pay any attention. I didn't know anyone—only the owner of the house, who came for the rent. He seemed nice, but he didn't speak Arabic." After Noura had given birth to her third child, her husband's drunken tantrums became more ferocious, and one night he threatened her with a pistol, beat his eldest daughter, and pushed Noura down the stairs. "That was too much. I had expected him to beat me. That's the way it is with Algerian men," Noura said matter-of-factly, "but my little daughter, never." Apparently, the landlord's son came the next morning for the rent and found her lying at the foot of the stairs and went for the police. Noura was not very clear. She was crying. "I don't like to remember this time in my life," she told me, but went on recounting her life. Later, she implied that she herself had gone to the police with her daughters. In either case, she refused to go back to her husband and managed to convey to the police that she was scared of her husband and wanted to be taken somewhere where he would not find her and her children. She was sent to the nearest town and then on to the city where I met her. There was a Harki *cité* there where the authorities wanted to house her. When she saw it, when she saw the barbed wire and the lookout tower, she said, "No, never here."

Whoever took Noura to the *cité*—she always referred to it as the camp— must have taken pity on her, for she was able to settle in a tiny garret in the center of the city. She found work as a cleaning woman. Dreadfully exploited, she was paid twenty centimes an hour and had to work fourteen hours a day. She did not have enough money to eat and often went without food so that her girls would not go hungry. She fell sick and was taken to a doctor who had connections in the mayor's office. He found her night work (so she could be with her children during the day) cleaning a school, where she worked for thirty-four years before retiring. Although she was entitled to support from her husband, she refused to apply for it, fearing he would find her. Noura worked hard, taking on extra jobs whenever she could. She learned to speak French—she is exceptionally fluent—but never learned to read more than a few words. "I learn the news from the TV," she told me. She is, in fact, very well versed in politics and sometimes digressed to talk about Chirac's treatment of the Harkis or how dreadful the situation was in Algeria. Once she tried to return to visit her family, but she was refused entry. My roots are there, she says, and angrily adds, "I'll never go back. I'm French."

Noura managed to put her three daughters through school. She was a hard taskmaster, telling the girls that she did not want them to have the same life she had. She made sure they went to a "European" school. They had only French friends. All three passed the *baccalauréat*. The two oldest went to university, one becoming a lawyer and the other a paralegal. The youngest became a secretary, married an Italian, and lives in Italy. The two oldest live with Frenchmen. "They would never marry an Arab," she told me proudly, laughing. In answer to my question, she said that they had been marked by their experiences but that she did her best to overcome this.

Despite stories like Noura's, the grim picture I painted is the one that the Harki children most often recount or against which they measure their own lives. It is their Harki story. What is clear is that they are entrapped in a seemingly irresolvable conflictual relationship with their fathers (and, particularly the Harki daughters, with both their fathers, violently so at times, and their mothers). Most of the ones I met accepted their fathers for what they were. Perhaps the most passionately forthright description of the ambivalence that the children feel toward their fathers is Zahia Rahmani's extraordinary autobiographical novel *Moze*, in which she recounts her attempts to come to terms with her father's death. A veteran of World War II, a Harki, a man who would not talk, Moze committed suicide, after wearing his old uniform to an Armistice Day ceremony, by throwing himself in a pond.[30] Rahmani (2003, 19) writes:

> Moze had died before his death.
> His tears, they're his death that groans.
> Standing, the night, outdoors, inside, alone or with us, an ailment,
>   an affection, of tears.
> A death that endures.
>
> He was only this outburst without voice.
> A groan, like the deaf with an open mouth.
> This unsustainable look, this extreme figure of guilt—
> I want to rid myself of it,
> I don't, however, want to render it innocent.
>
> What can one do with this error.
> That which I bear, which is not mine and which I cannot forgive.
> How to escape alone a shouldered guilt?
> This life given in the cradle.
> Moze's error, I have to say is my flesh and my custom.

Insofar as the their self-configuration is challenged as it challenges (at least, as they hope it challenges) the confidence, presumption, and empowerment of the French, the Harkis have to struggle continually for what seems to me a near-impossible identity. Psychological factors aside, they are confronted with an exclusion from French society—exacerbated by their being identified with North African Muslims and by contemporary events in the Middle East. They may be citizens of France, but they are also, indelibly, Harkis and must bear the weight of the racist, ethnic, class, and moral connotations of that identity. These can be insidious, entrapping not only them but also the French who are sincerely opposed to discrimination. They too are caught in the discriminatory idiom, as I tried to show in the previous chapter in my discussion of being a problem.

A few years ago, in Paris, I presented some of the results of my research to an academic audience. As it was open to the public, it seemed likely that some Harkis would be in attendance. I was cautious. I did not want to offend them. My discussant was a *pied-noir* who, though sympathetic to my approach, questioned my generalities. "You are doing a sort of psychoanalysis of the group," she said, somewhat puzzled. I was equally puzzled since I had no such intention. She went on to say that I had ignored individual differences among the Harkis and the range of responses to their situation. I agreed, saying that I had not had sufficient time to discuss individual differences. "There are Harkis," I said, "who are unemployed, who have menial jobs, who are politicians, bureaucrats, teachers, writers, historians, journalists at *L'express* and *Figaro*, and doctors. There's a urologist who has recently developed a new surgical procedure." As I was about to note that, despite individual differences, the Harkis I met were all attached to their story, she interrupted me. "Un urologue," she said, clearly surprised. "C'est pas vrai. Tiens, tiens" (A urologist. Is that so. Well, well). I am afraid that the English translation cannot do justice to her *Tiens, tiens*. What was extraordinary was that the audience seemed oblivious to her derogatory stereotypy.

The Harkis themselves make use of race, class, gender, and ethnicity with varying levels of sophistication, as we have seen in their understanding and publicizing their situation, but in many respects these are dismissive categories. They may function rhetorically—in their briefs, for example—with some success, but lying behind their use is a skeptical realism. They know that these social categories can never do justice to the pain they have experienced, the demands they make, and the hope they still have in even their most cynical moods. Children and grandchildren figure in the futureless ruminations of many of the old Harkis, however black their view of the world is.

In the early days of my research, I contacted several Harki activists whose names I had been given by French friends or discovered through the Internet. Some were in Paris, others in southern France. They were all enthusiastic and promised to help me. They immediately began listing the names of Harkis I should meet. They were scattered across France. One man spent more than an hour calling them for me. He seemed oblivious to the difficulties of working with such a dispersed community. When I pointed this out, he was surprised and then, with a certain reluctance, suggested several locations in the south of France where I could carry out my research. I attributed his surprise to his ignorance of anthropological methods, but later I realized that the Harki community is founded, not on place, but on shared memories. True, there are local communities in some areas, but these local communities are subsumed under the larger placeless community of memory, what the anthropologist Francesca Cappelletto (2003) calls a *mnemonic community*. Like the individual Harki stories, these local communities become exempla of *the* Harki story, and, though bearing specific memories, their uniqueness is drastically reduced. Here, too, is a double negation. The local communities lose their uniqueness, and, as they are usually close to the camps, hamlets, *cités*, and slums—places of suffering—their location is negative by association.

Harki history is a history of negated spaces. I recall the razed camps (Rivesaltes and Saint-Maurice-l'Ardoise), the abandoned forestry hamlets (Pujol le Bosc and Le Logis d'Anne), the dilapidated housing (Fureau near Aix-en-Provence and Bias), and the many rundown *cités* in Arles, Marseilles, and throughout France where the poorest Harkis are housed next to Algerians who fifty years earlier would have been their enemies. I think of their children, who, quite ignorant of what happened in Algeria, can still call up—in anger, derision, or humor—the word *collabo*. I think too of Algeria, to which the old Harkis cannot return and in which many of their children have little interest. A *pied-noir*, the former mayor of a rural commune in the Algerois, once compared the Harkis to the *pieds-noirs*. "They left something behind," he said, sympathetically. "Their roots are there, their families. But we—we left nothing behind, nothing. We had to begin our lives anew. Their situation was different."[31]

But was it? Certainly, many Harkis, their wives, and those children who were born in Algeria have left something behind, but what they have left behind they cannot recover. At the same time, despite their attempts to forget—if they should, in fact, try to forget—their present and future are in a surround of memory objects, which are not only ontologically irretrievable, as in Proust (or for any of us, for that matter), but also cut off from even the possibility, however magical, of recuperation that teases most memory. The cut is incisive. Some Harkis, especially the wives, will dream of returning to that past, but they know that, were they actually to return to "their" *douar*, the past would be lost to them in ways that are dramatically different from those of the Algerians who have lived there continuously. Still, most of the

Harkis I met are too realistic or too filled with regret or simply too angry even to dream of return. That past is dead for them. It is pure negation.

The old Harkis figure their story within the great sweep of a transcending history that they do not understand and know they can never understand. We can call it *destiny*. They call it *qdar*, figure it more concretely in terms of the writtenness—*mektub*—of the world, and attribute it to God's inscrutable will. Many of the old Harkis—those, at least, who have not succumbed to drink, drugs, and irredeemable despair—may find solace in such a view, a patient wisdom, and ultimate submission to God's will (*al-tawakkul*). I felt that some of them had found solace when I watched them gather in the afternoon to pray. I knew then that I would never understand the meaning of destiny as they did or experience what comfort it gave them.[32] But that was of little consequence. What I also knew was that the Harki children and their progeny had lost that sense of a transcending drama. They had been cast *by chance* into a world in which destiny had given way to chance and luck.[33] They have only their story, frozen as it is, to bind them together for the moment. The greatest of the many paradoxes in their lives may be that, were their demands for recognition, compensation, and apology met, their story would become irrelevant and their community an accident of a nasty history. Perversely, that community's future and the memories that bolster it depend, ultimately, on the stubborn refusal of the French to give them the recognition they deserve and the apology they long for with a hope intensified by skepticism.

Yamina, whom I had met at a protest in Paris, idealized her past in Algeria as she did her father. She left Algeria when she was a child, old enough, however, to remember her life there and the murder of her four brothers, one of which she witnessed. She spoke of the smell of jasmine, the odor of freshly baked bread, the colorful floor tiles in their home near Algiers, the fig tree growing in their courtyard, and the importance of hospitality. "There was always extra food for guests." She said that, three days before they were forced to leave Algeria, as she was returning home with bread from the local bakery, she had an experience she had never before had. She was suddenly overwhelmed by the beauty of the place and knew she would never see it again. She told her father. He said, "God has spoken to you, my daughter. We are leaving tomorrow[!]." "That experience was inscribed in my memory forever." Later in our conversation, she told me that half of her is still in Algeria. "It never leaves me."

Unlike many, but not all, of the Harki children, Yamina was able to visit Algeria. Her father refused. It is probable that he would not have been admitted in any case. In the French army, he was the only one in the family who was not in the FLN. Her family was clearly privileged. "We were a middle-class family." When she arrived in Algeria, one of her cousins, who is an important member of the judiciary, was there to meet her. She herself was stopped by an immigration officer. "I told him I was French, and I acted like a Frenchwomen. I told him he ought to be ashamed of himself, that he had no future aspirations." Another officer came over and asked what was wrong. "I told him how stupid the first officer was." "It was then that I saw an old Harki whom I had noticed on the plane. I can always tell a Harki. He was being turned back." It was at this point that her cousin came over and told the immigration officer to let her through. "I was overwhelmed [*bouleversée*]. Here I was given entry, and the old Harki was not. I had privilege, and he didn't. He would never see his home again. I asked my cousin if he could intercede, but he said it was too late. I watched the old Harki being escorted back to the plane." Yamina was terribly disappointed by Algeria. "Everything had deteriorated so much. There were people sleeping in the streets. I saw my old house. The house was there, but it was not the same. The jasmine did not have the same perfume . . ."

Yamina told her children about the Harki experience when they were eleven or twelve—old enough to appreciate it without being scared. She has pushed them to study hard "to be French but to remember what the Harkis had gone through." "We must let Europe see the dirty side of France," she told me later. "We are French. That is our responsibility. We are proud of being French." Her eldest son, about twenty, was also at the protest. It was he who introduced me to his mother. He had started to tell me the Harki story without much emotion, in a routine sort of way. It was when he realized that I knew something about it that he called his mother over. His father was there too, but he never joined us. He just watched from afar. It was clear that Yamina spoke for the family. Later in the day, as I was shopping in one of the Parisian department stores, I ran into another Harki woman who had been at the protest and had listened to Yamina for a while. She asked me whether I had learned anything from her. "She speaks for us all," she said. In many ways, Yamina reminded me of Celestine. "I never cry," she told me. "I have learned to control myself. It is my dignity. I walk proudly. We had our civilization." I noticed that she used the past tense, but I did not call her attention to it.

In Yamina's conversation, as in the conversation of many of the Harkis I spoke to, death figured importantly.[34] The Harkis were haunted not only by the massacres, or by the deaths of the children who were buried in the camps in unmarked graves, or by the suicides that almost everyone who had lived in the camps mentioned, or by the decease of the old Harkis. (Harkis rarely talked about the deaths they witnessed during their military service, although they did talk about the murders the FLN committed.) They were also haunted by the death of the past. That was the undersong of so much of what they told me. Yamina, who always spoke about particulars in an allegorical mode, told me that her father had wanted to be buried in Algeria, as did many old Harkis, some of whom somehow achieved their wish. "I told him, 'Papa you will be far from us. Who will take care of your grave? You are French.' 'You are right, my daughter,' he said."

I too have my allegory. I remember a roadside monument, barely noticeable, on a little-used road that runs by the camp at Rivesaltes. It was already there when I made my first trip to the camp with Belkacem and Azzedine in 2004. It consists of three stele, one next to the other, each with a bronze plaque in memory of the Spaniards, the Jews, and the Harkis who had been incarcerated there. As you approach the memorial—no doubt to distract attention from it—there is a sign with an arrow pointing away from the memorial to some windmills generating electricity. "Moulins-à-vent," it says. Of course, windmills can be seen from just about anywhere in that flat landscape. The arrow is a shoddy escape from memory—from what the French did in Algeria and what they did to the Harkis and to the others who were interned there. For me, there is something quixotic about the juxtaposition of windmills and memorials. We see the windmills and ignore the memorials, but others—the refugees, the dislocated, the victims of our cultural pretense—may well see the memorials and ignore the windmills. Such, perhaps, is the culling of colonialism and its aftermath.

NOTES

INTRODUCTION

1. Papon was responsible for the deportation of thousands of Jews to German death camps in 1942–43, for which crime he was finally convicted in 1998. He served less than three years of his ten-year sentence.

2. From 1960 to 2000, while France's population increased from 50 to 60 million, or roughly 20 percent, its Muslim population increased tenfold, from 500,000 to 5 million. Although the Muslim population is predominately North African, of which approximately 2 million are Algerian, it is quite diverse in terms of origin, ethnicity, education, and degree of religious piety. The largest number of Muslims (1.7 million) live in and around Paris. The majority are workers in low-paying jobs. Unemployment is very high, especially in the age group fifteen to twenty-nine (over 40 percent). Figures are from Laurence and Vaisse (2006, chap. 1).

3. Jason Throop (2010, 28–49) argues that basic correlates of experience, what I would call *structures of experience*, which are uncovered phenomenologically, are subject to cultural evaluation and articulation.

4. It would be interesting to compare Rahmani's description of her apartness with my wife's profile of a *pied-noir* family living in a village in the Vaucluse in 1972 (see Kramer 1980). The parallels are striking.

5. See Crapanzano (2004, 148–77) for a discussion of memory and memorialization.

6. See chapter 7 for a detailed discussion of generalization and stereotypy in social description.

7. The ubiquity of violence—its uncanny descent on a northern German village before World War I—is the subject of Michael Haneke's 2009 film *The White Ribbon* (*Das weiße Band*). Despite the speculation of the village schoolteacher, the cause of the violence remains inexplicable. Is Haneke suggesting that violence is so diffuse, so metaphysical, that any explanation inevitably falters?

CHAPTER ONE

1. Association, Justice, Information, Réparation pour les Harkis France. (AJIR is a homonym of the French *agir*, "to act.") The association was founded in 1998 by Mohand Hamoumou.

2. They were later joined by the AAAAS (Association des anciens des affaires algériennes et sahariennes) (*Paris-Normandie*, March 18, 2005).

3. The mayor, Frank Martin, was found guilty on March 28, 2008, of having publicly insulted the Harki community "en raison de son appartenance à la religion musulmane" in a case brought by AJIR. On March 24, 2005, as he was trying to calm the protesters, Martin said: "One begins this way, one burns books, and one finishes by sending out [*lancer*] fatwas. You are dictators, return home." Martin had been acquitted in December 2007 by the Tribunal correctionnel at Evreux. He vowed to appeal to the Tribunal de cassation. I should note that the Tribunal de grand instance d'Angoulême found a blogger guilty of insulting Benyoucef. See the story in the right-wing Rapatrié online publication *Bab el Oued Story*, available at http://www.babelouedstory.com.

4. See chapter 3 for a detailed discussion of the Harkis and other auxiliary units.

5. The official French definition of a Harki is "someone of Algerian origin who served in the auxiliary forces of the French army in Algeria between October 31, 1954, and July 2, 1962" (Benamou 2003, 220 n. 2).

6. Although sections of the law, to which the clause protecting the Harkis from defamation was attached, have been annulled, the clause itself has been retained.

7. Available at http//www.harki.com (copy in author's files).

8. The word *déshérence* is a legal term, *escheat* in English, that refers to the reversion to the state of property when there is no legal heir. It is difficult to see what Haddouche means by it in the present context. He may have meant *déshéritage*, "disinheritance." I have chosen to translate it as *alienating surrender*.

9. The French is awkward here: "Il poursuit sa démonstration par la négation de l'identité du fils, c'est-à-dire des Harkis et de leurs descendents qu'il affuble du nom SNP, pour mieux renaître toujours dans la peau d'un 'traître.'" The colonial administration tacked the initials SNP on to any of the colonized who did not have—or to whom it had not given—a patronymic.

10. *Letters to Jeanne* (Benyoucef 2002b) was produced as a play, *La mer blanche du milieu*, by Peyrotte's company, Baggage de sable, in 2001. *The White Sea in the Middle* is a literal translation of the Arabic for the Mediterranean, *El-bahr el-Abiadh el-Moutawwassit*. Peyrotte's discovery of a 1955 photograph of her class in Algeria was the inspiration for the book.

11. He was, in fact, troubled by Sartre's advocacy of violence in his introduction to *The Wretched of the Earth*.

12. Like the writer in *The Eagles*, the rapper speaks both from within and from without the action of the play. Though he is analogous to the prologue in European theater—the barker in Brecht's *The Resistible Rise of Arturo Ui* comes to mind—he also resembles the *meddah*, the storyteller, who both recounts and acts out the tales he tells, traditionally, in the marketplace and in the theater of the Algerian playwright Abdelkader Alloula. Like the rapper, the *meddah* actively engages his audience, who gather around him in a circle (*halqa*) (Alloula 1995). See also the beginning of *The Eagles*, where Aziz, an attendant in a psychiatric hospital, describes the *halqa* and its therapeutic potential to Fanon. Benyoucef himself characterizes the rapper's songs as in the manner of Brecht but with Arabo-Andalusian meter (see Théâtre online.com [at http://theatreonline.com] for May 17, 2005).

13. Lacan's punning here is impossible to translate into English as it plays on homophones in French. *Le nondupe erre* puns also, I believe, on the English *to err*. It may, perhaps, be related to Heidegger's (1952, 309) notion of erring (*irren, in dieser Wirre irren*)—to err in the realm of error, the space in which history unfolds. See also Arendt (1978, 191–92).

14. The confusion of political factions, both secular and Islamist, violent and nonviolent, in Algeria in the 1990s is reflected in SNP's contradictory allegiances and roles in the play. See Zaater (2003) and Roberts (2003) for discussions of the Algerian crisis and its factionalism.

15. A Frenchwoman named Christiane helps Abane escape from Algiers in *The Eagles*.

16. Benyoucef sacrifices historical chronology for dramatic reasons. There were no longer any Harki camps in France at the time the play is set. Many Harkis still live near the camps in which they had been incarcerated, and some still live in forestry villages.

17. See chapter 5.

18. SNP's friend and comic foil Dahmane alias Damien becomes Sakhr El Islam, the Rock of Islam, when he joins the Islamists. SNP (Benyoucef 2002a, 16) asks him whether he couldn't find a better name than a big rock. There are other plays with names and identities. The name of the French commander who recruits SNP, Zacharie, resembled the name of the Algerian commander, Zakaria, who recruits him later in the play.

19. See Rosello (2005, 128–64) for a discussion of the ghost in North African francophone literature.

20. I use *picaresque* with some hesitation. The arbitrary, autonomous sequence of events and the sudden recurrence of characters and situations remind me of the many stories I heard in Morocco. What seems important in the stories is, not a (final) denouement, but the recursive convergence of chance and seemingly unrelated events and characters—much like the overlapping of strands in an arabesque. The form of such stories highlights the contingency of existence—of a destiny that can be neither mastered nor explained but always produces wonderment, fascination, at times humorous pleasure, at times terror. One finds picaresque elements in North African literary genres like the *rihla*—itineraries—and in the stories recounted by the bard in the *maqamat* (public and familial meeting whose participants are entertained by a storyteller).

21. Although I distinguish between feelings of guilt and shame here, I am not invoking that simplistic dichotomy between shame and guilt cultures that anthropologists have promoted in the past. North African culture was, for them, a prime example of a shame culture (Peristiany 1966). The affective lives of individuals are far too complex for such generalizations.

22. It is, as Lacan sees it, the name of the father, his no (to the boy's desire for the mother during the Oedipal phase), the law he proclaims, that fixes signification by binding signifier to signified.

23. Benyoucef's focus on the name should not be seen simply as a figuration of identity. As we shall see, naming plays—and played—an important role for many Harkis.

24. In an interview with Véronique Hotte (Théâtre online.com [at http://theatreonline .com] for May 17, 2005), Benyoucef explained that it is the no of negation of the barred father, *le père barré*, that prevents "natural genealogical transmission." It is "a metaphor for the transmission of a memory that is missing."

CHAPTER TWO

1. It may also mean a fit of anger.

2. See Rousso (1991, 75–82) for a discussion of the role of World War II and the Vichy government in modeling the Algerian War. Many of the right-wing supporters of *Algérie française* saw Pétain as a guardian of empire; they were branded by the Left and the centrists as fascists. For the Pétainists, de Gaulle was the enemy. See also

Rothberg (2006) for a theoretically more refined discussion of the multidirectional-ity of memories of the Holocaust and the Algerian War.

3. One of the most harrowing depictions of how the violence of Franco-Algerian rela-tions has haunted the French since the war is Michael Haneke's film *Caché*. Tellingly, the film, which played for an exceptionally short time in Paris, was ignored.

4. During the war, 250 works appeared, roughly 20 percent of which were censured, including some of Frantz Fanon's. Research was and continues to be impeded by the ever-lengthening closure of French war archives, particularly those "sensitive ones" concerning people and national security. As Claude Liauzu (2004, 162) observes, the laws impede studies of the use of torture by the French. Liauzu suggests that de Gaulle's "turning the page of history" after the war was also responsible for the lull. He notes that schoolbooks in Algeria give considerable space to the "revolution." I myself found that most, if not all, French schoolbooks in history for the last year (*terminale*) of the lycée, in which twentieth-century history is taught, devoted less than two pages to the "war." The number of pages on the Algerian War has decreased significantly. In textbooks of between 350 and 400 pages, the approximately 2½ pages (1,500 words) and sixteen documents about the war were reduced in 1998 to 1½ pages (950 words) and eleven documents. One standard textbook, published by Hatier, decreased coverage from 3,500 words in 1983 to 600 in 1998. Teachers complained that they did not have time to discuss the war in any depth (McCormack 2006, 139).

5. Bourdieu (1965, 202) notes that, for the Kabyles, war—an agon—differed in func-tion and significance from modern wars in which total victory by any reasonable means is the aim. For the Kabyles, "Fighting was a game whose stake is life and whose rules must be obeyed scrupulously if dishonour is to be avoided; rather than being a struggle to the death, it is a competition of merit played out before the tri-bunal of public opinion, an institutionalized competition in the course of which are affirmed the values that stand at the very basis of the existence of the group and which assure its preservation."

6. *Barbarism* is one of the terms that military theorists use to describe those strategies that aim at harming noncombatants—rape; murder; torture; random, retaliatory kill-ings; etc. (Arreguín-Toft 2005, 31).

7. Paret (1964). See Talbott (1980, 7–8, esp. n. 11) for bibliography.

8. See Arreguín-Toft (2005, passim) for a discussion of asymmetrical wars. He argues that outcomes in such wars are determined largely by asymmetrical strategies (e.g., guerrilla vs. conventional warfare), not, as one might expect, by the relative size and strength of the engaged parties.

9. The *pieds-noirs*' stereotypic characterizations of *les Arabes* are vividly, if exaggeratedly, illustrated in the work of Antoine Porot, who dominated Algerian psychiatry from 1916 on and had significant influence in the colonial regime. He wrote of the mental inferiority and weakness of the *indigènes*, their tendency to give way to primitive in-stincts, their credulity, suggestibility, perseverance, stubbornness, rancor, vindictive spirit, narrow-mindedness, atonality, weak emotional and moral life, impulsiveness, and strong criminal tendencies. By 1939, he was arguing that the criminal tenden-cies of the *indigènes* were anatomical: "The Algerian does not have a cortex, or, to be more precise, as among lower vertebrates, domination is diencephalic. The cortical functions, if they exist, are very fragile, practically not integrated with the dynamics of existence. . . . The colonizer's reluctance to give responsibility to the *indigènes* is

not, therefore, racist or paternalistic but quite simply a scientific appreciation of the biologically limited possibilities of the colonized" (quoted in Berthelier 1994, 84 [see generally 71–85]). Although I have not heard any *pieds-noirs* refer to Porot, I was referred to him on several occasions by Moroccan *colons* when I was doing field research in Morocco in the late 1960s. They told me that, if I really wanted to understand *les Arabes*, I should read Porot. None of them were psychiatrists.

10. The reasons were far more complex. Aside from the dey's slap and his failure to acknowledge the debts he owed France, they included the desire of the then minister of war, the Count of Bourmont, to refurbish his name after having deserted Napoléon three days before Waterloo, Charles X's hope that the invasion would help support his fast-dwindling position against the liberals in the Chamber of Deputies, and English support of the dey.

11. Although, as the chapter epigraph indicates, Toqueville was critical of French policy in Algeria, he was, in fact, an advocate of colonialism.

12. Abd al-Qadir was, by his wish, buried in Damascus near his spiritual master, Ibn al-Arabi, the great Sufi philosopher. In 1966, his ashes were returned to Algeria, where they were placed, amid great fanfare, in the Square of Martyrs in the El-Alia Cemetery in Algiers. The return of the hero's ashes was politically motivated. Boumediene had seized power the year before and was, as François Pouillon (2004, 87) remarks, anxious to "be inscribed in a legitimate historical line." It should be noted that, for having saved a large number of Christians during the Druze-Maronite war of 1860, which had spread from Mount Lebanon to Damascus, the French awarded him a pension of four thousand louis and the Grand Cross of the Légion d'honneur. In 1949, France released a postage stamp that pictures both Abd al-Qadir and Bugeaud, the governor-general of Algeria.

13. Bugeaud, who came to Algeria in the early 1830s, became more and more ferocious in the 1840s. The principal cause for his call to Paris was the death of five hundred members of the Oulad Riah tribe who had taken refuge in a cave and were asphyxiated in an attempt to smoke them out (Sullivan 1983, 122–27).

14. During the Kabyle protests against the Algerian government in 2001, the protesters drew a parallel between those who were decapitated by Bugeaud in the 1830s and 1840s and the victims of the present-day Algerian government (Liauzu 2004, 170). Jordi and Hamoumou (1999, 28–29) also note, cautiously to be sure, a parallel between the war and the civil strife of the 1990s. They quote one of the Harki children, who, despite his inevitable reference to the Harki experience, acknowledges the parallel forcefully: "In the end, today, those who in Algeria organize militias in order to defend themselves against the horrors of the fundamentalists [*intégristes*], against the incursions of the army, or against those who profit from all this to settle old scores, yes, these Algerians who want to save their lives, to refuse to succumb to terror, are perhaps those who can best understand today how forty years ago one became a Harki." See Carlier (2004) for an interesting, if somewhat overblown, discussion of violence in Algeria.

15. Other estimates are much higher. Boulbina (2003, 26) claims that, by 1895, Algerians had lost the use of 5 million hectares and that, by 1936, the figure had risen to nearly 8 million. The discrepancy may, perhaps, be accounted for by Boulbina's inclusion of dominion lands or those in the Sahara. Such dramatic discrepancies are not, however, unusual. They depend on the political position of the writer or whether he or she is French, Algerian, or a *pied-noir*.

16. Despite this disparity in production, the Algerians paid higher taxes than the *colons*. Although, in 1909, the Algerians made up 90 percent of the population but produced only 20 percent of the country's revenues, they paid 70 percent of direct taxes and 45 percent of the total taxes collected.

17. Until independence, the Algerian Sahara was under military authority.

18. Ruedy (1992) argues that, from a sociological point of view, the Algerian nation came into existence between 1871 and 1920.

19. See Blévis (2001) and Lyons (2004, chap. 1) for details.

20. See Camus (1991, 1994) for literary descriptions of the *petits blancs*.

21. The predominantly European areas—the *communes de plein exercice*—were run on the French model with a mayor and an elected municipal council. Few Muslims were integrated into higher echelons of the administration. In 1956, they held less than 1 percent of these posts (Horne 1987, 34).

22. The leaders were members of the newly founded Comité révolutionnaire d'unité et d'action, out of which the FLN developed. The date was carefully chosen, not only strategically, since many *colons* would be in church, but symbolically, for All Saints' Day commemorates the persecution of Christian martyrs.

23. For details, see Servier (1955).

24. Well before the war, at least as far back as the 1930s, attempts were made to improve the lot of the Algerian population, but most of them were usually blocked or diluted by the *pieds-noirs* and the inertia of the French government. Reforms initiated by the French during the war proved ineffective. As the FLN became stronger among the Algerian poor in France during the war, the French did manage to initiate, as a countermeasure, reforms in welfare and housing for Algerians living in the métropole (Lyons 2004, passim).

25. The French response shocked Algerian soldiers serving in the French army. Many who had served in a highly disciplined manner in Indochina lost their discipline, and some joined the ALN (Armée de libération nationale, the military wing of the FLN), taking their weapons with them (Bodin 2005, 19). For an account of the trial of some of the supposed perpetrators of the El Halia massacre, see Halimi (1988).

26. After de Gaulle opted for an independent Algeria, Soustelle, who had served the general loyally, became a staunch supporter of the OAS. He had to flee France on December 18, 1961, in order to escape prosecution for attacking the authority of the state (*l'atteinte à l'autorité de l'état*). After seven years of exile, he was granted amnesty and returned to France on October 24, 1968. He took up a post at the École pratique des hautes études in Paris in 1969, reentered politics, becoming a deputy from Lyon in 1973, and was elected to the Académie française in 1983. He died on August 6, 1990. See http://www.assembleenationale.fr/histoire/biographies/IVRepublique/ Soustelle-Jacques-Emile-Yves-03021912.asp for details.

27. From April 1955, military operations in Algeria were understood in terms of a state of emergency.

28. See Meynier (2002, 219–20, 430–45, 492–94) for a discussion of torture in the FLN. Although prohibited by the Soummam document, execution by slitting the victim's throat was carried out throughout the war.

29. Valat (2004, 28) notes that, unlike the executions carried out in Algeria, two-thirds of those committed by the FLN in France were by strangling.

30. In 1974, the Algerian Association of Veteran Freedom Fighters estimated that, of the 336,748 civilian and military members of the FLN, 3.5 percent were women (Ibrahimi 2004, 285).

31. In a recent interview with Daniel Williams, the seventy-nine-year old Saadi, a senator for the FLN party, said that, though he does not approve of the way in which civilians are deliberately targeted today in Algeria and elsewhere in the Middle East, he is unrepentant about having done so himself during the war. "Our methods and theirs [the Algerian Islamists] are both cruel, but you must distinguish between an objective—ours—which was liberation and theirs, which is destruction." Saadi elaborated: "We killed women, yes, and took fetuses out of their wombs. But our [tactics] were for liberation. This was the only means against a cruel enemy" (*International Herald Tribune*, June 20, 2007).

32. Much of Pierre Bourdieu's Algerian fieldwork was carried out in these camps. Although Bourdieu has been criticized for not contextualizing this research, read carefully it provides a detailed picture of the consequences of camp life (see Bourdieu 1964). See the contributions to Goodman and Silverstein (2009) for an appraisal of Bourdieu's Algerian research and how it influenced his subsequent writings.

33. Challe had forced de Gaulle into agreeing to increase the number of Harkis by threatening to resign if he refused (Horne 1987, 333).

34. Challe has been criticized for using torture and for the conditions in the *regroupement* camps.

35. The *bachaga* Boualam was a notable exception. See chapters 3 and 5.

36. Challe, who had been sentenced to fifteen years of criminal detention, was pardoned in 1966. All the other officers involved in the plot and imprisoned were amnestied in 1968.

37. It is estimated that the OAS killed a total of twenty-seven hundred, of which twenty-four hundred were Algerians.

38. See Soufi (2004) for a detailed discussion of the Oran massacres.

CHAPTER THREE

1. Aside from the official and semiofficial names for Algerians, there is a long list of pejorative terms, such as *bicot* and *bougnole*, that the French have used in referring to them.

2. Before independence *Français de souche Nord-Africaine* was used in Algeria to distinguish the Muslim population from the Europeans, or *Français de souche Européene*. Among the terms used after repatriation are the following: in the early 1970s, *Français rapatriés de confession islamique*, which violated the secular principle (*principe de laïcité*) promulgated by the law of December 5, 1905, and *Français de souche indigène rapatrié d'Afrique du Nord*; in 1980s, *Rapatriés d'origine Nord-Africaine*; later, *Français-Musulmans rapatriés* (FMR), *Français Musulmans, Rapatriés Français Musulmans*, and *Rapatriés maghrébins*; and, since 2005, *Français rapatrié d'origine Nord Africaine*. See, among others, Whitol de Wenden (1990).

3. A *goum* was also a unit of two hundred men. See Chauvin (1995), Faivre (1995, 10–13), and Hamoumou (1993) for summary discussions of the recruitment of local auxiliary troops. See Lyons (2004, 35 n. 18) for bibliography.

4. See Richard Bouchareb's film *Indigènes* for a dramatization of the role of North African soldiers in the French army during World War II.

5. Though the *droit commun* is, in practice, equivalent to civil law, embodied in the civil code, it refers more generally, more abstractly, to the fundamental rights and liberties of the individual. As such, it serves as a referent for the construction of new norms. It is said to inspire every legal creation (*création de droit*) and every juridical development (*évolution juridique*).

6. My description of these auxiliary groups is based principally on Ageron (1995).
7. Members of the GMPR were popularly known as *goumis* and *jean-pierres* (from the pronunciation of the acronym by the Algerians).
8. See chapter 2.
9. Only about fourteen thousand Harkis had been granted this status by February 1962, as the war was drawing to a close (Ageron 1995, 6).
10. Throughout the war, the French administration complained about the cost of the Harkis and often refused requests for more funding. They considered the Harkis to be overpaid.
11. The term *harka* was first officially used on February 8, 1956, in an announcement of the army high command: "Des unités supplétives seront constituées dans chaque corps d'armée, à l'échelle 'quartier.' S'appuyant sur les unités de base (compagnie, escadrons, batteries), elles seront chargées de compléter la sécurité territoriale et de participer aux opérations loyales au niveau des secteurs. Ces unités porteront la dénomination de 'harkas' " (Hamoumou 1993, 115).
12. The *agha* had, in fact, been named a *chevalier* of the Légion d'honneur in 1953. See Boulhaïs (2002) for details, including the role of tribal feuding in the formation of this first *harka* and a critique by Pierre Rivière of Servier's account. Faivre (1995, 34–35) quotes a report by Captain Anglada, the founder of the Arris SAS unit, praising the *agha*. Anglada states that, by March 25, 1956, the *agha*'s *harka* had performed 63 full-day missions, 125 ambushes, and 6 fights. Twenty-three rebels had been killed, five taken prisoner, and eighteen weapons recuperated. Six Harkis had been killed, ten wounded, and forty-one citations awarded.
13. According to Fabbiano (2008b, 116), the Beni-Boudouane's engagement was dictated by the will to defend the honor of the clan rather than ideological reasons.
14. According to the Beni-Boudouane and the *bachaga*'s family, it was not Challe who asked the *bachaga* to form the *harka* but the *bachaga* who offered to form one.
15. As we have seen, in 1959, Challe had forced de Gaulle to increase the number of Harkis by threatening to resign if the general refused (Horne 1987, 333).
16. *Le monde*, December 13, 2007, in a review of Valat's (2007) *Les "calots bleus" et la bataille de Paris*. Valat suggests a figure of 300.
17. See chapter 2 for a discussion of the Café Wars.
18. The massacre was also part of Papon's continuing attempt to break the FLN's hold on the Algerian immigrant population in Paris. In all, 11,538 protesters were arrested that day, and, by the end of the week, their number had increased to 14,000, of which 1,005 were sent back to Algeria. It is noteworthy that no member of the French government was present on October 17, 2001, when the mayor of Paris, Bertrand Delanoë, placed a plaque commemorating the massacre on the Pont Saint-Michel. The perpetrators of the massacres were included in the amnesty laws of 1962, 1966, 1968, and 1982. See Cole (2006) and Valat (2007, 210–19) for details and bibliography.
19. The actual figures for France are 3,957 killed and 7,745 wounded, making a total of 10,223; for the Paris area, the figures are 1,433 killed and 1,726 wounded, making a total of 3,159 (Valat 2007, 27–28, 241–42). In 1960, there were roughly 150,000 Algerians, mostly men (115,000), living in France (Valat 2007, 16).
20. Again, these figures must be treated with caution. The French wanted to keep the number of deaths at a minimum. Other estimates are much higher.
21. Despite the FLN's official interdiction, slashing the throat was one of frequent means of assassination—one that calls to mind both sacred sacrifices and the butchery of animals in the Muslim world (Meynier 2002, 21).

22. Valat (2007, 22) has recently argued that the Harkis rarely used torture.

23. See Evans (1997) for an account of the *porteurs de valises*.

24. My discussion of the number of FMR is based primarily on Hamoumou (1993, 121–26). Faivre's estimates (see Faivre 1995, 137; and Faivre 2000, 131) are more conservative: seventy to eighty thousand auxiliaries and twenty-six to forty thousand troops on active duty on March 19, 1962. The discrepancy is indicative of the confusion at the war's end. It may also be a result of the status (active, inactive, absent) of the auxiliaries and regulars counted. See chapter 4.

25. In a recent study in which 169 households were interviewed across France, Soufflet and Williatte (2004, 121) found that, of the explanations given by the Harkis (in the extended sense of the word) for having become auxiliary troops, 23 percent claimed family reasons, 12.5 percent safety, 11 percent being drafted, 11 percent FLN exaction, 11 percent a pro-French stance, 9 percent the desire to make a military career, 9 percent pressure from the French army, and 8 percent economic pressure. The remaining 5 percent either gave no reason or claimed to have done so because they had been bureaucrats before the war or had converted from a nationalist position to a pro-French one. Their having lived for more than forty years in France, since their service, no doubt influenced their answers.

26. See Méliani (1993, 28–41) for a discussion of the importance of military honor and loyalty to de Gaulle and to France in the recruitment of auxiliaries. Méliani, a general, was the highest-ranking Algerian officer ever in the French army. A staunch patriot, devoted to the French army, his insistence on the French patriotism of those Harkis who had been veterans must be taken with caution.

27. Ferdi's two brothers lost their lives fighting with the FLN. Ferdi himself had carried messages for the FLN, but the French never discovered this.

28. See, with caution, Gaget (2000) for an account of the Commando.

29. That the Harkis' truncated speech was not simply the effect of their talking to me, a stranger, is attested to by many of the testimonies collected by Harki children, which are in the same terse and fragmented style.

30. Quotations are from military archives.

31. Faivre (1995, 132) notes that General Buis's position has been contradicted by his subordinates and successors.

32. Kerchouche's family story (2003b) as well as her autobiographical novel (2006) can be treated as documentation only with caution since, though, at least in the case of the former, she uses archival material, interviews, and observations made in her travels as she traces her father's trajectory in Algeria and France, she "colorizes" them for literary and, no doubt, rhetorical effect.

33. Reported in *La nouvelle république du centre ouest* (edition Loir et Cher), November 12, 2004.

CHAPTER FOUR

1. It was not clear whose heads, those of the adults, those of the children, or all of them.

2. There has been considerable debate among theologians over the difference between *qada* and *qadar*. *Qada* usually refers to divine decree perduring for all eternity and *qadar* to divine decrees operating existentially in time, setting limits to each and everything. The distinction reflects one often made between cosmic and local destinies. Combined, *al-qada wa l-qadar* refers to the decree of God. The Quran and the Hadith refer, on the one hand, to Allah's immutable will and, on the other, to the responsibility

humans have for their acts, on which they will be judged on Judgment Day. Despite Allah's unassailable will, efforts are frequently made to influence it through interme-diaries—saints or *waliyyin*—or by making a vow, sometimes modeled on prevailing contractual arrangements. See Crapanzano (2009b) and chapter 7 below for a more detailed discussion of destiny.

3. To make my point here, I refer to the distinction German historiographers make between *Geschichte* (roughly, what actually happened) and *Historie* (the narratives about what actually happened). I am, in fact, not particularly satisfied with the dis-tinction since it fails to account for the interchange between the two: the postulation of a chain of events that exists independently of its construction.

4. See Rahmani (2003, 124) for her father's attitude toward the word (*parole*): "He who had committed by his acts his word as a man never went back on this word. For him the word was indivisible. It had only one meaning, that which was attributed to it. . . . It did not belong to the world of the lie or of the truth; it was the word."

5. Again, there are marked discrepancies in the figures. See Hamoumou (1993, 121–26) and chapter 3 above. In the autumn of 1961, it was thought that increasing the number of Harkis in the GMS could provide a basis for local forces, but the idea was quickly abandoned (Roux 1991, 186).

6. Hacène is the founder and president of Coordination Harka, one of the most impor-tant Harki associations. In 1992, he was a member of one of the government's *mis-sions de réflexion*, one headed by Roger Romani. His participation was taken as a sign of his personal ambition by some Harki activists, though he is generally respected by the Harki community as a whole.

7. See chapter 5 for a continuation of Hacène's story.

8. The relevant section of Article 2 reads as follows:

   Nul ne pourra faire objet de measures de police ou de justice, de sanctions disciplinaires ou d'une discrimination quelconque en raison
   —D'opinions émises à l'occasion des événements survenus en Algérie avant le jour du scrutin d'autodétermination
   —D'actes commis à l'occasion des mêmes événements avant le jour de la proclamation de cessez le feu.
   Aucun Algérien ne pourra être constraint de quitter le territoire algérien ni empêché d'en sortir.

9. So, at any rate, was the final Declaration of Principles of the Agreement interpreted: "France and Algeria will resolve the differences that may arise between them by peaceful means of settlement" (Horne 1987, 521).

10. See Lyons (2004) for a discussion of Algerian families and the French welfare system.

11. Here is a rough translation, which does not do justice to the nuanced syntax of the original: "The early demobilization of the troops certainly cuts with the little will-ingness the public powers demonstrated for repatriating the auxiliaries and their families. A posteriori, the massive dismissal of troops and their often expeditious demobilization appears as proof that the army wittingly sought to rid itself of those men it nevertheless knew were threatened while obviously taking back their weap-ons. In reality, the confused circumstances at the end of the conflict render the situa-tion less readable than a retrospective view leads one to believe. The FLN's reassuring declarations, the period of calm that followed the signing of the Treaty of Evian, the Harkis' representation at the time of their commitment to the French side: the hope of a peaceful conclusion to the conflict was during several weeks still permitted."

12. Charbit does not qualify the much smaller number of deserters as "limited." See Roux (1991, 214) for details.

13. In fact, OAS actions continued. See Angelelli (2004) for an account of the brutality during the war and its aftermath perpetuated by OAS sympathizers, like Angelelli himself, in the military. Angelelli, a *pied-noir* who was enlisted in army intelligence, does not hesitate to describe war atrocities and the viciousness of his unit's response, including his own, to captured *fellaghas*, especially those who had killed members of his unit. Though he admires many of the Harkis with whom he served, he, among others, shot deserters. Angelelli (2004, 240–41) writes: "One evening, it was necessary to kill. I didn't like that, but what's the good of searching for excuses? It was necessary to do it without hatred and without joy, duty and necessity. . . . It was the law. The tons of ink spilled on it will change nothing. They [the *fellaghas*] had chosen to be outlaws, calm killers; they worked for a sense of history with the satisfaction of having accomplished it." Angelelli wrote his book immediately after the war but could, he told me, find no publisher who was willing to risk government seizure of it. It was finally published forty years later. Its tough depiction must be treated with caution, but it is revealing of the anger and disgust of the *pieds-noirs*.

14. See Roux (1991, 199–203) and Hamoumou (1993, 246–51) for detailed discussions of the various calculations used in these estimates.

15. One of the ways in which anger is dissipated, Aristotle observed in the *Nicomachean Ethics* (1126a), is through revenge. See Crapanzano (2008) and chapter 7 below for a discussion of the relation between anger and outrage as it was and is played out among the Harkis.

16. Clearly, one must distinguish between the rural Algerians and the urban ones, who had a far more sophisticated notion of nationhood, independence, and the consequences of colonialism.

17. Even the foreclosure (*Verwerfung*) of an event—its being thrust from consciousness, leaving only an absence, a hole—is not without effect. See Laplanche and Pontalis (1973, 163–67) for a discussion of foreclosure (*forclusion*).

18. I am not referring to the torture carried out by the ALN members who may still have thought they had the need to gather information.

19. See Nedjadi (2001, 111–24) for a description of the various modes of torture carried out by the French. Nedjadi makes no mention of the tortures carried out by the ALN or those directed at the Harkis. The literature on the French use of torture is now enormous. See, e.g., Alleg (1958), Vidal-Naquet (1958, 1983), Beauvoir and Halimi (1962), Vittori (1980), Maran (1989), Stora (1998), and Branche (2004). See Aussaresses (2001) for an unapologetic justification of torture by one of Massu's officers that caused outrage when it was published in France. For the most part, the French have concentrated on the tortures they carried out, not on those carried out by the Algerians. Does this self-centeredness rest on racism? "What can we expect from *les Arabes?*"

20. The conversion of the abstract enemy into the personal enemy, my enemy, does not necessarily make him human; it is, rather, a mode of possession—a focusing.

21. See Gray (1959, 141–69) for four principal ways in which the enemy is abstracted.

22. The corpses of Harkis who lived in France but wanted to be buried with their families in their home villages have usually been refused entry into Algeria, and, if permitted entry, they would probably not have been buried in village cemeteries. Many of the Harki children I talked to mentioned, at one time or another, that Harkis were not allowed to bury their dead in Algeria (see chapter 7). Alive or dead, they

were not permitted reentry by the Algerian immigration authorities. Mehdi Charef (1999) described one such occasion in his novel *Le Harki de Meriem*. (See Rosello [2005, 139–47] for commentary.) As Scheele (2006) notes, cemeteries, at least among the Kabyles, with whom she worked, reflect changing village social relations. Since independence, they also reflect the role of the deceased in recent Algerian history. The *shuhada*, the "martyrs" who died for Algerian independence, are buried in white, man-sized concrete blocks, reminiscent of saints' tombs, that are meant to last. Though they have personalized inscriptions, these have faded over the years and are practically illegible. They do act, according to Scheele (2006, 867), as "physical markers of the new social order established by the war of independence." Traditionally, Kabyle grave sites were marked anonymously by a pile of stones.

23. An official document published in an article by Jean Lacouture in *Le monde* on November 13, 1962, noted that, as the number of auxiliaries seeking refuge in French garrisons was increasing daily and was already more than six thousand, it was necessary to interrupt this "current of threatened Muslims" since the Algerian government was taking umbrage at "our centers open largely to their opponents" (cited in Roux 1991, 218).

24. The priority could be and was justified on the grounds that, unlike the *pieds-noirs*, who were citizens of France, the Harkis as Algerians had an ambiguous legal status. See Blévis (2001), Miège (1992), Saada (2003), and Whitol de Wenden (1991), among others, for discussion of the legal status of the Algerians and, by extension, the Harkis and other repatriated or repatriatable Algerians.

25. Morelle (2004) suggests that the French were simply overly optimistic at the time. Her position has been contested.

26. See Roux (1991, 208–12) for details.

27. Some officers, as well as sea captains, did carry on despite the risk of imprisonment, but these were exceptional. Before ships from Algeria could land, radios in Marseilles asked whether there were any Harkis on board. If there were, the captain was automatically sentenced to eight days in prison (Charbit 2006, 53, 55).

28. On May 23, 1962, *Le figaro* reported that fifty-five Harkis from the region of Palestro were turned back on their arrival in France (cited in Roux 1991, 216). It seems that others were turned back in Marseilles, apparently because their papers were not in order. The Communist dockers' union, which had supported the FLN, has been blamed.

29. Joxe's phraseology is tellingly awkward here: "mais ce qu'il faut surtout obtenir, c'est que le gouvernement ne soit plus amené à prendre une telle décision." In a meeting in Parliament on June 28, Joxe commented on "secret orders" sent by General Le Roy to his officers concerning the relocation of Harkis to France: "The officers who want to bring back their men demonstrate a condemnable proprietary instinct directed at people [*un condamnable instinct de propriétaire exerce sur des personnes*], which violates their freedom of choice in order to institute in France subversive groups" (Faivre 1995, 169).

30. Years ago, at a reception in Paris, before introducing me to Pierre Joxe, my hostess took me aside to tell me he was Louis Joxe's son. Clearly, she wanted to make sure that I would not mention his father's connection to Algeria. Her clear embarrassment suggests that Pierre was not altogether immune to the effect of his father's involvement in Algeria. The sins of the father . . .

31. That is, about four thousand auxiliaries. In April 1962, the French army estimated that there were about 9,400 Harkis whose lives were seriously threatened. In June, the Ministry of the Army reduced the number to 4,931 (Roux 1991, 214).

32. In 1972, it was estimated that around twelve thousand were still detained in Algeria (Heinis 1977).

CHAPTER FIVE

1. There was a Foreign Legion post at Zeralda.

2. The settlement of Harkis in France was designed to prevent the creation of *douars* (villages) and other communities based on origin by dispersing Harkis from the same region (Saliha 1984).

3. See Abdellatif (1990).

4. In accordance with the Treaty of Evian, the Déclaration recognitive de la nationalité française—Article 2 of an ordinance of July 21, 1962—gave the Harkis the right to (retain) French citizenship by means of a simple declaration in front of a *juge d'instance*. See Heinis (1977) for detailed figures by year for Algerians who declared themselves French. The total registered between 1962 and 1970 was about sixty thousand, though, by some estimates, it was more. In 1963, they were given repatriate status, but it was not until November 21, 1974, that they were recognized as veterans and became eligible for pensions and other benefits.

5. Unfortunately I cannot give page numbers in my references to Heinis's thesis since the copy I have has no pagination.

6. He was, in fact, taken to a French hospital, where he was treated.

7. A derogatory term for an Algerian.

8. Despite the interdiction on privately settling auxiliary troops in France, the French army took charge in September 1962 of flying sixty-seven members of the *bachaga*'s extended family to Mas Thibert. Over the next few years, more Beni-Boudouanes arrived, sometimes from Rivesaltes and La Rye. By 1968, there were seven hundred repatriated French Muslims living in Mas Thibert (Fabbiano 2006, 486). Their living conditions were as poor as those in the Harki camps. In 2000, houses built by the government, each worth roughly 300,000 francs, were given to the Beni-Boudouane, thereby arousing the ire of other Harkis (Fabbiano 2008b, 121).

9. Despite the sense of community, the Mas Thibert Harkis are divided along lineage lines (Fabbiano 2006, 144–45).

10. Though some of the Harkis would have liked to be buried in Algeria, the Algerian government would never, they told me, allow it. "We're on the list." Others had no desire whatsoever to be repatriated, though they regretted not being able to attend the funerals of their relatives in Algeria. The children and certainly the grandchildren expressed no interest in being buried there. See chapter 7.

11. See also Boulhaïs (2002, 307–403) for a detailed account of one of the Chaouia tribes from the Aurès in the Bassin de la Sambre.

12. See Faivre (1994, 219–24) for more details. Most of the general's book, based largely on military records, is concerned with wartime conditions and maneuvers in the Bobor Region. Other Harki communities were less successful. A former Kabyle senator arranged for about a hundred members of his tribe, the Iflissen, to settle in Poix in the Somme, but, as there was not enough work in the area, they soon left (Abdellatif 1984a, 63).

13. Brahim Sadouni (2001, 131), a Berber who had enrolled in the French army at the

age of seventeen and arrived in France in 1964, describes in his heated autobiography the medical examination that he and the other auxiliaries underwent before they were able to leave Marseilles. He claims that they were divided into two groups—the healthy and the sick—and that the sick were sent back to Algeria to face imprisonment, torture, and death. None of the Harkis I talked to ever mentioned this triage, nor have I read any reference to it.

14. The military camp, the largest in southern France, encompassed more than 600 hectares, of which 165 were used for internment.

15. Of the 6,784 interned in Rivesaltes, 51.4 percent were adult men; 81.9 percent of the adult population was married, but their spouses were not necessarily in the camp; 20.8 percent of the men and 15.4 percent of the adult women were unmarried. These figures contrast with those for all the camps at that date: 56.9 percent were adult males; 72.2 percent of the adults were married; 48.4 percent of the residents were children; 37.3 percent of the men were bachelors; 62.7 percent of the men were married; 15.2 percent of the women were unmarried. Roughly 75 percent of the married were living in the camp. The average family had 2.6 children.

16. According to Moumen (2008, 133), who is in charge of historical research at Musée-mémorial du camp de Rivesaltes, the number of Harkis incarcerated at Saint-Maurice reached a maximum on January 5, 1963, of 5,542, of which about half were children. The number of occupants decreased to 4,028 by the end of March, under 2,000 on July 25, and 908 November 9. The camp was meant to hold 400. Detailed figures for the end of March 1963 indicate that 65.1 percent were male, that 47.7 percent of the men were married; that 87.9 percent of the women were married; that 43.3 percent of the population were children, and that the average family had 2.5 children. See Charbit (2006) for details.

17. Jordi and Hamoumou (1999, 54), citing Moinot (1997, 224). A colonel in the French army, Moinot reconstructs the life of Ahmed in a loose literary form, making it difficult to evaluate the work's content. Curiously, the work is cited as evidence by a number of writers on the Harkis.

18. Though conditions were worse at Bias than at Saint-Maurice and other camps, it was organized along the same military lines. Until 1973, when a reduction of the incarcerated began, it housed between 800 and 1,000. In 1973, there were still 103 families (or a population of 690, of which 104 were under four and 432 under twenty). In 1980, four years after its official closing, there were nearly 300, mostly children, living there, and, in 2004, there were about 30 families (Jammes 2008, 150). For descriptions of the camp, see Roux (1991, 296–98), Kerchouche (2003b, 119–68), and Azni (2002, 97–133).

19. See also Azni (2002, 119ff.). See Kerchouche (2006) for a semifictionalized account.

20. "An associative logic," Heinis (1977) writes, "permits taking account, by way of symbolic explanations, of the deep meaning of appearances, even contradictions in a phenomenon."

21. Possible work fell into three categories: seasonal agricultural labor, work in a camp atelier (after 1970), and maintenance of the camp itself.

22. Heinis (1977) reports that older Harki men, particularly those married to younger women, frequently asked doctors for drugs to increase their potency. "To prove that they were still men," Heinis comments.

23. See Noura's comments in chapter 7. Mixed marriages usually created family problems on both the Muslim and the European sides, reflecting racist and inverse-racist

attitudes. Muslim fathers, I was told, also objected because, in mixed marriages, there was no bride wealth.

24. In the fall of 1973, Paul Feuilloloy, the prefect of the department of the Lot-et-Garonne, also noted the bitterness of the young people at Bias (Choi 2007, 227).

25. See chapter 7 for Noura's story.

26. In *Mon père, ce Harki*, Kerchouche (2003b, 69–82) describes her meeting with a Juliette who showed similar kindness to her mother. She also mentions a social worker who helped her family avoid being sent to Bias, for at least a time (81).

27. Heinis (1977) describes a similar case in a discussion of Harki relatives who thought they were French when they were, in fact, legally citizens of Algeria.

28. According to Jordi and Hamoumou (1999, 95 [see generally 94–96]), the AAAA could not single-handedly have been responsible for the creation of the forestry hamlets, though it played a "nonnegligible role in supervision [*encadrement*] of the Harkis after the camps were created."

29. Seventy-five represents the total number of camps constructed during the 1960s. The most there were at any one time was sixty (Roux 1991, 247 n. 25).

30. Bourdieu and Sayad (1964, 25) argue, somewhat facilely, that both positions were really not that different. The segregationists "invoke differences of fact in order to deny legal identity [*l'identité de droit*], and the assimilationists deny differences of fact in the name of legal identity."

31. The settlement was started by Nicolas d'Andoque, a former SAS officer who strongly believed that the Harkis should be able to live in a milieu in which they would not have to abandon their customs: "How can we soften the transition, attenuate the effects of the disruption? As much as possible, we must avoid cutting off their habits. They were peasants. They must remain so" (d'Andoque 1977, 183). He claims that, having assembled a group of auxiliaries at Larzac, they went to Pujol on their own before he could arrange matters officially. At the time, only one shepherd lived there. D'Andoque continued to promote the forestry hamlets through the AAAA, which he helped found. Devoted to the auxiliaries, his position was not based on rendering them invisible, as the isolationists wanted to do.

32. Belkacem asked me to stop the car and take some photographs as evidence of the way in which the Harkis had been treated. After I took them, he told me pointedly that he had taken the son of *pieds-noirs*, who worked with the Harkis, to the camp six months earlier. "He could not bring himself to photograph the camp," Belkacem said. "He was too moved by the sight." Though Belkacem's hostility toward me on this occasion was evident, his trapping me also reflected the ambivalence he felt: the rage, the shame, the desire to show and not show what he had lived through. This occasion was the only time that he expressed any hostility toward me.

33. Kerchouche (2003a, 172–73, quoting Abi-Samra and Finas 1985) reproduces an anonymous letter written to the secretary of state for the repatriated by a Harki who had been sent to Pujol in which are described conditions much the same as Belkacem recalled. The author noted that, if you did not give the military personnel bottles of liquor, they would turn on you. To obtain clothes donated by the Red Cross you had to give the head of the camp chickens or a bottle of champagne at midnight. Instead of using a car furnished by the prefecture to take the sick to a hospital, the head used it for himself. The author asked that the head be replaced by an "honest Frenchman." The letter apparently led to an investigation, which resulted in the discovery of the identity of the writer, who was then sent to another camp, probably Bias. A French television program on the Harkis shown in 1963 includes a section on Pujol that

paints an altogether different picture of the camp. A woman, a recent arrival from Rivesaltes, tells the reporter how much she likes the camp. He asks her whether this is because she has her own home here; she readily agrees.

34. In fact, the remuneration that Harki forestry workers received was from the state *au titre de l'action sociable*, which meant, in effect, that they did not have the same rights as salaried workers (Abdellatif 1990, 33).

35. In fact, they had all served in the Affaires musulmanes et sahariennes (Jordi and Hamoumou 1999, 98).

36. See Crapanzano (2008) for a discussion of anger, rage, and outrage.

37. Jordi and Hamoumou (1999, 102) noted a similar nostalgia in the former residents of the camp.

38. See Langelier (2009, 186–207) for a discussion of the various laws and policies concerning the construction of Harki housing.

39. In order to avoid *reclassements sauvage*, the Ministry for the Repatriated asked employment services to find work for only those Harkis who had been recommended by the Service d'accueil et de reclassement des Français d'Indochine et des musulmans (Roux 1991, 248).

40. In 1990, the last figures that I have found, their number was eleven thousand (out of fifteen thousand). The Algerian workers also numbered eleven thousand (Souida 1990, 59). Those readers who like detective stories may find the description of Roubaix and the conflict between Algerians and Harkis in Belaïd (2000) entertaining.

41. See also (Colonna 2007), a documentary, in which one of the Harkis makes the same observation.

CHAPTER SIX

1. *L'express*, May 15, 1997. According to other accounts, he was placed in a rest home. See also Besnaci-Lancou (2010, 78–79) and Muller (1999, 50–51). Muller's book must be read with caution since it is filled with errors of fact. Muller also gives an account of Kletch's life.

2. On at least one of these occasions, Hacène was protesting the diversion of Harki funds to the Office national de l'action sociale, éducative, et culturelle.

3. Other Harkis I talked to about the protests did not mention Hacène at all. "We just couldn't take it anymore," one of them said. "We had to do something." One Frenchman who was living in Saint-Laurent at the time told me that the cause of the riots was the murder of a Harki child by a group of drunken Frenchmen from a neighboring town. "They were out to get an Arab." The discrepant stories are symptomatic of the factionalism among the Harki activists.

4. My account is indebted to Roux (1991, 344–49).

5. Two secretaries were also taken hostage, but they were immediately released.

6. It is noteworthy that one of the first public demonstrations of the plight of the Harkis was also carried out by an ex-deputy from French Algeria. On March 19, 1971—the anniversary of the signing of the Treaty of Evian—Laklouf Galhem immolated himself on the boulevard Raspail in Paris. None of the Harkis I talked to ever mentioned Galhem's suicide.

7. See Choi (2007, 217–27) for a discussion of changing employment policies. During the years immediately following the war, policy was determined in part by the fear that the employment of immigrant labor would promote FLN influence—indeed, violence—in France. It was also feared that, by living side by side, the Harkis and the immigrants would end up sympathizing with each other. Two surveillance or-

ganizations specializing in North African workers—the Service de coordination des informations nord-africaines and the Service d'assistance technique (SAT), a subsidiary of the Prefect of Police—were particularly concerned with FLN infiltration and influence in France. Though mistrusting both populations, the SAT opted to support the Harkis.

8. See chapter 5.

9. The CFMRAA was active until the 1980s and ended with Laradji's death in the 1990s. Boussad Azni (Azni 2002, 129) argues that, from the start, Laradji had been manipulated by the OAS and the *nostalgiques,* who armed and incited the protesters, as they made it clear to the French authorities that it was with them that they had to deal. In a recent and somewhat sentimental memoir, Mohammed Hadouche (http://harkis .com), the president of AJIR who had led the protest against *The Name of the Father,* sees Laradji as a hero in the Harki cause. He recalls how taken he was by Laradji when he saw him for the first time on television: "I remember admiring the man who, with a single blow [*coup*], exited the Harkis and their families from the oblivion in which they were immersed for sixteen years." Hadouche stresses Laradji's role in the development of Harki associations. He notes, sadly, how few attended his funeral. Azni and Hadouche's divergent appraisals of Laradji reflect, I am afraid, their respective political positions within the Harki community rather than an objective view of the man who, manipulated as he may have been by the *pieds-noirs,* did, in fact, spur Harki activism.

10. See Whitol de Wenden (1990, 11) for a listing of offices that were designed to help the Harkis after the closing of the camps.

11. See chapter 5, n. 18, for details.

12. Single people were given 600,000 old francs.

13. See Silverstein (2004) for discussions and bibliography of race and racialization of immigrants in Europe. See, among others, Hargreaves (1995), Noiriel (1996), Pierret (2008), Silverstein (2004) for France.

14. It is not clear how many Harkis actually support Le Pen's Front national (see Doghmane 2008). As a group, the Harkis are said to support the right-wing Union pour un mouvement populaire. They have never forgiven the Left, particularly the Communists, for its support of the FLN and its condemnation of them. Many Harki Web sites insisted during the last presidential election that there was not "a Harki vote."

15. Tixier Vignancourt, the far Right onetime general assistant secretary of information in the Vichy government, defender of Salan, and candidate for president in 1965, is one of their heroes (Bouclier 2003).

16. The march was to protest the marginalization of North African immigrant children born in France, or Beurs. *Beur* is a syllabic inversion of *Arab* in the Beur argot (*verlan*). It is of significance that Kletch and other Harkis marched along with the Algerian immigrant youths. Born in France, the Beurs are, unlike their parents, French citizens.

17. The law (no. 356, 2003–4, no. 104) had already been adopted by the National Assembly. No mention is made in the official record of the Harki protest, and, when I tried to see the Senate press officer, the receptionists refused, telling me that nothing unusual had happened in the Senate that day. The protest was seen, however, by both a friend who lives across from the Senate and the man who sells newspapers in the kiosk in the square in front of the Senate. He "got a kick out the way the Harkis outfoxed the CRS" by refusing to stop singing the *Marseillaise.*

18. The debate reflects French ambivalence toward the Harkis. The use of *événements,* it was argued by several of the senators, suggested a return to France's refusal to

acknowledge the struggle for independence as a war until 1999. *Événements* was, as we have seen, commonly used until then. Other amendments were rejected on the ground that they belonged to the realm of history and were not suitable for legislation.

19. One of them in October 2008 included historians and other scholars and a number of Harki activists. Judging from the invitations I received, the two groups understood the purpose of the conference differently: as a scholarly meeting and as a protest. I decided not to attend.

20. The full text of the award reads: "Pour rappel, cette association était aux côtés de tous les partis et associations qui ont répondu à l'appel du Comité du 17 octobre et qui s'étaient rassemblés la semaine dernière pour demander, entre autres, l'abrogation de l'article 4 de la loi du 23 février 2005 (voir *Soir d'Algérie* du 17 octobre). L'intéressée a été à l'origine, en septembre de l'année 2004, du manifeste commun d'enfants de Harkis et d'immigrés algériens, dans lequel les signataires appellent à 'la réappropriation des mémoires confisquées' car, disent-ils, 'nos parents, par choix, hasard ou nécessité, se sont trouvés dans des camps différents durant la guerre d'Algérie' et le manifeste de condamner 'la dualité simpliste qui veut qu'il y ait des bons d'un côté et des mauvais de l'autre.' "

21. More than a thousand historians, writers, and intellectuals signed a petition demanding the repeal of the law. They condemned the law as "imposing an official lie on massacres that at times went as far as genocide, on the slave trade, and on the racism that France has inherited" (Henley 2005).

22. Article 4 was, apparently, the result of an unnoticed amendment added by a group with close ties to the *pieds-noirs* (Henley 2005). The full French text reads: "Les programmes de recherche universitaire accordent à l'histoire de la présence française outre-mer, notamment en Afrique du Nord, la place qu'elle mérite. Les programmes scolaires reconnaissent en particulier le rôle positif de présence française outre-mer, notamment en Afrique du Nord, et accordent à l'histoire et aux sacrifices des combattants de l'armée française issus de ces territoires la place éminente à laquelle ils ont le droit. La coopération permettant la mise en relation des sources orales et écrites disponible en France et à l'étranger est encouragée."

23. The other associations (and their presidents) are Unir (Ali Aissaoui), Association des Harkis et des rapatriés d'Algérie et de leurs enfants de Bourgogne (Khadra Safrioune), Responsables des Harkis de Rosans (Amar Assas), Association étoile d'espérence (Mohammed Bouzid), Collectif justice pour les Harkis et leurs familles (Abdelkrim Kletch), Association génération mémoires Harkis (Smaïl Boufhal), and Association des jeunes du Logis d'Anne.

24. I certainly do not want to suggest that the violent protests are ritualized or orchestrated.

25. Of course, Harkis who live in public housing do not take the same pride in their homes. For the most part, the homes I visited in the *cités* were kept up. Like the Harkis' houses, they were furnished with European furniture. Some of them did have Orientalist paintings or lithographs of a desert scene, but there were usually no other objects that suggested the North African origin of their inhabitants. The memories they evoke would probably have been too painful. See Silverstein (2004, 76–120) for a discussion of houses of Berbers living in France.

26. All figures are from Chabi (2007), whose report for the Conseil économique et social goes into far greater detail than I have indicated here. See also Langelier (2009).

27. Similar societies were started by Berber immigrants to France in the 1980s. They defined their mission in cultural terms, which—given their situation—was impossible for the Harkis.

28. The case was based on the press law of 1881.

29. Although Sedira changed the subtitle that was in question, in her interview with Bernard Geniès in *L'express*, she again referred to the Harkis as collaborators. She agreed that the subtitle had provoked their anger but went on to say: "But I think the entire content of the exhibition troubled [*dérangé*] the Harki association as well as certain members of the military and the *pieds-noirs*. My mother talked about rapes, thefts, and torture committed by the French army, and she spoke of the Harkis since they collaborated with the French army." She questioned the freedom of speech in France. At the end of May 2010, the Tribunal administratif of Nice ordered the reopening of the exhibit.

30. For example, Boussad Azni, the *conseiller au ministère pour la communauté Harki*, criticizes Sarkozy for not keeping his promise to improve employment opportunities for the Harkis. The interview with Azni by Jacky Sanudo took place on February 1, 2009, and was originally published in *Sud Ouest*. It was accompanied by a list of Internet sites making similar points. There is, of course, nothing new about broken promises by elected officials. Broken promises are noted regularly on Harki Web sites after elections.

31. At the meetings they organize, the Harkis, especially newcomers, attempt to situate one another in terms of family connections, place of origin, and, especially, the camps in which they had been incarcerated.

32. On January 27, 2007, a few months before my meeting with Kletch and his friends, Frêche was forced out of the Socialist Party for having noted that the composition of the French soccer team—nine blacks out of eleven—was disproportionate to the number of Africans in France, concluding that the "the whites are worthless" (*les blancs sont nuls*).

33. See Choi (2007, 234–53) for a summary discussion of the promises political candidates for the presidency of France have made to the Harkis for their vote.

CHAPTER SEVEN

1. This is true, not only when the anthropologist's informants are literate and can access his or her writings, but also, phantasmatically, penetratingly so, when they are illiterate and can have no such access.

2. Though I do not share Felman and Laub's (1992, 15, 57) psychoanalytic approach, at least with regard to the Harkis, I note their observation that the listener to (painful) testimony "comes to be a participant and a co-owner of the traumatic event[s]" recounted. The Harkis' legalism and their insistent political goals often diminished the intensity of my participation in their pain.

3. Compare Skultans (1999, 169, quoted in Eastmond 2007, 257–58), who found that Latvian men and women wanted their lives to bear witness to the wrongs that they had experienced—collectivization, deportation, and exile—and the injustices of their history. Their stories were directed toward a wider audience than the researcher and, as such, affirmed a sense of collective identity and nationhood. Unlike the Harkis, who had no sense of lost nationhood, the Latvians mingled their memories of past brutalities and state violence with folk-cultural elements. These features were strikingly absent from the Harki stories. Their ties with the Algerian nation, but not necessarily with Algeria, were simply cut.

4. Brillet (2001), citing the philosopher Olivier Abel (Abel 1993, 62), argues that, under such circumstances, the "wisdom [*sagesse*] of the pardon is a practical wisdom that offers, not deliverance from the tragic, but a deliverance in the tragic itself: the pardon is the virtue of a compromise because it accepts the difference [*differend*]."

5. "It is necessary, it seems to me, to begin from the fact, yes, there is the unforgivable. Is this, in truth, the only thing to forgive? The only thing that calls for forgiveness? If one is only prepared to forgive what appears forgivable, what the church calls 'venial sin,' then the very idea of forgiveness would disappear. If there is something to forgive, it would be what in religious language is called mortal sin, the worst, the unforgivable crime or harm. From which comes the aporia, which can be described in its dry and implacable formality, without mercy: forgiveness forgives only the unforgivable" (Derrida 2001, 32–33).

6. By referring to *trivial and serious acts*, rather than *venial and mortal sins*, I want to avoid, as best I can, the culturally specific (Christian) presuppositions of much of the theorizing about forgiveness and the postulation of the requisite spiritual condition (e.g., repentance) for its success.

7. Oliver (2004, 195–200) argues—from within her idiosyncratic social psychoanalytic perspective, which stresses the role of forgiveness in the constitution of subjectivity—that colonial oppression deprives the colonized of the "space" for forgiveness and, in consequence, of the sublimation and idealization necessary for the formation of subjects and subjectivity. Aristotle might have argued that anger, outrage, and revenge can be as liberating as forgiveness, as constitutive of subjectivity, but such a position would require a rethinking of the role of sublimation (less so idealization) in consociation.

8. Strictly speaking, just as forgiveness is impossible in Derrida's idiosyncratic understanding, so is the giving of a gift (*don*) since the exchange of gifts would put the receiver of the gift in a debt relationship with the gift giver. It would not be unconditional. The present (*présent, cadeau*), like the excuse, is possible because it assumes—or does not deny—the debt relationship, its conditionality (Derrida 1991, 51–94; Caputo 1997, 160–61).

9. Arendt's metaphor is far more penetrating than she realized. Forgiveness does not necessarily "[release us] from the consequences of what we have done." It undoes neither the irreversibility of time nor the deeds done, though it may, magically, as it were, diminish the psychological consequences of those acts and facilitate their burial in forgetfulness. It gives us at least the illusion that we are rid of the past and, thereby, open to the future. Forgiveness relates to notions of atonement, expiation, contrition, and redemption, all of which, in Arendt's terms, serve to release us from the witting and unwitting harmful consequences of our acts—to undo or give the illusion of undoing history. See Hertz (1988), who understands expiation as an attempt to undo history.

10. See also Brillet (2001), whose approach, following Abel (1993), is mechanical, abstract, centered on pardon from within a system of exchange, and opposing debt and amnesia. He argues that the "logic of the debt participates in the crystallization of the memory of the wrong-doing [*tort*] in the victim." The debt—the wrongdoing—is, for the victim, "obsessionally objectified" through resentment and fixation. As such, it has a shattering effect on him or her. Everything is understood in terms of the debt. It becomes impossible to react to other things. The victim is rendered incapable of reacting anew.

11. Arendt (1958, 237) notes that forgiving "enacted in solitude or isolation remain[s] without reality and can signify no more than a role played before one's self." Is self-forgiveness ever possible? Arendt suggests, rather too facilely, that "just as the extent and modes of self-rule justify and determine rule over others—how one rules himself, he will rule others—[so] the extent and modes of being forgiven . . . determine the extent and modes in which one may be able to forgive oneself" (238). I am not at all certain that this mirroring of rule and self-rule can ever lead to the possibility of self-forgiveness. Derrida's aporia seems pertinent here in both grammatical and experiential terms. Whether or not the possibility of forgiveness or self-forgiveness requires the unforgivable, the aporia points to an unbreachable schism in all forgiveness. Forgiveness in itself can never be fully achieved. Does the efficacy of forgiveness then lie in a you'd-better-believe-it style?

12. Arendt (1958, 237) adds: "Without being bound to the fulfillment of promise, we would never be able to keep our identities; we would be condemned to wander helplessly and without direction in the darkness of each man's lonely heart, caught in its contradictions and equivocations—a darkness which only the light shed over the public realm through the presence of others, who confirm the identity between the one who promises and the one who fulfils, can dispel." "Condemned to wander helplessly and without direction in the darkness of each man's lonely heart" is reminiscent of SNP's situation in *The Name of the Father*. See Ricoeur (2000, 633) for a critique of Arendt's postulation of "a symmetry in terms of power between the pardon and the promise." Ricoeur stresses the fact that the pardon has a religious aura that the promise does not have. What both Ricoeur and Arendt fail to consider is the religious aura that surrounds some promises (e.g., vows).

13. In the same declaration, the Algerian government was asked to permit the free circulation of the Harkis and their children and to allow them "to find a tomb [*sépulture*] in the land of their ancestors."

14. The French sociologist Réagis Pierret's (2008) study of Harki children, who were, for the most part, younger than those of the hinge generation, stresses their connection with the Algerian immigrant generation (see also Fabbiano 2006). Pierret describes their situation as "between double rejection and triple belonging [*entre double rejet et triple appartenance*])," that is, their being rejected by both the French and the Algerians yet being at once French, Algerian, and immigrant Algerian. There is no doubt that the Harkis were—and are—rejected by the French and the Algerians, but they were also rejected by the immigrant Algerians. Their relationship with each of these groups is, as we have seen, complex. Most of the Harki children I worked with were quite adamant in preserving their difference from the immigrants. Older than the forty Harki sons and daughters Pierret interviewed, they had lived through the period in which their relations with the immigrants, particularly those affiliated with the FLN, were violent, at times murderous. It is certainly true that, with the passage of time, some of them have begun to recognize commonalities with the immigrant population, particularly the racist marginalization they have both suffered.

15. Many Harkis I talked to equated the transition camps with German concentration camps. Celestine, among other Harki daughters, described the fear she felt when she entered the collective showers. She had seen a film about the death camps.

16. The portraits of sixty-two Harkis that Besnaci-Lancou (2010) provides illustrate the diversity of the Harki population. She focuses primarily on the Harki children and does not include the many children who have succumbed to their past.

17. I do not accept the argument that some authorities have made that the Harkis became Harkis only when they arrived in France. They were referred to as *Harkis* long
before they came to France, and, certainly, those who have remained in Algeria bear
all the consequences of that denomination. Yet it cannot be denied that their identity
has been reformulated over the years since they came to France.
18. The reader will recognize an implicit critique of Pierre Bourdieu's (1977) notion of
habitus, which he and his followers render so mechanical as to preclude recognition
of the conflictual—and the creative—space to which I am referring.
19. Muller (1999) seems to have found more overt anger among Harki children toward
their fathers than I did.
20. Azzedine seemed close to his wife and kept telling me I should talk to her—she was
the daughter of a Harki—but the occasion never seemed to arise. She was at work,
busy with the children, or cooking. She served us but ate separately with the children
in the kitchen. Although, traditionally, Algerian men and women ate separately—a
tradition that is upheld by some Harki children—I am certain that this was not the
normal arrangement in Azzedine's family but was done so that the children would
not disturb us. Azzedine was very affectionate with his children, but he paid more
attention to his son than to his daughter. His wife was not shy. What little she said to
me was astute. During the night, I heard her arguing quietly with Azzedine. I should
add that most of the Harki children I met *en famille* shared Azzedine's views and related to their spouses much as Azzedine and his wife did to each other. Their attitude
toward women and the family differentiated them, as more than one implied but
never said directly, from the Algerian immigrants. There are, however, some Harkis,
particularly in northern France—and mainly of the third generation—who have
been recruited by the Islamists and lead more traditional lives.
21. I use *responsibility* rather than *obligation* since requirements of responsibility are less
passive than those of obligation.
22. See chapter 6.
23. This is a frequent complaint among all young North African men living in France.
24. The indefinite pronoun *on/one* is used far more frequently in French than in English.
It is both impersonal (exclusive, in linguistic terms) and personal (inclusive) insofar
as it substitutes for *we/nous*.
25. I have avoided using *trauma* in my discussion of the Harkis' experiences in order to
steer as clear as possible of the articulation of their suffering in a psychiatric idiom
that deflects its political dimension (Fassin 2008). One of the most striking examples of this deflection was the near-instantaneous response to the terrorist attack on
the World Trade Center as traumatizing. Within hours, psychiatrists, psychoanalysts,
and psychologists volunteered their services—in good faith, to be sure—to care for
the "traumatized." I have preferred to use *wound* in order to avoid the psychiatric
connotations of *trauma* and to stress the real and symbolic carnal nature of what the
Harkis experienced. I should note, however, that several of the more educated Harki
children, like Azzedine, often used *trauma* to describe their and their parents' experiences. As I have argued (see Crapanzano 2009b), the contemporary use of *trauma*
correlates with the contingencies of the modern world, which are understood in
terms of chance and luck rather than destiny.
26. One of the most recent examples of the pain a father's silence caused his daughter is
Saliha Telali's heated autobiography *Les enfants des Harkis* (2009). Silence figures so
insistently in the book that it becomes a trope that loses both its referential and its
rhetorical power.

27. Bougrab was appointed president of the Haute autorité de lutte contre la discrimination et l'égalité on April 16, 2010.

28. Here, I part company with those psychologists who assume, all too facilely, that claiming a narrative inheritance, claiming an absent memory, and telling a story are healing (see McNay 2009). They may well be, at times, in those cultures that give therapeutic value to confession and storytelling, but they may also perpetuate the suffering, the emptiness, that lies behind those narratives.

29. See Besnaci-Lancou (2006a) for accounts by Harki women of their lives.

30. Rahmani (2003, 129) comments on Moze's suicide: "Moze saluted the monument to the dead. Surrounded by the elite, he, the ghost [revenant] of an unknown war, he, the unknown soldier, saluted the absent monument of a war that had taken place. Moze saluted the monument to the absent dead in a war that had buried him. He saluted the monument of the victims of a war before killing himself, before dying from a war that should not have taken place [d'une guerre qui n'aurait pas eu lieu]. From a war for which he would not die as a soldier." As Susan Ireland (2009, 308–9) notes, this passage evokes the need for recognition, the idea of commemoration, and the theme of death and burial. The image of the known unknown soldier killing himself before a monument to an unknown soldier is one of the most haunting in Rahmani's book.

31. Later in our conversation, however, the former mayor told me that he sometimes goes to meetings of an association of pieds-noirs. He insisted that it was not a political but a cultural one. "We talk about our lives there with a lot of nostalgia," he said with surprising distance. He had lost a vegetable farm of over a hundred acres on which a hundred journeymen, peasants, and three sharecroppers worked. They had two crops per year. His was one of the first farms in his area to be burned down by the FLN. It was random, he said, again with surprising distance. They had nothing against me. They just wanted to scare us. I learned later that the deputy mayor, an Arab, was murdered at the end of the war, as, he thought, were several other Arabs who worked for him in the town hall. There were several colons who were murdered and still more who were abducted. He never heard what had happened to them. Algeria has been emotionally absented for him. All that seemed to remain was an objectified nostalgia and a scrapbook containing newspaper articles on him and his mayoralty. See Kramer's (1980, 171–217) portrait, written in 1972, of a pied-noir family that had settled in the Vaucluse for the contradictions in their relationship to Algeria and France. See Silverstein (2004) for a discussion of the root as metaphor and immigration.

32. See Crapanzano (2009b) for a discussion of the role of destiny in the lives of both the Harkis and their children. I do not mean to imply that the Harkis' sense of destiny necessarily protected them from the wounds they suffered or prevented the distortion and repression of those wounds and what responsibility they themselves had for them. Clearly, drunkenness, depressions, idées fixes, and suicides suggest otherwise. What I am questioning is the adequacy of the biomedical understanding of these and other symptoms—in terms of trauma and posttraumatic stress disorders—which does not take account of the existential and ethical orientations that constitute a person's sense of self, environment, and history and that influence, if they do not determine, his or her responses to the contingencies of life. As Sherine Hamdy (2009) reminds us, fatalism—an accommodation to destiny—need not be passive. Forbearance, as she translates sabr, and reliance on God (al-tawakkul) require cultivation through prayer, reflection, and, I would add, collective recitation (dhikr).

33. See Hacking (1990), Becker (1997), and Giddens (1990, 29–31) for discussions of chance in modernity.
34. See Mireille Rosello (2005, 128–64) for a discussion of death as a figure of loss in Maghrebian francophone literature. On my first visit to Mas Thibert, I was taken to see the grave of the *bachaga* Boualam.

REFERENCES

Abdellatif, S. 1984a. "Être Français-Musulman en Picardie." In *La France au pluriel*, 100–109. Paris: L'Harmattan.

———. 1984b. "Les français musulmans ou le poids de l'histoire à travers la communauté picarde." *Les temps modernes*, nos. 452–54:1812–38.

———. 1990. "Le Français Musulman ou une entité préfabriquée." *Hommes et migrations*, no. 1135:28–33.

Abel, O. 1993. "Ce que le pardon vient faire dans l'histoire." *Esprit* 193:60–72.

Abi-Samra, M., and F. Finas. 1987. *Regroupement et dispersion: Rélagation, réseaux et territories des Français-Muselmans*. Rapport pour la Caisse d'allocations familiales. Lyon: Université de Lyon II.

Abrial, S. 2001. *Les enfants de Harkis, de la révolte à l'intégration*. Paris: L'Harmattan.

Addi, L. 1995. *L'Algérie et al démocratie: Pouvoir et crise du politique dans l'Algérie contemporaine*. Paris: Editions La Découverte.

Agamben, G. 1998. *Homo Sacer: Sovereign Power and Bare Life*. Stanford, CA: Stanford University Press.

Ageron, C.-R. 1979. *Histoire d'Algérie contemporaine: De l'insurrection de 1871 au déclenchement de la guerre de libération*. Paris: Presses Universitaires de France.

———. 1995. "Les supplétifs algériens dans l'armée française pendant la guerre d'Algérie." *Vingtième siècle* 48:3–20.

al-Ghazali. 1989. *The Remembrance of Death and the Afterlife*. Cambridge: Islamic Texts Society.

Alleq, H. 1958. *La question*. Paris: Gallimard.

Alloula, A. 1995. *Les généreux, les dires, le voile*. Arles: Actes-Sud.

Angelelli, J.-P. 2004. *Une guerre au couteau: Algérie, 1960–1962, un appelé pied-noir témoigne*. Paris: Jean Picollec.

Arendt, H. 1958. *The Human Condition*. Chicago: University of Chicago Press.

———. 1978. *The Life of the Mind*. San Diego: Harcourt Brace.

Aristotle. 1941. *Nicomachean Ethics*. In *The Basic Works of Aristotle*, ed. R. McKeon, 927–1112. New York: Random House.

Arreguín-Toft, I. 2005. *How the Weak Win Wars: A Theory of Asymmetric Conflict*. Cambridge: Cambridge University Press.

Aussaresses, P. 2001. *Services spéciaux: Algérie, 1955–1957*. Paris: Perrin.

Azni, B. 2002. *Harkis, crime d'état: Généalogie d'un abandon*. Paris: Editions Ramsay.

Baillet, F. 1976. *Les rapatriés d'Algérie en France*. Notes et études documentaire, nos. 4275–76. Paris: La documentation français.

Baussant, M. 2002. *Pieds-noirs, memoires d'exil*. Paris: Stock.

Beauvoir, S. de, and G. Halimi. 1962. *Djamila Boupacha*. Paris: Gallimard.

Beck, U. 1992. *Risk Society: Toward a New Modernity*. London: Sage.

Becker, G. 1997. *Disrupted Lives: How People Create Meaning in a Chaotic World*. Berkeley and Los Angeles: University of California Press.

Behr, E. 1962. *The Algerian Problem*. New York: Norton.

Belaïd, L. 2000. *Sérail killers*. Paris: Gallimard.

Benamou, G.-M. 2003. *Un mensonge français: Retours sur la guerre d'Algérie*. Paris: Robert Lafont.

Bensmaïa, R. 2003. *Experimental Nations; or, The Invention of the Maghreb*. Princeton, NJ: Princeton University Press.

Benyoucef, M. 2002a. *Dans les ténèbres gîtent les aigles*. Nointel: Embarcadère.

———. 2002b. *Lettres à Jeanne*. Nointel: Embarcadère.

———. 2005. *Le nom du père*. Nointel: Embarcadère.

Berthelier, R. 1994. *L'homme maghrébin dans la literature psychiatrique*. Paris: L'Harmattan.

Besnaci-Lancou, F. 2003. *Fille de Harki*. Paris: Les Editions de l'Atelier/Les Editions Ouvrière.

———. 2006a. *Nos mères paroles blessées: Une autre histoire des Harkis*. Paris: Zellige.

———. 2006b. *Treize Chibanis Harkis*. Paris: Editions Tirésias.

———. 2010. *Des vies. 62 enfants de Harkis racontent*. Paris: Les Editions de l'Atelier.

Besnaci-Lancou, F., and G. Manceron. 2008. *Les Harkis dans la colonisation et ses suites*. Paris: L'Atelier.

Besnaci-Lancou, F., and A. Moumen. 2008. *Les Harkis*. Paris: Le Cavalier Bleu.

Blévis, L. 2001. "Les avatars de la citoyenneté en Algérie coloniale ou les paradoxes d'une catégorization." *Droits et société* 48:557–80.

Bodin, M. 2005. "Le retour d'Indochine." In *Sortie de la guerre*, ed. J. Frémont and M. Battesti, 11–20. Paris: Ministére de Défense.

Boissieu, Alain de. 1982. *Pour servir le général: 1946–1970*. Paris: Plon.

Boualam, B. 1962. *Mon pays, la France*. Paris: Editions France-Empire.

———. 1963. *Les Harkis au service de la France*. Paris: Editions France-Empire.

———. 1964. *L'Algérie sans la France*. Paris: Editions France-Empire.

Bouclier, T. 2003. *Tixier Vignancour: Une biographie*. Paris: Perrin.

Boulbina, S. 2003. "Présentation." In *Tocqueville sur l'Algérie*, ed. S. Boulbina, 7–41. Paris: Flammarion.

Boulhaïs, N. 2002. *Des Harkis berbères de l'Aurès au nord de la France*. Villeneuve d'Ascq: Presses Universitaires de Septentrion.

Bourdieu, P. 1964. *Le déracinement: La crise de l'agriculture en Algérie*. Paris: Minuit.

———. 1965. "The Sentiment of Honour in Kabyle Society." Translated by P. Sherrard. In *Honour and Shame: The Values of a Mediterranean Society*, ed. J. G. Peristiany, 191–242. London: Weidenfeld & Nicolson.

———. 1977. *An Outline of a Theory of Practice*. Cambridge: Cambridge University Press.

Bourdieu, P., and A. Sayad. 1964. *Le déracinement: La crise de l'agriculture traditionnelle en Algérie*. Paris: Minuit.

Branche, R. 2004. "La torture pendant la guerre d'Algérie." In *La guerre d'Algérie*, ed. M. Harbi and B. Stora, 549–79. Paris: Hachette/Pluriel.

Brillet, E. 2001. "Les problématiques contemporaines du pardon au mirroir du massacre des Harkis." *Cultures et conflits* 2:47–73.

Buis, G. 1975. *Les fanfares perdues: Entretiens avec Jean Lacouture*. Paris: Seuil.

Butler, J. 1997. *The Psychic Life of Power*. Stanford, CA: Stanford University Press.

Camus, A. 1951. *L'homme révolté*. Paris: Gallimard.

———. 1958. *Actuelles III*. Paris: Gallimard.

———. 1991. *L'étranger*. Paris: Gallimard.

———. 1994. *Le dernier homme*. Paris: Gallimard.

Cappelletto, F. 2003. "Long-Term Memory of Extreme Events: From Autobiography to History." *Journal of the Royal Anthropological Institute* 9:241–60.

Caputo, J. D. 1997. *The Prayers and Tears of Jacques Derrida: Religion without Religion*. Bloomington: University of Indiana Press.

Carlier, O. 2004. "Violence." In *La guerre d'Algérie*, ed. M. Harbi and B. Stora, 499–548. Paris: Hachette/Pluriel.

Chabi, H. 2007. "La situation sociale des enfants de Harkis." *Paris: Avis et rapports de Conseil économique et sociale* 2 (January 22): 1–110.

Chapsal, J. 2006. *Harkis à vie*. Trézélan and Paris: Filigranes Editions.

Charbit, T. 2006. *Les Harkis*. Paris: La Découverte.

Charef, M. 1999. *Le Harki de Meriem*. Paris: Mercure de France.

Chauvin, S. 1995. "Des appelés pas comme les autres: Les conscrits français de souche-nord-africaine." *Vingtième siècle* 48:21–30.

Choi, S.-E. 2007. "From Colonial Citizen to Postcolonial Repatriate: The Reintegration of the French from Algeria after Decolonization." Ph.D. diss., University of California, Los Angeles.

Cohen, W. B. 2006. "The Harkis: History and Memory." In *Algeria and France, 1800–2000: Identity, Memory, Nostalgia*, ed. P. M. E. Lorcin, 164–80. Syracuse: Syracuse University Press.

Cole, J. 2006. "Entering History: The Memory of Police Violence in Paris, October 1961." In *Algeria and France: Identity, Memory, Nostalgia, 1800–2000*, ed. P. M. E. Lorcin, 117–34. Syracuse: Syracuse University Press.

Colonna, Marie. 2007. *Harki—un traître mot*. Paris: Play Films. Colonna wrote the screenplay for and directed this documentary.

Cornaton, M. 1967/1998. *Les camps de regroupement de la guerre d'Algérie*. Reprint. Paris: L'Harmattan.

Crapanzano, V. 2004. *Imaginative Horizons: An Essay in Literary-Philosophical Anthropology*. Chicago: University of Chicago Press.

———. 2008. "De la colère à l'indignation: Le cas des Harkis." *Anthropologie et sociétés* 32:121–38.

———. 2009a. "The Dead but Living Father, the Living but Dead Father." In *The Dead Father: A Psychoanalytic Inquiry*, ed. L. J. Kalinich and S. W. Taylor, 163–73. London: Routledge.

———. n.d. "Half-Disciplined Chaos: Thoughts on Contingency, Fate, Destiny, Story, and Trauma." In *Violence, Memory, Symptom, and Recovery*, ed. A. L. Hinton and D. Hinton. In press.

d'Andoque, N. 1977. *Geurre et paix en Algérie, 1955–1962: L'épopée silencieuse des SAS*. Paris: Société de Production Littéraire.

Dante. 1970. *The Divine Comedy: Inferno*. Translated by C. S. Singleton. Princeton, NJ: Princeton University Press.

Deming, H. 2006. "Language and Politics: A New Revisionism." In *Algeria and France, 1800–2000: Identity, Memory, Nostalgia*, ed. P. M. E. Lorcin, 181–98. Syracuse, NY: Syracuse University Press.

Derder, P. 2001. *L'immigration algérienne pendant la guerre d'Algérie et les pouvoirs publics dans le department de la Seine*. Paris: L'Harmattan.

Derrida, J. 1991. *Donner le temps: Le fausse monnaire*. Paris: Galilée.

———. 2001. *Cosmopolitanism and Forgiveness*. New York: Routledge.

Doghmane, S. 2008. "Le prétendu soutien des Harkis de Provence au Front national." In *Les Harkis dans la colonisation et ses suites*, ed. F. Besnaci-Lancou and G. Manceron, 193–95. Ivry sur Seine: L'Atelier.

Eastmond, M. 2007. "Stories as Lived Experience: Narratives in Forced Migration Research." *Journal of Refugee Studies* 20, no. 2:248–64.

Eliot, T. S. 1964. "Hamlet and His Problem." In *Selected Essays*, 121–27. New York: Harcourt, Brace, & World.

Entelis, J. 1982. *Algeria: The Revolution Institutionalized*. Boulder, CO: Westview.

Evans, M. 1997. *The Memory of Resistance*. Oxford: Berg.

Evans-Pritchard, E. E. 1949. *The Sanusi of Cyrenaica*. Oxford: Clarendon.

Fabbiano, G. 2006. "Des générations postalgérienne: Discours, pratiques, recompositions identitaires." Ph.D. diss., Università degli studi di Siena and Écoles des hautes études en sciences sociales.

———. 2007. "Écritures mémorielles et crises de la représentation: Les écrivants descendants de Harkis. *Amnis*, no. 7. http://amnis.revues.org/831.

———. 2008a. "Devenir-Harki: Les modes d'énonciation identitaire des descendants des anciens supplétifs de la guerre d'Algérie." *Migrations et sociétés* 120:155–72.

———. 2008b. "Les Harkis du Bachaga Boualem: Des Beni-Boudouanes à Mas Thibert." In *Les Harkis dans la colonisation et ses suites*, ed. F. Besnaci-Lancou and G. Manceron, 113–24. Ivry sur Seine: L'Atelier.

Faivre, M. 1994. *Un village de Harkis*. Paris: L'Harmattan.

———. 1995. *Les combattants musulmans de la guerre d'Algérie: Des soldats sacrifiés*. Paris: L'Harmattan.

———. 2000. *Les archives inédites de la politique algérienne, 1958–1962*. Paris: L'Harmattan.

Fanon, F. 1972. *Sociologie d'une révolution (l'an V de la révolution algérienne)*. Paris: François Maspero.

Fassin, D. 2008. "The Humanitarian Politics of Testimony: Subjectification through Trauma in the Israeli-Palestinian Conflict." *Cultural Anthropology* 23, no. 3:531–58.

Felman, S., and D. Laub. 1992. *Testimony: Crises of Witnessing in Literature, Psychoanalysis, and History*. New York: Routledge.

Ferdi, S. 1981. *Un enfant dans la guerre*. Paris: Seuil.

Fine, E. 1988. "The Absent Memory: The Act of Writing in Post-Holocaust French Literature." In *Writing and the Holocaust in French Literature*, ed. B. Lang, 41–57. New York: Holmes & Meier.

Foucault, M. 1980. "Two Lectures." *Power/Knowledge: Selected Interviews and Other Writings, 1972–1977*, ed. C. Gordon, 78–108. New York: Pantheon.

Fytton, F. 1961. "War in the 18th Arrondissement." *London Magazine* 1:66–73.

Gaget, R. 2000. *Le Commando Georges: Renseignements et combats*. Paris: Grencher.

Giddens, A. 1990. *The Consequences of Modernity*. Stanford, CA: Stanford University Press.

Goodman, J., and P. Silverstein. 2009. *Bourdieu in Algeria: Colonial Politics, Ethnographic Practices, Theoretical Development*. Lincoln: University of Nebraska Press.

Gray, J. G. 1959. *The Warriors: Reflections on Men in Battle*. New York: Harper & Row.

Green, L. 1994. "Fear as a War of Life." *Cultural Anthropology* 9, no. 2:227–56.

Griswold, C. L. 2007. *Forgiveness: A Philosophical Exploration*. Cambridge: Cambridge University Press.

Gross, J. T. 2000. "Themes for a Social History of War Experience and Collaboration." In *The Politics of Retribution in Europe*, ed. I. Deák, J. T. Gross, and T. Judt, 15–35. Princeton, NJ: Princeton University Press.

Habermas, J. 1990. *Strukturwandel der Offentlichkeit: Untersuchungen einer Kategorie der bürgerlichen Geselschaft*. Frankfurt a.M.: Suhrkamp.

Hacking, I. 1990. *The Taming of Chance*. Cambridge: Cambridge University Press.

Halimi, G. 1988. *Le lait de l'oranger*. Paris: Gallimard.

Hamdy, S. 2009. "Islam, Fatalism, and Medical Intervention: Lessons from Egypt on the Cultivation of Forbearance (*Sabr*) and Reliance on God (*Tawakkul*)." *Anthropological Quarterly* 82, no. 1:173–96.

Hamoumou, M. 1993. *Et ils sont devenus Harkis*. Paris: Fayard.

Hamoumou, M., and A. Moumen. 2004. "L'histoire des Harkis et Français: La fin d'un tabou." In *La guérre d'Algérie*, ed. M. Harbi and B. Stora, 455–95. Paris: Hachette/Pluriel.

Harbi, M. 1998. *1954: La guerre commence en Algérie*. Brussels: Editions Complex.

Harbi, M., and B. Stora, eds. 2004. *La guerre d'Algérie*. Paris: Hachette/Pluriel.

Hargreaves, A. 1995. *Immigration, "Race," and Ethnicity in Contemporary France*. London: Routledge.

Haroun, A. 2008. "Effacer les séquelles de la guerre en Algérie." In *Les Harkis dans la colonisation et ses suites*, ed. F. Besnaci-Lancou and G. Manceron, 201–4. Ivry sur Seine: L'Atelier.

Heidegger, M. 1952. "Der Spruch des Anaximander." In *Holzwege*, 296–344. Frankfurt a.M.: Vittorio Klostermann.

Heinis, A. 1977. "L'insertion des Français-Musulmans: Étude faite sur les populations regroupées dans le Midi de la France dans les centres ex-Harkis." Thèse de troisième cycle, Sciences Économiques, Université Paul Valérie, Montpellier.

Henley, J. 2005. "French Angry at Law to Teach Glory of Colonialism." *Guardian*, April 15.

Hertz, R. 1988. *Le péché et l'expiation dans les sociétés primitives*. Paris: Jean Michel Place.

Horne, A. 1987. *A Savage War of Peace: Algeria, 1954–1962*. London: Macmillan.

Ibrahimi, K. T. 2004. "Les Algériennes et la guerre de libération nationale: L'émergence des femmes dans l'espace public et politique au cours de la guerre et après-guerre." In *La guerre d'Algérie*, ed. M. Harbi and B. Stora, 281–323. Paris: Hachette/Pluriel.

Ireland, S. 2009. "Facing the Ghosts of the Past in Dalila Kerchouche's *Mon Père, ce Harki* and Zahia Rahmani's *Moze*." *Contemporary French and Francophone Studies* 13, no. 3: 303–10.

Jackson, M. 2002. *The Politics of Storytelling: Violence, Transgression, and Intersubjectivity*. Copenhagen: Museum Tusculanum Press.

Jammes, P. 2008. "Être médicin au camp de Bias." In *Les Harkis dans la colonisation et ses suites*, ed. F. Besnaci-Lancou and G. Manceron, 147–50. Ivry sur Seine: L'Atelier.

Jaulin, A. 2005. "L'épilogue à la Christiane." Théâtre online.com, May 17. http://theatre-online.com.

Jordi, J.-J., and M. Hamoumou. 1999. *Les Harkis: Une mémoire enfouie*. Paris: Editions Autrement.

Kara, M. 1997. *Les tentations du répli communautaire: Le cas des Franco-Maghrébins en general et des enfants de Harkis en particulier*. Paris: L'Harmattan.

Kemoum, H. 2003. *Mohand le Harki*. Paris: Anne Carrière.

Kerchouche, D. 2003a. *Destins de Harkis: Aux racines d'un exil*. Paris: Editions Auturement.

———. 2003b. *Mon père, ce Harki*. Paris: Seuil.

———. 2006. *Leïla: Avoir dix-sept ans dans un camp de Harkis*. Paris: Seuil.

Kramer, J. 1980. *Unsettling Europe*. New York: Random House.

Kripke, S. *Naming and Necessity*. Cambridge, MA: Harvard University Press.

Lacan, J. 1966. *Écrits*. Paris: Seuil.

Lacouture, Jean. 1962. "Atteintes aux accords d'Evian." *Le monde*, November 13.

Langelier, E. 2009. *La situation juridique des Harkis: 1962–2007*. Poitiers: Université de Poitiers.

Laplanche, J., and J.-B. Pontalis. 1973. *Vocabulaire de la psychanalyse*. Paris: Presses Universitaires de la France.

Laurence, J., and J. Vaisse. 2006. *Integrating Islam: Political and Religious Challenges in Contemporary France*. Washington, DC: Brookings Institution Press.

Lévi-Strauss, C. *The Raw and the Cooked: Introduction to the Science of Mythology*. Translated by L. Wrightman and D. Wrightman. New York: Harper & Row.

Liauzu, C. 2004. "Mémoires croisées de la guerre d'Algérie." In *La guerre d'Algérie dans la mémoire et l'imagination*, ed. A. Rosenman and L. Valensi, 161–72. St. Denis: Bouchène.

Lyons, A. H. 2004. "Invisible Immigrants: Algerian Families and the French Welfare State in the Era of Decolonization (1947–1974)." Ph.D. diss., Department of History, University of California at Irvine.

Malkki, L. H. 1995. *Purity and Exile: Violence, Memory, and National Cosmology among Hutu Refugees in Tanzania*. Chicago: University of Chicago Press.

Maran, R. 1989. *Torture: The Role of Ideology in the French-Algerian War*. New York: Praeger.

Mauss, M. 1990. "Essai sur le don: Forme et raison de l'échange dans les sociétés archaïques." In *Sociologie et anthropologie*, 145–279. Paris: Presses Universitaires de France.

McCormack, J. 2006. "Memory in History, Nation Building, and Identity." In *Algeria and France, 1800–2000: Identity, Memory, Nostalgia*, ed. P. M. E. Lorcin, 135–49. Syracuse, NY: Syracuse University Press.

McNay, M. 2009. "Absent Memory, Family Secrets, Narrative Inheritance." *Qualitative Inquiry* 15, no. 7:1178–87.

Méliani, A.-E.-A. 1993. *La France honteuse: Le drame des Harkis*. Paris: Perrin.

Meynier, G. 2002. *Histoire intérieure du FLN: 1954–1962*. Paris: Fayard.

Miège, L. J. 1992. "Legal Developments in the Maghrib: 1830–1930." In *European Expansion and the Law: The Encounter of European and Indigenous Law in Nineteenth- and Twentieth-Century Africa and Asia*, ed. W. J. Mommsen and J. A. De Moor, 101–10. New York: Berg.

Moinot, Bernard. 1997. *Ahmed? Connais pas . . . le calvaire des Harki*. Paris: Godefroy de Bouillon.

Montagnac, L. F. D. 1885. *Lettres d'un soldat*. Paris: Plon.

Montagne, R. 1930. *Les Berbères et le Makhzen dans le sud du Maroc: Essai sur la transformation politique des Berbères sédentaires (group Chleuh)*. Paris: Félix Alcan.

Morelle, C. 2004. "Les pouvoirs publiques et le rapatriement des Harkis en 1961–1962." *Vingtième siècle* 83:109–19.

Moumen, A. 2003a. *Entre histoire et mémoires: Les rapatriés d'Algérie*. Nice: Editions Gandini.

———. 2003b. *Les français musulmans en Vaucluse, 1962–1991: Installation et difficultés d'intégration d'une communauté de rapatriés d'Algérie*. Paris: L'Harmattan.

———. 2008. "Du camp de transit à la cité d'accueil: Saint-Maurice-l'Ardoise." In *Les Harkis dans la colonisation et ses suites*, ed. F. Besnaci-Lancou and G. Manceron, 131–45. Ivry sur Seine: L'Atelier.

Muller, L. 1999. *Le silence des Harkis*. Paris: L'Harmattan.

Nedjadi, B. 2001. *Les tortionnaires de 1830 à 1962*. N.p., ANEP.

Noiriel, G. 2004. "Histoire, mémoire, engagement civique." *Hommes et migrations*, no. 1247: 17–26.

Oliver, K. 2004. *The Colonization of Psychic Space: A Psychoanalytic Social Theory of Oppression*. Minneapolis: University of Minnesota Press.

Paret, P. 1964. *French Revolutionary Warfare from Indochina to Algeria: The Analysis of Political and Military Doctrine*. London: Pall Mall.

Péju, P. 1961/2000. *Ratonnade à Paris précédé de les Harkis à Paris*. Paris: La Découverte.

Peristiany, J. G. 1966. *Honour and Shame: The Values of Mediterranean Society*. London: Weidenfeld & Nicolson.

Pervillé, G. 1987. "Guerre d'Algérie: L'abandon des Harkis." *L'Histoire* 102:30–34.

———. 1991. "La tragédie des Harkis." *L'histoire* 140:120–23.

———. 2004. "La guerre d'Algérie." In *La guerre d'Algérie*, ed. M. Harbi and B. Stora, 693–716. Paris: Hachette/Pluriel.

Peyroulou, J.-P. 2004. "Rétablir et maintenir l'ordre colonial: La police française et les Algériens en Algérie française de 1945–1962." In *Le guerre d'Algérie*, M. Harbi and B. Stora, 137–86. Paris: Hachette/Pluriel.

Peyrfitte, Alain. 1994. *C'était de Gaulle*. Vol. 1, *La France redevient la France*. Paris: Fallois/Fayard.

Pierret, R. 2008. *Les filles et fils de Harkis: Entre double rejet et triple appartenance*. Paris: L'Harmattan.

Pouillon, F. 2004. "Abd el-Kader: Icône de la nation algérienne." In *La guerre d'Algérie dans la mémoire et l'imaginaire*, ed. A. Rosenman and L. Valensi, 87–102. St. Denis: Bouchene.

The Qur'an. 2004. Translated by Yusuf Ali. New York: Oxford University Press.

Rahmani, Z. 2003. *Moze*. Paris: Sabine Wespieser.

———. 2006. *France: Récit d'une enfance*. Paris: Sabine Wespieser.

Ricoeur, P. 2000. *La mémoire, l'histoire, et l'oubli*. Paris: Seuil.

Roberts, H. 2003. *The Battlefield: Algeria, 1988–2002*. London: Verso.

Rosello, M. 2005. *France and the Maghreb: Performance Encounters*. Gainesville: University Press of Florida.

Rothberg, M. 2006. "Between Auschwitz and Algeria: Multidirectional Memory and the Counterpublic Witness." *Critical Inquiry* 33 (Autumn): 158–84.

Rousso, H. 1991. *Le syndrome de Vichy à nos jours*. Paris: Seuil.

Roux, M. 1991. *Les Harkis: Les oubliés de l'histoire, 1954–1991*. Paris: La Découverte.

Ruedy, J. 1992. *Modern Algeria: The Origins and Development of a Nation*. Bloomington: Indiana University Press.

Saada, E. 2003. "Citoyens et sujets d'empire française: Les usages du droit en situation coloniale." *Genèse* 53:4–24.

Sabeg, Y., and F. Besnaci-Lancou. 2004. "France-Algérie: Les voies de la reconciliation." *Le figaro*, August 14, 10.

Sadouni, B. 2001. *Destin de Harki: La témoignage d'un jeune Berbère, enrôlé dans l'armée française à 17 ans*. Paris: Cosmopole.

Saliha, A. 1984. "Les Français-Musulmans ou le poids de l'histoire à travers la communité picarde." *Les temps modernes* nos. 452–54:1812–38.

Sartre, J.-P. 1958. Introduction to *The Question*, by H. Alleg. New York: Braziller.

Sayad, A. 1999. *Le double absence: Des illusions de l'émigré aux souffrances de l'immigré*. Paris: Seuil.

Scarry, E. 1985. *The Body in Pain: The Making and Unmaking of the World*. New York: Oxford University Press.

Scheele, J. 2006. "Algerian Graveyard Stories." *Journal of the Royal Anthropology Institute*, n.s., 12, no. 4:859–79.

Servier, J. 1955. *Dans l'Aurès sur le pas des rebelles*. Paris: France Empire.

Shephard, T. 2006. "Pieds-Noirs, Bêtes Noirs." In *Algeria and France, 1800–2000: Identity, Memory, Nostalgia*, ed. P. M. E. Lorcin, 150–63. Syracuse, NY: Syracuse University Press.

Shoeb, M., H. M. Weinstein, et al. 2007. "Living in Religious Time and Space." *Journal of Refugee Studies* 20, no. 3:441–61.

Silverstein, P. A. 2004. *Algeria in France: Transpolitics, Race, and Nation*. Bloomington: University of Indiana Press.

———. 2009. "Of Rooting and Uprooting: Kabyle Habitus, Domesticity, and Structural Nostalgia." In *Bourdieu in France: Colonial Politics, Ethnographic Practices, Theoretical Developments*, ed. J. E. Goodman and P. A. Silverstein, 164–98. Lincoln: University of Nebraska Press.

Skultans, V. 1999. "Weaving New Lives from Old Fleece: Gender and Ethnicity in Latvian Narrative." In *Ethnicity, Gender, and Social Change*, ed. R. Barot, 169–90. New York: Palgrave.

Smith, J. I., and Y. Y. Haddad. 2002. *The Islamic Understanding of Death and Resurrection*. New York: Oxford University Press.

Sophocles. 1959. *Oedipus at Colonus*. In *The Complete Greek Tragedies*, ed. D. Grene and R. Lattimore, 2:77–155. Chicago: University of Chicago Press.

Soufflet, A. A., and J.-B. Williatte. 2004. "Harkis, hier et aujourd'hui." In *La guerre d'Algérie dans la mémoire et l'imaginaire*, ed. A. Rosenman and L. Valensi, 110–29. Paris: Bouchene.

Soufi, F. 2004. "L'histoire face à la mémoire: Oran, le 5 juillet 1962." In *La guerre d'Algérie dans la mémoire et l'imaginaire*, ed. A. Rosenman and L. Valensi, 133–48. St. Denis: Bouchene.

Souida, A. 1990. "Roubaix, les 'Rona' dans la cité." *Hommes et migrations*, no. 1135:59–68.

Stora, B. 1998. *La gangrene et l'oubli: La mémoire de la guerre d'Algérie*. Paris: La Découverte.

———. 2004. "Guerre d'Algérie: Les instruments de la mémoire." In *La guerre d'Algérie dans la mémoire et l'imagination*, ed. A. Rosenman and L. Valensi, 215–24. St. Denis: Bouchene.

Sullivan, A. T. 1983. *Thomas-Robert Bugeaud, 1784–1849: France and Algeria, Politics, Power, and the Good Society*. Hamden, CT: Archon.

Talbott, J. 1980. *The War without a Name: France in Algeria, 1954–1962*. New York: Knopf.

Telali, S. 2009. *Les enfants des Harkis: Entre silence et assimilation subie*. Paris: L'Harmattan.

Thénault, S. 2004. "La justice dans la guerre d'Algérie." In *La guerre d'Algérie*, ed. M. Harbi and B. Stora, 107–36. Paris: Hachette/Pluriel.

———. 2008. "Massacre des Harkis ou massacres de Harkis? Qu'en sait-on?" In *Les Harkis dans la colonisation et ses suites*, ed. F. Besnaci-Lancou and G. Manceron, 81–91. Ivry sur Seine: L'Atelier.

Throop, C. J. 2010. "In the Midst of Action." In *Toward an Anthropology of the Will*, ed. K. M. Murphy and C. J. Throop, 28–49. Stanford, CA: Stanford University Press.

Tocqueville, A. de. 2003. *Tocqueville sur l'Algérie*. Paris: Flammarion.

Turnaturi, G. 2007. *Betrayals: The Unpredictability of Human Relations*. Chicago: University of Chicago Press.

Valat, R. 2007. *Les "calots bleus" et la bataille de Paris: Une force de police auxiliaire pendant la guerre d'Algérie.* Paris: Michalon.

Vidal-Naquet, P. 1958. *L'affaire Audin.* Paris: Edition de Minuit.

———. 1983. *La torture dans la République.* Paris: La Découverte.

Vittori, J.-P. 1980. *Confessions d'un professionnel de la torture.* Paris: Ramsay.

Whitol de Wenden, C. 1990. "Qui sont les Harkis? Difficultés à les nommer et à les identifier." *Hommes et migrations*, no. 1135:7–12.

———. 1991. "Harkis: Le paradoxe identitaire." *Regards sur l'actualité* 175:33–43.

Yahiaoui, R. 1990. "Amiens, la cité de la Briquetterie." *Hommes et migrations*, no. 1135:46–49.

Zaater, M. 2003. *L'Algérie de la guerre à la guerre* (1962–2003). Paris: L'Harmattan.

Zirem, Y. 2002. *Algérie: La guerre des ombres.* Brussels: Editions Complexe.

INDEX